PENGUIN BOOKS

THE GOOD WORD AND OTHER WORDS

Wilfrid Sheed, twice nominated for the National Book Award in fiction, has written the novels *A Middle-Class Education, The Hack, Square's Progress, Office Politics, The Blacking Factory and Pennsylvania Gothic, Max Jamison, People Will Always Be Kind,* and most recently, *Transatlantic Blues.* He has also published an earlier collection of essays, entitled *The Morning After.*

The Good Word

and Other Words

Wilfrid Sheed

PENGUIN BOOKS

Penguin Books Ltd, Harmondsworth, Middlesex, England
Penguin Books, 625 Madison Avenue, New York, New York 10022, U.S.A.
Penguin Books Australia Ltd, Ringwood, Victoria, Australia
Penguin Books Canada Limited, 2801 John Street, Markham, Ontario, Canada L3R 1B4
Penguin Books (N.Z.) Ltd, 182–190 Wairau Road, Auckland 10, New Zealand

First published in the United States of America by
E. P. Dutton 1978
First published in Canada by
Clarke, Irwin & Company Limited 1978
Published in Penguin Books 1980

LIBRARY OF CONGRESS CATALOGING IN PUBLICATION DATA
Sheed, Wilfrid.
The good word & other words.
I. Title.
[PR6069.H396G6 1980] 824'.9'14 79-26559
ISBN 0 14 00.5497 9

Printed in the United States of America by
Offset Paperback Mfrs., Inc., Dallas, Pennsylvania
Set in Fairfield

All of the essays in Part One ("The Good Word") first appeared in *The New York Times Book Review.* The following reviews also appeared in *The New York Times Book Review:* V. S. Pritchett's *Midnight Oil, Letters of E. B. White,* Ring Lardner, Jr.'s *The Lardners: Remembering My Family,* and Norman Mailer's *Miami and the Siege of Chicago.* "America and the Movies," "Toward the Black Pussy Cafe," "I Am a Cabaret," "Ernest Hemingway," and the review of Mary Gordon's *Final Payments* first appeared in *The New York Review of Books.* "The Twin Urges of James Baldwin" first appeared in *Commonweal.* The review of Graham Greene's *A Sort of Life* originally appeared in *Life.* "F. Scott Fitzgerald" appeared first in *Harper's Bazaar.* "Chicago on My Mind" first appeared in *Chic.* "Miami: 1972" first appeared in *Saturday Review.* "Now That Men Can Cry . . ." first appeared in *The New York Times Magazine.* The author is grateful to the editors of these publications for permission to print the essays in this volume. "The Interview as Art" first appeared in *Writers at Work,* published by The Viking Press, copyright 1976. The essay on James Thurber first appeared in James Thurber's *Men, Women and Dogs,* published by Dodd, Mead, copyright 1975. The essay on P. G. Wodehouse first appeared in P. G. Wodehouse's *Leave It to Psmith,* published by Random House, copyright 1975. The author is grateful to the editors at the above publishing houses for permission to print these essays.

To my father,
who put me on to all this

CONTENTS

INTRODUCTION

Wilfrid Sheed the critic and Wilfrid Sheed the novelist have been played off against each other for so long that I had myself come to believe they were two different people, whose ups and downs I followed with fitful interest. Until, that is, I began collecting the pieces for this book, which showed me how surprisingly much I had in common.

Fiction is an extension of criticism by other means, and the subjects chosen here come from the same, common stock of obsessions as Sheed's novels. All the writers discussed are English and American, not because I like them best, but because they are facts in my life, like relatives, that have to be confronted. The particular adventure of an Englishman becoming American in this century meant finding faces like Hemingway and Ring Lardner at the dock, and the queer chalky mask of the old *New Yorker,* that turned out to be Thurber and E. B. White hiding behind a scrim. These were to be my literary guides to America c.1940, that vulgar, subtle sprawl, but more than that, they were experiences in themselves, as real as baseball and fistfighting and the strange sounds in the street. And I only wish I could introduce them all: James M. Cain, who has never received his due; Damon Runyon, that trap for foreigners;

Thorne Smith, John Tunis, Joe Mitchell; and the whole crazy chorus of American letters and subletters.

These people were history before they were literature, and I wanted to know how they got that way. How in the world did Runyon, H. Allen Smith, and Gene Fowler all manage to come from *Denver?* Was there a tiny replica Manhattan out there? And how about Ben Hecht's Chicago? Did the reporters there really hide escaped murderers in their desks? My father told tales of Al Capone beating rivals to death with baseball bats at ceremonial dinners, and I made no fine distinctions between this and, say, Dashiell Hammett's novels. The gore ran out of *Red Harvest* and into the streets where a gorgeous pageant of long cars and machine guns and boys on rafts was in full swing; and later, this would be joined by Gershwin playing all night in penthouses, while George Kaufman fired one-liners into the guests and Harpo scrambled eggs in their hats. America hit me all of a piece just before adolescence did, and the result is subject matter for a lifetime, cashable in fiction and nonfiction both.

Returning to England in 1946, I found new faces at the dock, but they didn't match the country as the Americans had. England had just been through an experience of a kind that is said to age one overnight, and there were no writers yet to express the sourness and shock in the air, only isolated druids of an earlier time, whose traditions I couldn't trace at all. For instance, why was this fellow Orwell, with his decency and humanity, more forbidding than Evelyn Waugh, with his swinishness? Where were the comfy people I remembered, like Wodehouse and Chesterton? Had they died in the war? Or had they only shrunk? Listening to the BBC, one heard the remnants of that world chattering about the literary life as if nothing had happened. Yet a smoking chasm lay between them and their memories. In that pre-Amis, pre-Sillitoe lull, there seemed to be nothing to do but stare at the chasm and make patterns with one's hands: Bloomsbury must have looked like this; Cyril Connolly in a feather boa, like that. Although the old bridges may have since been rebuilt, one sensed in 1946 a discontinuity in the English imagination more drastic than anything that had happened in America.

So much for travel. When I got back to America and found the Beats in full swing, I saw that the discontinuity was partly in the traveler, and that I would keep finding new countries every time I went away and came back. If I wanted bridges, I would have to build them myself. My two essays on the Beats in this book are a particularly conscious attempt to do this: to show that the changes the eye picks up may be superficial, compared with the slower music of social history. From Whitman to Kerouac is a leap, of course, but not as great as the electric banging and flashing of fashion would make one suppose.

If I were to try to link English writers in this way, it would feel like guesswork. America, true or false, had proposed itself as a single experience, from book to highway to jazz band, and I feel at home with it now and can pontificate with the natives (i.e., I don't hear "only an Englishman could make that mistake" as much as I used to). With England I feel, in Joe Heller's phrase, as if "something happened" in my wartime absence, and I can't quite put my finger on it. I am absolutely terrified of Virginia Woolf.

Insofar as this America of mine was a literary and theatrical creation (pretty far, I think) I find my reviews still cross-referencing literature with life more than criticism should, even tracing such purely aesthetic matters as narrative technique and rhetorical convention to region and circumstance. "Combining and separating"—as Thomas Aquinas described the business of thinking. The doodles on the back of my imagination might read: Wilson and Fitzgerald at Princeton, so what? President Woodrow, dining clubs, southern girls? Zelda vs. Patriotic Gore (not Vidal). Better forget for now. Gertrude Stein, if only she could draw, she would draw like Thurber and Sherwood Anderson meet E. B. White and Thoreau at Algonquin Hotel. Host, Harold Ross of Aspen, Colorado, who hated women schoolteachers. Hemingway's "wimmies" vs. Thurber's unbaked cookies. Lardner, Fields, Philadelphia, why not Groucho, T. S. Eliot, and W. S. Gilbert instead? Mrs. Rittenhouse? And so on. This is the game behind the criticism, an orderly sort of *Finnegan's Wake* in which real and spurious associations do their own mad dance, and the winner goes into the review.

I am perfectly happy not to call this criticism at all, but just one of the things one can do with literature (and there should be many more of these, outside the critical liturgy). My own subject in college was history, not letters, and history demands connections: it would be lost without them. No poem is an island for a historian—or if it is, he can't do anything with it. The invention and testing of links is his business. Shakespeare, Italy, dark ladies: he is forever sorting out these bundles and matching strips of color until everything is tied to something else. Even in history proper, the resulting chain can look sturdy and last a long time (see Gibbon, or anything written about the Boston Tea Party) and still fall apart at a touch. In literature, it happens so often that critical theories must mostly be admired for their looks and audacity.

But though I believe that good textual criticism is usually worth a dozen of these historians' farragos, I find the patterns and groupings irresistible. If Conrad, James, and Ford Madox Ford really did sit up late now and then talking bawdy, I want to know about it, even if it leads nowhere. The image of these three portraits shaking gently over some lapse of, say, George Gissing, is its own reward.

History is the most dreamy and self-indulgent of studies, if you're any good (bad historians tend to miss the jokes and have a thin time), and it is a natural way station to writing. Because its other great pleasure is a most practical one: namely, holding one's own experience against history and trying to decide what one could validly imagine and what one could not: how much of one's brain one would have to change or lose to write Homer, or to follow Muhammad, or to collaborate with Hitler. What about the texture of a firing squad, poison gas, a shower of arrows? An hour on the rack, an evening with Dr. Johnson, a night with Queen Victoria? A cross-cultural upbringing enriches these exercises to madness, because alienation is our racket. We are connoisseurs of strangeness.

Such a childlike approach can lead only in one direction: the writing of fiction. Whether it should also lead to reviewing is another question. In the days when I grabbed and stamped movies, plays, and novels off a rotating band, I used to fear that I was the most inventive of critics, making up whole stories and interpretations that nobody else could see. In this book, I also make up whole people, like Henry Luce, and movements, like the peaceniks, and flatly deny the existence of others, like the New Journalism, mainly to be cantankerous. I try to stake claims for White and Thurber and wind up maddening their fans. (In championing a writer, you have to concede the indefensible. But try telling that to a fan.)

This kind of reviewing is imprecise, speculative work like fiction, and its truths are the truths of fiction. The books are events that happened to me and are as open to misinterpretation as my neighbors or the Siege of Chicago in 1968. Along with one's novels these pieces form a mosaic of someone coming of age at a certain time and place, and what he made of it.

PART ONE

The Good Word

1 / EDMUND WILSON

1895-1972

Don't let them intimidate you, Edmund Wilson once said to me, and I thought, if you don't, sir, *they* certainly won't. My fund of personal Wilsoniana is extremely modest, and I won't attempt to stretch it here. Claiming close friendships with the recent dead is a knavish trick, and in Wilson's case there will be a lot of it because he had, behind his hedge of crotchets, an extraordinary gift for friendship in all its degrees, from the exchange of funny postcards to the complete opening of his mind. My own degree, pitched somewhere between the two, was, I know for a fact, shared by many.

It began because Wilson was interested in something I wrote—there was no telling what would catch his ravenous interest—and he just rang up and said, "Hello, I'm Edmund Wilson. What would you say to lunch?" His lunching was as direct as his invitation. After negotiating like a Vietnamese over the size of our table at the Princeton Club (they always put people too far apart, he said), he began to talk like a very old friend, possibly even a classmate. What did I make of so-and-so (a famous writer)? A bit of a fraud don't you think? When I, rather hysterically, quoted some lines of his own, he accused me of cribbing up for the meeting. He couldn't believe that anyone actually knew his stuff by heart and seemed boisterously embarrassed by it, like an English schoolboy squirming under a compliment.

The lunch went well enough, heaven knows how, for him to ask us up to the Cape that Christmas. Whether he meant it or not, there was no way he was going to get out of it. He met us at the Hyannis Airport and seized our bags immediately, although he was all of seventy-four and stiff with arthritis, and set off in his defiant waddle, refusing to hand them back, even when his hat flew off in the wind, obliging him to reroute his waddle.

As luck had it, we were snowed in for about five days, and we cursed the thaw when it came. If Wilson had a gift for friendship, his wife, Elena, seemed to have a genius for it. The evenings were riotous, Early Princeton Triangle as one dreams it, with Wilson singing snatches of English music hall songs and shaking with laughter at everyone's jokes, filling the glasses every few seconds, and burning up his own Johnny Walker Red with sheer boyish exuberance. I even began to wonder whether Scott Fitzgerald had ever had to put *him* to bed. But his head was Churchillian. One night he slipped on the bathroom floor and bellowed like a bull when offered assistance. But this was on the order of carrying our suitcases, a matter of simple pride. I never saw him the worse for booze, which is probably more than he could have said for me after that visit.

In the morning he would come harrumphing past our door, indicating that he was up and ready to talk. Another harrumph came about an hour later, and if we held out against that, a final "I say, Sheed, I'm going downstairs now." He had a terrible time putting the brain to sleep, and by dawn he was burning to share his thoughts with someone.

At that time, he was wallowing in one or other of his majestic controversies, so he allotted some morning time to firing off his mock-indignant letters and postcards. If people took them seriously so much the better. He was at heart a trickster, and his bathroom walls were lined with books on magic. If he and that other cut-up Nabokov could draw a crowd of gapers with their stagy barroom brawls, he was pleased as Houdini. Not that he wasn't serious about his Russian verbs—he was serious about everything—but he was also an entertainer with a special love of theater. (In fact, I believe he was prouder of his many unproduced plays than all his criticism put together, and even the latter can sometimes be read as a play of voices, like the interview he once conducted with himself.)

The famous crankiness was as comforting as a bulldog's roar if you were on the right side of it. Toward the people at hand, he could be almost alarmingly respectful, assuming that they knew at least as much as he did and might easily teach him some vital new thing. "I say, Sheed, what do you make of Meredith?" If you passed Meredith, you got Peacock, and indeed on one shirt-drenching afternoon virtually the whole nineteenth century.

"Well, Sheed and I took care of the nineteenth century," he said over supper. "We don't think much of it, eh?" Food bored him, and as he poked at it despondently the talk seemed to turn moodier than usual. "If you've got past thirty-five you should be all right till fifty-one," he said. "Then watch out." He supposed he should be writing memoirs at his age, but he didn't feel much like it; he'd rather tackle a new field, possibly another language or two.

Still, the past was there, in a vibrant, impatient sort of way. One felt that Scott Fitzgerald had just left the room and Edmund was still not sure what to make of the rascal. "I'm sorry he lost his faith at Princeton. It gave him something he needed." Still, it didn't do to worry about Scott. He was a mercurial Celt like Oscar Wilde: By the time the reader was crying over *De Profundis* or *The Crack-Up* the author had forgotten all about it and was off making jokes in some bar.

When I told him that my first novel was almost as bad as *This Side of Paradise,* he said, "You're too modest." He was fond of Fitzgerald in his elder brother way, but so much had happened to him since then that he didn't want to hang out with Scott's ghost indefinitely. "Scott believed that Ring Lardner had caught a touch of the clap as a boy, which made him prudish": from which slander we went into Lardner (whom he admired enormously) and from Lardner into Benchley and Perelman and from that into. . . .

Wilson's friendship was a continuous workout. One-on-one conversation with him was always *about* something, and he didn't give you the breather of an occasional monologue. He really wanted your opinion, so every minute or so you found yourself pretending desperately that you'd read Meredith or glumly confessing that you hadn't. To make matters worse, he was courteous though puzzled about these lapses in your obviously vast scholarship. The only time I ran into his famous crustiness was at a party in New York sometime later when I flunked Islam, and he said, "I don't want to monopolize you," a dismissal I associated with Victorian aunts. But by then he was riddled with pain and very likely couldn't bear to talk to anyone whether they knew their Islam or not.

He did turn to religion toward the end, not for consolation like most people but for amusement. He was not scornful about it as he once had been, but quite gentle and bemused. He simply found it incomprehensible and fascinating that people could believe those things. He lived under an earth sign himself and found life itself all the consolation he needed. His extraordinary wife, Elena, made the texture of his days as festive and tranquil as they could possibly be. The rest he did himself, reveling with his stoical willpower in the joy of new ideas and discoveries to the end. If some of his later work seems disappointing, it was certainly through no failure of mind. He might have lost whatever he had ever had of a young man's eagerness to please, the necessary minimum of intimidation. But his brain as I encountered it was good for another fifty years.

"How are you? I feel rotten." Our last conversation, over the phone, was cheerfully lugubrious in the style that the gapers took for pessimism. One last joke on them. Yet he was terribly ill by then, quite palpably dying. He distressed those close to him by talking matter-of-factly about his death—he was not going to evade a fact of that importance. But he worked as if he was immortal, and the brain blazed like a blast furnace until the body gave out.

To use a Wilson locution—what did one finally make of him? He was much funnier than I expected, in curious combination forthright to the point of gullibility and alertly mischievous, so that I imagined his life as one long leg-pull going and coming. He was, as painted, aristocratic, beyond any writer I've met, but in a Jeffersonian-American way that was so sure of itself it brooked no artificial distinctions. There was no cheap way you could impress him. At the same time, no one was faster or firmer with a compliment.

This lordly democracy of spirit could have quaint effects, as in a letter he wrote to me which began, "Where you and Tolstoy both go wrong. . . ." He saw no reason why one of his friends shouldn't share at least Tolstoy's mistakes. It was a particular strength of his as a critic that he was not even impressed by the Dead as such. He could write of living authors in precisely the same tones, and applying the same standards, as he used for the Classics. Beyond that, one remembers especially his voice with its high pitch that seemed to be pushed up there by his exuberance, and its ripe cadences that reminded one of an eighteenth-century squire raised on Virgil and Cicero. He spoke as he wrote, using his full measure of perfects and pluperfects and his stately "thises." "I had expected him to have noticed this"—that kind of sentence. With a lesser man such prose would have seemed fusty and unmanageable; but he wielded this superheavy instrument with the ease and naturalness of a titan swinging a sword that no one else can lift—or, to use a simile from the only field where I could top him, like Babe Ruth flushing a 44-ounce bat as if it were a toothpick.

There will be plenty of time to assess Wilson's contribution to letters: in particular those audacious raids of the amateur gentleman on the scholarly preserves, rescuing the princess from the ivory tower, and slipping past the pedants who ooze around in the moat. Sometimes he may have been too cocky to get away with it completely, but meanwhile he set a standard of scholarship-as-adventure that has vivified even his enemies and helped liberate academic diction from the slithy pedants for the next generation.

For now, though, I would rather remember things like one's first encounters with him in *The New Yorker*—his attack on detective stories that had my family in an uproar for days and his genial blast at Evelyn Waugh's tory Catholicism that had us in two minds—what other book reviewer ever made a whole family shout at once? Or later, the long essays on Dickens, Kipling, Housman that showed how criticism could be a breathtaking art in itself, and then *Axel's Castle* and then and then. Finally, Wilson himself autographing his own books, scribbling into *Patriotic Gore*, with that underground chuckle of his, "Sometime you ought to read this one. It is very informative." Myself, almost too moved to speak, as I find myself now when I think of it.

1972

2 / *The Art of Reviewing*

The author chokes as the wheel spins. Somewhere he will be called "one of our finest since . . . in his greatest yet," and somewhere else he will be called a tasteless baboon —but where? If the blow strikes in *The Hoboken News,* he may be spared in *The New York Times Book Review.* His luck either way is capriciously rationed. What he will not be called anywhere is probably what he is—"our most middling author in his most middling achievement."

These words come hard to a reviewer warming himself by his twig fire and trying to feel his work is important. All those hours of imaginative re-creation, of bringing a book stuttering to life in his head, and nothing to say at the end but "so-so" or "not too bad"—it's a lot to ask of an assistant professor. Besides, excessive opinions excite the average reader to madness, or at least to attention. A critic of fine discriminations like John Simon only draws a crowd when he snarls his famous "viles" and "loathesomes." And you might suppose Pauline Kael had reviewed nothing all year but *Last Tango in Paris,* her liberating yell of the season. Our best critics are known for their hammiest moments.

So a reviewer who would rise must learn to roar and gush and roll on the stage in mirth and pain, making of book and self a single spectacle, a Main Event. Excess (in moderation) is good for business. In England, criticism used to be so understated that you might as well be reading tombstones. A slight carnival atmosphere is better than that, with the clowns bawling and offering to guess your weight and squirting you in the eye with their wax flowers. Authors would rather take their chances in that slapstick world than be called "one of our more encouraging fifty-year-olds"—*Nottingham Post;* and the reader can always choose his favorite clown.

Still, in the uproar certain decencies should be observed. Older authors who've been through before and collected their tin stars and stuffed pandas know how little most praise and blame actually mean. If properly arrogant, they marvel at these young puppies (teaches English *where?*) who presume to tell them their craft, and only fret about the possible effect on sales. Their heads are too old and stiff to be turned by praise or bent by grief. If they could cash reviews at a pawnshop, they'd be down in the morning with a sackful of the best.

Young authors, though, may be taken in by the trumped-up noise and glare, and reviewers for the only time may actually have a chance to influence them a little. Hence, more precision is called for. Overpraise can lead to bad habits, some of them incurable—trying to repeat that thing you did so marvelously. Blame hurts and confuses. A talented beginner like Alan Lelchuk (author of *American Mischief*) must wonder if he can do anything right and whether it's worth going on at all. Owing to some garish pretrial publicity (largely of his own making—but what does Literature care about that?), he was set upon as an elder and not as a first novelist. His novel was read for the most part without care or sympathy and consigned to the pit. A writer with a large advance is assumed to be able to take it.

Conversely, a veteran like Jerzy Kosinski finds bad reviews, as he finds most things, a source of bitter amusement. "At least they can't arrest me for it," he says saturninely. They can't in fact lay a glove on him. When a review makes Kosinski sound like the village idiot, the reader's curiosity is only mildly aroused: what did the reviewer miss? (In the last case, *The Devil Tree,* he missed Kosinski's fiendish impersonation of an Ivy League student writer's sensibility and thought those clichés were coming from Kosinski himself.)

Established writers will reach their audience somehow, so it's quite in order to rough them up a little. But some bloodbaths are almost too painful to watch, as when Helen Vendler made the mighty Allen Tate's whole career sound like a waste of time (a gamble the best poets take, all or nothing. Still, it hurts to be thought to lose), and some are downright implausible, as when Richard Poirier in a recent *New Republic* refused to see any merit whatever in Alfred Kazin. Famous writers bleed when they're cut, like anyone else, if you manage to puncture the thick skin. Or maybe it's knowing that somebody out there wants to hurt you that does the trick.

Anyway, these are occupational risks in a very rough game, and according to Lord Byron, nobody ever died of them: not while cirrhosis is around to compete with. There is a much deadlier reviewing device making the rounds these days, debasing the whole literary transaction, and let's call it with suitable banality the ratings game. To read that Sven Angst may be the number-two Swedish novelist, surpassing even Igmar Klutz, may be O.K. It means we have five minutes to take in the Swedish scene before the guests arrive. But to find this applied to our own writers is to wonder where tourism ceases.

When a reviewer says that Malamud is second only to Bellow, it means he isn't really thinking about either of them. When he's reading Malamud he's thinking about Bellow, and when he's reading Bellow he's thinking about Roth. This is the essence of the ratings game: distraction. Children play it all the time. "Is this the biggest bridge in the world?" "No, it's the third biggest." "Oh." They lose all interest in the bridge.

Malamud is a pleasure unto himself, and Bellow has nothing to do with it. You don't rate sunsets, you enjoy them or curse them on their own merits. But a reviewer will do anything to avoid looking a text in the eye. He will drag in authors from Malaysia and the Cinque Portes. "A bit like the early Waugh . . . the late Firbank . . . dare one say Chekhov?" he babbles. Anything but the unique experience of the book before him.

And when he runs out of apples and pears, he starts playing the banana against itself. Perhaps so-and-so's finest to date. Or else, a decided disappointment after his classic *Nonesuch.* In his fever to place the book next to its right number, he forgets to tell you which scenes work and which don't, and whether the writer has honored his intention —which may be a harder one to pull off than the theme of his classic but facile *Nonesuch.* E. M. Forster regarded all his books as quite distinct tasks well or ill done and not as sinister indices of growth or decline, and reviewers should at least see what he meant before proceeding.

Of course, books do illuminate each other and Fashion had to bounce back from the New Criticism, with its divinization of the Text and nothing but the Text. But you get no illumination from the ratings system, only the gloomy bangings of a playground seesaw. Item. The gifted Don DeLillo is currently being punished for not writing *End Zone* again. His new book, *Great Jones Street,* is a fascinating attempt to do something entirely different, but it won't relieve him of his albatross. If he wrote a seed catalogue, he'd be told it wasn't as good as *End Zone.*

All this tends to confirm something cramped and anxious about our reading habits, which probably traces back to schooldays. "Milton was the greatest poet in the seventeenth century. His greatest achievement was. . . ." Enough. Eventually you have to tell your son that this is not the longest ball game ever played or maybe even the best. It is fatally flawed in the ninth inning. However, it's the only game we happen to have right now, and it fills the moment as full as a great game would, even sharing some of the same textures. If you don't enjoy it, you wouldn't enjoy a great game either, except for its damn greatness.

Something like this should be brought to the season's books, replacing our customary *Guinness Book of World Records* approach. After reeling and gasping from the reviews, I was surprised to find that this spring's masterpieces were not all that far from the disasters. A reviewer may have his reasons for raving—nobody would pay to read the kind of sober assessments authors think they want—but that's no excuse for taking him seriously. Enjoy the show, if you can. If he's a professional like Kazin or Simon, you get a little more. You'll know his standards, his code language, and his high competence and can steer by that. Yet even the best critics have been heard to say in real life, "I wish you'd read it and tell me what you think." Omniscience is on the calling card, along with the tricks and novelties; but between trash and Shakespeare, there is much uncertainty. Just buy a "deeply flawed" novel this week and see for yourself.

1973

3 / *Howe's Complaint*

"This is the novel the author always wanted to write, and we should now be glad he's gotten it over with and can get on with the ones he doesn't want to write." This kind of sentence has been going around a lot lately and is a menace to health. The particular example is plucked from my own past—probably one of the silliest sentences I ever committed. (Note especially the glib fatuity of "doesn't want to write," as if that insured a good book.)

It all comes under the chopped-liver heading: Reviewer's Instructions to Author. In the bracing tones of a juvenile magistrate, we tell the shivering wretch out there to forget his nasty little mistake as quickly as possible and get on with the book we all know he can write. The mistake in question may have cost him his last pint of blood, his wife, and his self-respect, and he may seriously doubt he has the strength for another assault. Never mind that: this sunken-cheeked ruin shall not be spared his pep-talk and his hearty slap on the butt from us.

Probably no one has received more such cumbersome advice than Philip Roth. Roth was cursed early with "promise," which Cyril Connolly once compared to "the medieval hangman who, having settled the noose, pushed his victim off the platform and jumped on his back."

With the precocious promise of *Goodbye, Columbus,* Roth embarked on a career of disappointing people indefinitely.

Recently, the estimable Irving Howe put it all together in a kind of "Best of Philip Roth Advice" piece in *Commentary.* Being lectured by Howe is no joke. He not only argues mordantly—bites like a bulldog in fact—but with a note of grouchy integrity which suggests he isn't doing it for fun. You feel you must have done something very bad to have aroused this decent, serious man.

Much of what Howe says is just, not to say wearyingly intelligent. Yet it finally comes down to the kind of criticism a writer can only stare blankly at—the kind that doesn't speak to his real possibilities, but seems to be about somebody else altogether. For instance, Mr. Howe accuses Roth of dealing superficially with Jewish life, with not exploring, say, the real pathos of Mrs. Sophie Portnoy. But what would have happened to the book's manic drive, its unique tone, if he had done that? *Portnoy* would have been a more sensitive book under Howe's guidance but sensitive books are a dime a dozen. Roth tried a couple himself in *Letting Go* and *When She Was Good,* and Mr. Howe himself admits they were not very successful. Yet those are the very books he seems to want Roth to write again and again, never mind whether he does them well or not, simply because they are a superior kind of book.

Are funny books of any value at all? Howe uses the donnish phrase "amusing, but" a couple of times, which suggests that humor had better watch its step around him. It had, for openers, better tell us something about the human condition and all that great stuff. But unfortunately, much first-rate humor tells us nothing at all about the human condition, unless to lie about it, and is chronically superficial to boot: Mr. Portnoy's bowel movements, if humor they be, may have a tragic explanation, but we don't want to hear it. Not in this book.

Humor also demands quick recognitions or stereotypes, than which nothing could be more superficial. Howe chides Roth for making Mrs. Patimkin (in *Goodbye*) a Hadassah lady, which he likens to writing about blacks in the watermelon patch. Well, admittedly Hadassah is a frowsy epithet by now—for which Roth may be partly to blame (when *Goodbye* first appeared, Howe found it "ferociously exact"; now he finds it full of comic hand-me-downs. Handed down by whom?). But the kind of nuanced Jewish satire Howe would presumably prefer would be lost outside the Jewish community. So too, a Catholic or Mason must stick to the known, if he wants to make a public joke. Does this mean that public jokes have to be, in Howe's word, vulgar? Of course. His definition of vulgar, "the impulse to submit the rich substance of human experience, sentiment [etc.] to a radically reductive levelling or simplification," takes in just about every joke I know.

But of course, as Howe rightly says, Roth comes on as something more than a comedian and cannot be granted full Woody Allen immunity. I agree. What I don't understand is why Howe can't see this as a real artistic problem for the author rather than a moral defect. Roth is a comedian as well as a novelist, and the novelist must make his fictions out of the clown's simplicities. Roth has tried every way he knows to get his Panza and Quixote onto the same horse, but one of them usually falls off. Without his clown, as in *When She Was Good,* Roth doesn't quite make the weight. With Sancho up, as in *Portnoy,* the woeful knight slides gracefully off the horse's rump.

Howe accuses Roth of choosing an "audience" rather than "readers," and certainly his reputation as a baby tycoon suggests opportunism of a sort. Yet the striking thing about Roth's career is his vagrant choice of subjects, almost as though he were trying to shake off his audience. *The Breast,* for instance, reads like a most earnest attempt to shed any easy popularity he'd gained from *Portnoy.* Likewise, where another writer might have exploited the vein of *Goodbye, Columbus* unto 70 times Singer, he abruptly abandoned it, on the admirable Kipling principle that when you've mastered something, you should do something else. Perhaps he goes for the big money to insure against failure.

Portnoy itself might be taken for something of a hustle, except I'm told that the author had reason to believe it wouldn't be published at all. Perhaps for this reason he sold it piecemeal to magazines at no great profit, the book acquiring thereby its major defect, a lack of growth and development. Roth was obliged to set the table and trot out the characters again and again, with all their crotchets relabeled, until they did begin to look like stock comic figures. Maybe a more saintly craftsman would have written over the cracks for book form, but it would have meant throwing out some great material, which is a lot to ask of a writer, and it might have damaged the delicate structure of the monologues. Critics should look to these technical problems before they reach for the moral ones.

Roth's one complete aberration was *Our Gang,* and I can't begin to explain it. It seems like the kind of snappy idea one might have at a party, which the great god Pan usually erases mercifully by morning. But it points up the problematic nature of Roth's gift: he is not precisely a satirist, nor exactly a pure humorist, just someone who has to keep on looking for things he can do.

People talk about talent as though it were some neutral substance that can be applied to anything. But talent is narrow and only functions with a very few subjects, which it is up to the writer to find. In this respect, Philip Roth's career is both honorable and adventurous. His new book, *The Great American Novel,* struck me as happy material for Roth. The opening depends too much on verbal virtuosity which, surprisingly, Roth hasn't got in great quantities. ("I am a plodder," said Scott Fitzgerald. For all his dazzle, Roth strikes me as a plodder too.) But the myth that follows, of a missing baseball league like Atlantis, gives scope to his galloping imagination, driven humor, cold heart. (His other heart, the warm one, just never works as well.) The delicate boy with the dirty mouth has found himself another Subject.

In the humor section of the same *Commentary,* Roth was accused of being anti-American, but this is like calling Dickens anti-English. There is no other frame of reference for Roth, no world outside America. It is his Universe, his Good and Evil. Howe says he lacks a culture, but we all lack one these days. That is his very material: the first generation to try winging it without a culture. And for it he can hardly pitch his voice in the sonorous tones of a major writer. An anxious wise guy, a quintessential punk with a fast, shallow mind is more like it. And don't think it doesn't take craft and hard work and real literary intelligence for Roth to achieve that effect.

Anyway, Howe would know better than to call Roth anti-American himself. What really saddens Howe is that Roth has lost Europe, a sadness we all share in our different modes, the Assimilation Blues. Like an immigrant father confiscating comic books, Howe dismisses the culture that the Roths have put together over here, out of old box scores and radio shows and B movies, a barbarous culture perhaps but rich in legend and catch-phrase for the novelist to transmute if he can. The title *Great American Novel* is one more gag for the punk to throw at the elder. Can one make a great novel out of such flashing surfaces and carnival geegaws and neon strips? Who knows? As Tommy Dorsey once said to the serious conductor, after a gorgeous trombone tremolo, "It's the way we do it in Roseland."

1973

4 / *The Company of Writers*

A recent correspondent accused Capricorn here of having a lazy mind, and God knows it's true. This month, I'm not even going to try to think, but will talk instead about the plight of the writer—which can be done while cracking nuts and whistling the "Grand Canyon Suite."

"Toil, envy, want, the patron and the jail," is how Sam Johnson, blues singer, described the writer's life. Then there was Joseph Conrad, comparing writing to carrying heavy bales under a low rope on a hot day. (I'll admit *reading* Conrad can be like that, for all that it's worth it. If "easy writing makes damn hard reading," your hard writing can be a real mother.)

Writers are never more impressive than when moaning their own fate. To the general public, this may seem like the journalists who gripe about the toilets at the Royal Yacht Club—you're lucky to be there at all, Jack. O.K. Yet allowing that the lonely road of the writer has points over the crowded road of the commuter, and that there's no substitute for sleeping late, Dr. Johnson's list still holds up fairly well. Let jail be an English department and toil what they make you do there—brushing away students' tears, gagging over their prose, etc.—the rest can be taken fairly straight.

Envy? Oh yes. Wanton. "Every time a friend succeeds I die a little." Only a writer could have said that. In fact, I thought I'd said it myself, only to learn that Gore Vidal had beaten me to it by years—the upstart. And in a sense La Rochefoucauld beat us both, when he said "it is not enough to succeed; a friend must also fail."

One reason the human race has such a low opinion of itself is that it gets so much of its wisdom from writers. No foreclosing banker ever said anything more mean-spirited than La Rochefoucauld's "in the misfortune of our best friends, we find something which is not displeasing to us." Is that so, you old toad? Does that include terminal diseases or just minor fractures?

Never mind, it's just a writer talking. I asked one of the most generous ones I know how he felt when a friend's book was panned, and he told me his heart leaped like a fawn. You should hear the others; or hear for contrast the hollow congratulations on a triumph, and the murmurs of "why *him?*" along the rim of the room.

There are solid reasons for this professional vice, beyond the ego that art normally and naturally builds to protect itself. Painters apparently despise other painters as a matter of course, and think no more about it. (I'm told it's the very devil to get a painter to propose a colleague for an award. Writers do it all the time.) Musicians bad-mouth each other with vigor but are not called on to review each other's performances.

It is the special curse of writers that they need each other in the tawdriest way and are smart enough to know it. Besides the unseemly scuffle for jacket quotes, there is the endless Guggenheim grope and the NBA crawl and finally the academic one-step, all the bits and scraps of livelihood which depend on the recommendations of other writers. Think of it: a writer in a million like you having to crawl to a burned-out old pot like so-and-so, it hones your malice to diamond sharpness.

Then again, as La Rochefoucauld might have said, if one cannot prevent a rival's success, one can at least try to seem responsible for it. So you get the occasional grotesque reversals where a writer overpraises a friend to the point where the friend begins to seem like a protégé, leading to mutual resentments that only a writer could love. For never forget: a maker of fictions lives on mischief and can find it in a desert, like an aborigine sensing the next meal. "Writers perpetuate trouble like nobody else," said Thurber, and Thurber knew.

But behind all this devilment lurk want and the patron. In my maundering researches, I asked a well-known songwriter whether there was much envy in *his* profession, and he said, "No—we were all too rich." True. When a song is played on the jukebox, the creator collects his tithe, whether he's Cole Porter's estate or Tex Outhouse. When a book is borrowed from the library, unto seven times seven, the author gets nothing but the price of one copy and a sniveling note from a reader saying he doesn't understand women. And he will be looking for teaching jobs in New Mexico in his seventies while Tex plays golf in Bermuda.

Writers would probably talk about money anyway, because money's every movement is dramatic and its stillness downright terrifying, but they mightn't talk about it quite so much if they had any. (For instance, I'm told businessmen think about it less than writers.) Money-talk is also a demure form of boasting, as a shorthand for "how'm I doing?—better than you, I trust." But more than that, it represents steadily leaking anxiety. There is no pension plan for writers, no talent depletion allowance—in fact some of them can't even get credit at Bloomingdale's. "No writer leads a charmed life," said Edmund Wilson; but you don't have to tell writers that. A fellow I know wrote a best seller in the forties and can't get published at all now, in his Golden Years. He looks like a ragpicker. And one of the more famous names in American letters recently startled a roomful of people by half shouting, "Why don't you all phone me? I'm home all day. I'm in the book."

For vintage bitterness, brewed to a fine vinegar, you can't match an aging, over-the-hill writer. The charming Edwardian poet Alfred Noyes used to read bus tickets to his students and pretend they were written by T. S. Eliot. "You see—you couldn't tell the difference, could you, could you?" he cackled. But in fact, you need be neither old nor over the hill to achieve this state. No amount of success is enough for some writers: the most brutally petty remarks have come from the Hemingways and Tolstoys, the uneasy kings, suspicious even of the dead, not to mention young pretenders. There is only room for one on the Magic Mountain.

As for age—our skittish reading and publishing habits have turned many young writers to vinegar while still on the vine. Calling a kid a "major new talent" may be all in the day's work to a flap-jawed blurb writer. But the kid will take it too seriously; and when his second book is rejected and his third, he will wither like a crone. Eventually he may go festering off to some English Department with a heart full of hate and write letters like the one I got recently saying, "Goddam it, Sheed, why have you gone downhill like that? Why has everyone gone downhill?"

Meanwhile, to keep authors' eyes green and shiny, there are the unexplained successes: an amiable lightweight book like Dan Jenkins's *Semi-Tough,* festooned with back-slapping quotes from the boys at the literary Athletic Club, which rises on the charts like an air bubble. The same year a fine novel, Gilbert Sorrentino's *Imaginative Qualities of Actual Things,* slipped out almost unnoticed. Sorrentino's subject was, ironically, the fervid envies and betrayals that circulate among fringe writers, and it probably cost him a couple of friends who thought the book was a betrayal (which it probably was—it being part of its own subject matter), and if it paid for a new typewriter and dinner for two at Horn & Hardart, it did better than some. Bitter, baby. And there are so many others: but to name them is to make them sound like losers. Yet put them in a room with Irving Wallace and old Irving won't feel like a winner.

What I've completely omitted in this piece, because it's no fun to write about, is the extraordinary amount of honest admiration there is in this profession, and how much disinterested help you can reasonably hope for. I won't list the twenty kindest writers, because they don't want to be bothered, but it would be a cinch and a pleasure. The only thing is, once they help you up there, don't be surprised if they say, "What's so good about him? I thought his latest was a disappointment, didn't you? And talking of latests, have you seen mine?" It is our nature, like scorpions. Otherwise, you couldn't ask for a nicer bunch.

1973

5 / *New York Blues*

To judge from various snarls and whimpers coming in on the west wind, anti-New York fever is getting worse out there by the minute. It has always puzzled me that hulking agglomerates like Detroit and Cincinnati, many times the size of ancient Athens, don't have their own distinctive cultures. But it seems that New York is in some way preventing them from this, and I'd like to know why.

"You think you're so hot," says a heckler in Chicago (a city that ought to know better), but actually few New Yorkers give it a thought. Would it help if we were humbler and thought more about the Midwest? Is there anything we can do? I hate to be responsible for keeping Cincinnati down.

Meanwhile, there probably is a New York, but it is not what it seems. In a recent book on the subject called *The End of Intelligent Writing,* Richard Kostelanetz makes it sound like a tale of intrigue in an old folks' home, with wizened literati scheming behind locked doors, but this (unless I've missed something) is much too lively. It leaves out the randomness and drift, the sheer, as it were, deadness.

One of Kostelanetz's ace Machiavellis, Jason Epstein (who draws huge crowds by protesting his innocence), can usually be found in Sag Harbor, tending his plants and working on a history of Eastern Long Island. Impossible to tell what the man is really thinking. Here at the Power Center, the vagueness is downright English: a conspiracy theorist would go slowly mad looking for a design in *The New York Times Book Review.* And yet it might seem like the German High Command compared with *The New Yorker,* where, one suspects, one is ushered down various corridors and into a broom closet (read Brendan Gill's jolly book *Here at The New Yorker* for details).

As for the famous feud between *Commentary* and *The New York Review of Books,* it is political, not literary (Kostelanetz is right about this, I think), and besides which, it is quite dead. It serves only as a prime example of how small, serious matters can be teased into pop entertainment for the out-of-towners. In his breezy, gum-snapping book, *Intellectual Sky Writing,* Philip Nobile managed to make it sound like a spat between *Playboy* and *Penthouse.* The personal falling out of Epstein and Norman Podhoretz was made central, because personalities are everything in the magic of Gotham. The heavy political issues could thus be animated, Luce-style, for the sake of the busy reader.

Actually, if you tread between the smartcracks, you will find a sad story even in Nobile's book. This was no hair-pulling contest, but a battle of political principle that broke more than one good friendship. The counterculture popped up as an issue, but only symbolically (*The New York Review* never really liked the damned stuff). The real wedge was Vietnam, and perhaps behind that Israel. What it emphatically was *not* was Epstein's manners or Podhoretz's vanity. These are, for better or worse, serious men.

But as soon as it was presented as a colorful clash of egos, of talented babies, the nation could fling into its favorite stance of feverish condescension toward New York intellectual life. How parochial, the cry goes up, and how basically unimportant! In fact hundreds of people write in to say how unimportant it is, all the way from Fiji. One should do so well with important subjects. At *Commonweal,* where I used to work, a breakthrough article on Latin America usually drew one letter, perhaps from the ex-president himself. A dull subject, like Burton and Taylor (or its theological equivalent), drew stacks of mail from all over.

Kostelanetz contributes something more to the mythology of New York—adding a Godfather touch that is more intriguing than anything I've found in real life. If he is right, your reporter has been wandering like some Lemuel Pitkin through Mafia gunfire without knowing it. I have contributed to both *The New York Review* and *Commentary* (until a falling out with Podhoretz that got some silly ink in its own right); was I being co-opted by the Mob as a token Youth? or as Catholic window dressing? Then again, since I have also written for *The New Yorker* and *The New York Times,* I may be at the very heart of the Mob. In which case I would of course deny its existence (see *The End of Intelligent Writing,* page 80). Yet I am disappointed to find I don't make Kostelanetz's establishment chart even as an outer onion skin

Could this be because his book is published by Sheed & Ward, my parents' former firm? Well, you can see where conspiracy theories lead you if you're not careful. Kostelanetz himself admits that New York is much more complicated than his single-Mob theory permits. At one point, he talks of "two literary New Yorks." And in another he suggests a town brimming over with establishments—some consisting of no more than one husband and wife (no names please). An establishment of One may not be altogether out of the question when the husband or wife dies.

That is the point. You can only beat New York with another New York; you can only beat an establishment with another establishment. In the second half of his book, Kostelanetz takes us on a useful tour of the avant-garde and the underrated, and it stretches for miles. No book editor could possibly cope with it. Someone will have to do what the author himself hesitates to do—winnow it, cut it to size, cram it into one or two magazines: then wait for the stuffiness and backbiting to set in.

If such a new establishment does form, it had better not leave out Kostelanetz. This is what finally makes his book interesting—the desolate feeling of outsidedness, even though he claims to have hundreds of young writers on his side, and readers too. Couldn't they all simply bypass New York and set up their own fruitstand?

They do, of course, all over the place—more people seem to be founding magazines than reading them—but still the noses are pressed against the windows of the old people's club, the old *Partisan Review* club, which may be dying but is still felt to run New York like some withered Tammany. And if this is how it looks from a few inches away, how must it look from the outback?

New York may just be a national obsession like London or Paris, a place you have to conquer even if it's rotten, a place where wondrously evil things *must* be going on. I know that when writers exile themselves from it, moving only so far as Connecticut, they develop horrible fantasies in no time flat.

"What are they saying about me? You mean—they're not saying *anything* about me?" Forgotten are the cocktail parties where the same free-loaders hunt in packs while the top people stay home watching *Kojak;* forgotten too the new secretary who sends your book out to the wrong reviewer, or the lazy reviewer who doesn't get round to reading it in time. "The *Times* has it in for me," croaks your man, conjuring visions of Ochses and Sulzbergers drawing fingers across their throats at the mention of his name. Magazines take on personalities out there, and one pictures nothing less than a full board meeting setting their Chumley policy, or whatever your name is, for the year.

In fact, what you actually get is often a tired young woman from Jersey who doesn't know or care what the magazine's editorial policy is (she might feel she had to resign if she knew), confronted with an ever-fresh mound of first novels by unknown authors and no instructions —unless you call "we're very high on this book here at Rhomboid" instructions. Her job is simply to get literate reviews at bargain prices, free of spite and logrolling ("You mean you didn't know they fought a duel at Vassar?") from unpredictable amateurs or reliable hacks. She is not, whatever the results, out to get you.

This is your dreaded New York power, for the most part—and even the famous powerhouses are not so much more impressive. And if Cincinnati feels inferior to that, it should be ashamed of itself.

1975

6 / *Four Hacks*

Are all the blockbusting best sellers written by the same person? Not necessarily. The fact that all their authors give the exact same interview should not blind one to exotic varieties of plumage and even character. For instance.

Picture, if you will, the worst: four major hacks passing through New York at the same time—passing through the same hotel room in fact—celebrating their latest smasheroos. Their interlocutor is a pale literary man with a business suit and a heartful of hate because he has to work for a living. The others look so much like authors you could eat them.

First, Irving Trustfund dressed in regulation poncho and love beads, sucking thoughtfully on his meerschaum. *How goes it, Irving? Did you read those lousy reviews? Aren't you ashamed of yourself this time?* "Not at all," says Irving with his famous strained smile. "Dickens and Zola were despised by the critics of their day, you know. I'm happy to leave the verdict to the people—the *real* people, that is. Dickens was just too popular for the self-appointed pseudo-intellectuals of the day—I don't mean you, sir. You look like a *real* intellectual." Irving's poncho is suddenly drenched. He hates to make enemies. "I have enormous respect for real intellectuals," he ends miserably.

Now for Peaches Smedley, concocter of sexy gothics, swathed for town in see-through vinyl. *I hear your crap is coming back, Miss Smedley. How do you account for this sickening lapse in public taste?* "Why, I believe my so-called crap was never really gone, Mr., er, Snead. People, I mean the people *out there,* have always relished a good yarn told at a crackling pace and with lots of real characters. That's the tradition I place myself in—the robust storytelling tradition of Dickens and, er, others."

Is it true that your stuff is also dirty as hell? "If you think that the love of a man for a woman is dirty, Mr., er, yes, my stuff is dirty, gloriously, life-enhancingly dirty. I myself happen to think that the real pornographers are the munitions makers and the politicians who poison our air and that we shouldn't be ashamed of our bodies."

"Effing A-OK to that, sweetie," says our third, Percy Fang, in captain's hat and Castro fatigues, biting down hard on his corncob. "I don't know why we're wasting time on this loser anyway, Peaches. How much money you make last year, Jack? Not as much as Dickens, I'll bet. That's what you people forget about effing Dickens every time. The guy was mad for the moola. Couldn't get enough of the long green. That's a real artist, baby. No one ever wrote a great book in a garret. Charlie knew that. Yet would you believe, Mr. Pale-faced Loser, that the guy the critics went for in those days was a certain Colly Cibber?"

Sharply. *What do you know about Colly Cibber?*

Guardedly. "Plenty."

Next, Aldershott Twilley, the English hack laureate, half-buried in tweed, puffing on his briarpatch: "Oh Lord yes, how they hated Dickens. Because the chap was first and last a born storyteller, you know. They can't stand that. These youngsters today have completely forgotten how to tell a story. They slap down whatever comes into their bally heads, if that's the portion of the anatomy they use, whurf whurf, and expect busy people with real concerns to take them seriously."

By youngsters, I guess you mean Joyce and Stein?

"Yes, yes, all that lot. Joyce was absolutely potty, of course. And as for Stein—what's that marvelous limerick about her: With my Rumpty tittlety. . . ."

Peaches Smedley: "I happen to have terrific respect for James Joyce. In fact, I sometimes think of myself as belonging to that tradition in a way. Joyce, Flaubert. . . ."

Jesus.

Trustfund: "I happen to agree wholeheartedly. I learned a lot from Joyce, and from Kafka too and from all those great writers. And do you know why? Do you know what they were writing about? They were writing about *people!*"

Twilley: "Absolutely potty."

Fang: "Joyce is A-OK with me. He told it like it is in the sack, and that's the name of the game. The sack is where it's at for a real writer."

Trustfund: "I absolutely agree. If by sack you mean all the inexhaustibly multifaceted aspects of. . . ."

Fang: "By sack I mean sack. What do you think Keats was writing about, fella, and Gerard de Nerval and all those guys? S-A-C-K. Ever hear of Gerard de Nerval, paleface? He was pretty far into sex, I hear."

Fang has a reputation for turning interviews into shambles at this point, so the interlocutor changes the subject nimbly.

Hobbies, Ms. Smedley? "Well, people, mostly. For instance, I'd love to be interviewing *you* right now."

Muttered. *You would be, if there was any justice.*

Smedley: "And books, of course. I'm never without a book. Bishop Andrewes, Mrs. Gaskell, anything at all."

Working methods, Mr. Twilley?

Twilley: "Well, old Dickens had the answer to that as to so many things. Four, five thousand words a night. Work your arse off, dear boy, it won't kill you."

Trustfund: "It's true, modern writers do tend to coddle themselves. Genius is a robust flower, all the giants knew that instinctively."

What about Joyce and his four books?

Trustfund: "Well, there are giants and giants of course."

Twilley: "Joyce was a bloody little twit if you ask me."

Fang: "He was too busy in the sack, which is where I'd be myself if I had any sense."

Eyes Smedley, who turns away in undisguised horror. Fang is bent on his shambles: it's only a question of time now.

Critics, Ms. Smedley?

Smedley: "To be frank, I don't read them. They're such sad little people. So full of envy."

I read somewhere that bad reviews make you cry?

Smedley (uncertainly): "Well, as I say, I don't read them."

Twilley: "Neither do I. I'm much too busy writing novels myself. Do you know the old Welsh saying that goes, 'Those who can do. . . .' "

All (roaring): ". . . and those who can't, teach."

Twilley: "Oh, you'd heard that one?"

Hobbies, Mr. Trustfund?

Trustfund: "Merovingian porcelains, anything bearing on the Icelandic comic spirit. . . ."

Working methods, Ms. Smedley?

Smedley: "Five or six thousand words a day. Work your arse off."

Twilley: "Dickens."

Trustfund: "Dickens and *Zola,* I tell you.

Fang (pouncing on Smedley): "Here I come, ready or not."

You're nothing but a pack of cards. You're nothing but. . . . The cat, which had been Peaches Smedley only a moment before, stares at me levelly. I have been shaking the bejasus out of her ever since I stepped into Jacqueline Susann's looking glass a few weeks back in *The Times Magazine* and had my head straightened out by Humpty Dumpty. (Incidentally, that guy Lewis Carroll certainly knew how to get out of a dream sequence, and I'd like to acknowledge my debt to him and Theodore Dreiser right now.)

Some conclusions now from a pseudo-elitist. Although hacks vary enormously in quality, such that a Herman Wouk might reasonably reject the title and a Mickey Spillane can barely claim it, they seem to share a certain turbid homogeneity of thought and phrase which perhaps explains their popularity. Since, by me, straight oompapa storytelling is a perfectly respectable craft, I hate to see its artisans driven to these monstrosities of defensiveness. At the same time, they must know in their sweetbreads that their line traces from Dumas and Rider Haggard and not from the grand masters of language and social observation and felt madness. Dickens in particular has earned his rest from this kind of talk.

We could certainly use a good analysis of the pops in terms of their own function—but no more, please, from the hacks themselves: solemn Jack Bennys all, who think that owning a Stradivarius and a townhouse makes you Isaac Stern, and makes of "Love in Bloom" a worthy successor to Beethoven's "Pastoral" and the other rattling good tunes that made the West.

1973

7/ *The Novel of Manners*

Joe Heller writes in: "I was already seriously considering a novel of manners until you just pronounced the novel of manners dead. Maybe, though, I'll continue with it *because* it's dead."

That sounds about right. In fact, Heller has already written such a novel. *Something Happened* is precisely that—a dead novel of manners. Its characters maneuver for status like ghouls in a mausoleum. One poor wretch signals his failure, as with a leper's bell, by invariably wearing the wrong clothes. The hero, Bob Slocum, claws his way through the web of power and fear known as "manners" in order to give a three-minute speech at the company convention.

The bit players are called things like Mr. Brown and Mr. Green, indicating pieces in a game, and this is perhaps a little *too* dead. People who work in such organizations are actually named after long and interesting numbers.

But, anyway, we bookfolk will not settle for last year's satire, however pertinent. We've already done dehumanization (like pollution) and we can't do it again. We want a satire for the future, however aimless and untrue.

Heller, a book person himself, seems to have felt the same thing. (His career maps cultural history like the traces of a glacier.) Back in the Pleistocene Age, when the book began, office satire was very much the thing. But since we all moved to Stamford, the Family took over, and so Heller changed his crawl to that direction, producing to my mind an extraordinary piece of work.

The subject is still manners, the tearing down and building up of protocols, and the application of management techniques to living people. Slocum tries the same silky manipulations and power grabs at home, but his son is too good for them, and his wife too slyly vague, while his daughter resorts to anti-manners, the paralyzing weapon of the young. Slocum is rendered helpless by her lethal blasts of rudeness. Love, the alternative to manners, is unfortunately beyond him, buried under layers of performance. Or else lost in the mail room.

Reactions to *Something Happened* have been so disproportionate that one senses some nonliterary nerve being tapped. Heller's droning repetitions obviously have something to do with it—yet these match the set phrases people actually use and the set thoughts behind the phrases: those obsessions lined up like toothaches which one's tongue returns to maddeningly. In Heller, manners is what you do while playing with your toothaches, to keep you from boring and maiming other people, and some readers may feel that a whole book about this is just too damn cute and nerve-racking.

Well, so is life, according to Heller and I daresay to many people. Amy Vanderbilt's sad death prompted me to check out the sales of her etiquette book, which is as airless and obsessive as any Heller, and I was mildly astonished to hear that some 2,750,000 are in print and moving —especially around June. (How many people in novels still get married in June?)

Which leads one to suppose that the fusspots are still out there as numerous as ever, although keeping a low profile for now. The tyranny of temperament in this country distorts these perspectives. When I was a kid, everybody had to be funny and laconic, with some truly excruciating results. Then came the mystic-sincere takeover, and people dropped Wit with a clatter.

In each case, maybe a tenth of the populace was calling the tune for the rest; and, in each case, it was hard times for etiquette. When Vanderbilt's last edition appeared, *The New York Times* reviewer summed up both temperaments: he laughed at it the old way, and then he said that, what with Vietnam and all, manners really seem pretty trivial. Such a reader hits you both ways like the Alka-Seltzer villains. Facetious and earnest, programmed equally for Bangladesh and The Scene—the reviewer spoke for all of us just then.

Meanwhile, the flower arrangers have gone quietly about their business, raking in a fortune from June brides and other extinct creatures. They too have had their season on top, when everyone bent to their whims. To judge from the publication dates, the great heydays of etiquette books came in the Gilded Age and again after the two wars. Leaving aside waves of immigration and social climbing, etc., the common factor would seem to be the promise of leisure, which etiquette promptly expands to fill.

By any rational standard, Jane Austen's characters had nothing to do; yet no one has ever put in a more hectic day, writing letters, deciding who should pay the first visit, sneering. And in Henry James, the in-between, cigarette-lighting bits that novelists still have trouble with are crammed with protocol: should he send his calling card or wait for theirs? And how long? This was not make-weight stuff, stuck in to keep the dialogue apart, but variously voluptuous and dramatic, depending on who had the whip hand.

It doesn't look as if that kind of leisure is going to come back, though we may get another kind, which will breed its own etiquette. (Who will write the first novel of manners about welfare?) But manners remains the preeminently American subject in good times and bad. The need to live and trade with strangers has forced it on us, and Americans are often surprised, in contrast, by the gut rudeness of Europeans. ("Bunch of bloody incense burners" I had my religion described to me by some young gentleman at Oxford. Or how about this, same place: "You're not having tea with that smelly black man are you?" Poignant, because my questioner had not bathed in at least two weeks.)

The American alertness to manners can still produce at least one sort of novel—the novel of bad manners. After all, only the descendants of Wharton and James could have produced a whole counterculture devoted to this subject. And no dowager ever made one more conscious of saying the wrong thing or expressing the not-quite-right attitude as a hippie in full feather. "Oh, man, you just don't *know*"—the strains of Emily Post still linger in that one. Remember: it wasn't just that you could have whatever manners you chose, good or bad; you had to have *none* and the right kind of none. "Man, those beads are too much."

Small wonder the next generation couldn't stand the strain and have gone to law school.

Meanwhile, one awaits an exquisite novel of manners from a hippie commune, where they must in effect have reinvented manners from scratch—both as traffic direction (passing the yogurt cannot *always* be an existential decision based on love) and as the ritual which mankind routinely attaches to eating, drinking, coupling. For instance, I've heard several complaints about the ceremonial smoking of pot—the moans of "mmm, good grass," the dreamy passing of the joint, geared to the most bovine member. There have been good nonfiction accounts of this, but there is still room for some apostate to get his stuff together and do us a real Marquand about how Ms. So-and-so wouldn't wash the dishes and laughed at exorcisms.

Meanwhile, back to Amy Vanderbilt. Recent promo material suggests that the latest edition is really into all this and now deals with such spicy matters as sex in college and, Lord have mercy, "snooping." But "dealing with" would be putting it a bit strongly. It turns out that sex in college can be cured by a mature approach, while snooping (which means reading over someone's shoulder!) is best parried by looking at the bounder "with raised eyebrows." This really is her world, the raised eyebrow and the icy frown, and I entered it with a sort of desolate pleasure, as with Heller. "He [a gentleman] does not poke her [any her, I guess] in the ribs to make a point—nor does he do this to a man either if he has any sensitivity." That's talking. "Playful gestures of pushing or punching he might do with another man he should never indulge in publicly with his wife." Right on. I don't want to hear about pot smoking from Amy Vanderbilt.

And the same goes for Emily Post, or whatever passes under that name these days, whose latest volume features *inter alia* "human relationships." That stuff we can get in the street. The only relationships we want from Miss Post are the grueling ones between knife and fork, glove and mustache. We want to know that Mrs. Rittenhouse lives, materializing majestically at weddings and funerals, telling us, like Ecclesiastes, when and how long to weep.

If she doesn't live, except as a well-thumbed manual, and we are now a nation of Grouchos forced to go it alone, one reason may be found in a fascinating book called *The Ordeal of Civility* by John Murray Cuddihy. Cuddihy concentrates on the phenomenon of "Jewish rudeness," but his description applies equally to all tribal peoples, including Scottish clansmen, French peasants, Alan Sillitoe's bicycle workers in Nottingham—in short, most of the world. Such people are inured to loving or hating, but not to the neutral condition known as politeness. Jewish intellectuals, Freudian and Marxist, have simply spearheaded the tribal attack on commercial civility, the treating of even loved ones as strangers.

Hence "doing one's thing" and smelling like a goat. Yet as a Jewish friend points out to me, tribal codes of civility can be just as suffocating as Wasp-cult; and if you think Emily Post is hard to cope with, you should try Confucius. We cannot make do forever with novels about hospitals, where everyone dresses alike and politeness is unknown. The manners-people will be back, in who knows what hideous form. Meanwhile a greedy writer looking for subject matter might consider Post's and Vanderbilt's sales and be wise. That's quite a piece of America, virtually a lost continent, and the world's funniest subject is there for the taking.

1975

8 / *Genre Writers*

In movies, they're called genre writers; in real life they're called hacks. If Alfred Hitchcock wrote novels, he would be herded into a roundup, and thrown in the caboose at the back of the book section. If Agatha Christie made films, she would be the toast of France.

Occasionally some ingenious rogue tries to smuggle a genre hack into literature. In recent months, P. G. Wodehouse, Ross Macdonald, James Cain, and others have all turned up on the front page of *The New York Times Book Review* with prodigious references. Hacks never enter literature in the middle; they can only come in as geniuses. Each of these writers has, in fact, some interesting claims: yet they have it in common that when they are approached as major writers they lose all their strength and don't even seem as good as they are. The first extravagant praise kills them like frost. Whom the gods would destroy, they first oversell.

In the characteristic hack-transfiguration rite, the reviewer himself seems stumped what to say after he's said "genius." Colin MacInnes argued that Wodehouse had created a whole world of his own, but it really seems more of an old world with a fresh coat of words. All these comic servants, fuddled noblemen, and goofy juveniles were staples of the old musical comedies, and Wodehouse is the first to say so. "Musical comedies without the music," he calls his novels. Genre writers are maddeningly unpretentious; it's part of their survival kit.

As a genre recedes, the survivors begin to look unique against the skyline. Whatever Wodehouse may have learned from George Ade or his pal Guy Bolton or from the *Boy's Own Paper* is all his own now. In the economy of pop scholarship one name is easier to remember than twelve: so a Darwin, a Freud, a Wodehouse picks up all the marbles and the surrounding sages and hacks shuffle off to oblivion.

I believe that Wodehouse reigns supreme over a special category: the hacks of genius, whose main characteristic is to melt away under serious discussion. He is probably the most derivative writer since T. S. Eliot. His characters, like W. S. Gilbert's, were imposed on him by the resources of theater repertory. Casting problems make hacks of us all. For instance, Gilbert's obsession with fat, middle-aged ladies has been queried darkly by nontheater-minded critics—yet what else do you do with your contract contralto? Similarly, Wodehouse's characters are so far from being original that the precursors of Arthur Treacher and the late A. E. Matthews probably were playing nothing else long before Wodehouse was born. As to plots, the quasi-Wodehousian *No, No, Nanette* indicates not only P. G.'s banality but his transcendence.

For hackwork done purely enough comes closer to classic art than romantic expressionism even tries to. The Wodehouse types, in their timeless masks, strolling their endless summer lawn—and above all, the author's own rigorous tough-minded artificiality—have the sturdiness of Japanese No theater, while Thomas Wolfe's "feelings" expire like a scream. Sturdiness may not be everything, but it's something. If Wodehouse ever spoke in his own voice (supposing he has an own voice) or inserted a real emotion, his work would die on the instant. Statues live longer than warm-blooded mammals; and even the romantic characters who survive the years tend to have a bit of the statue about them.

Still, he defeats us, because there's nothing to say about him. In the academic astrodome where we all live now, there is no place for the undiscussable writer. The best hacks can't even talk about themselves; they usually sound like plumbers in interviews. I have heard ugly talk about college courses in Kurt Vonnegut—if so, they will zero in on Vonnegut's weakest feature, his explicit thought—but Wodehouse serenely defies the barmiest course deviser. As it stands, his fellow writers love him, being as sick as painters of all this talk *around* art, but the discussable, the writers whose homes you can visit and whose characters you can trace, remain the darlings of the uncreative.

For such, there is at least one trivial fact about Wodehouse to browse on: he went to the same school—Dulwich, near London—as Raymond Chandler. Dulwich criss-crosses class lines interestingly and may be the only English school that could produce masters of both the high and low colloquial. Chandler has practically nothing else to recommend him. His plots and people smell of cheap paper from the pulp magazines where he began life, and his only principle of composition seemed to be the old Edgar Wallace stream of meaningless surprise. His powers of invention were so slight that, on more than one occasion, he retreaded the same humpbacked story and sent it limping out once more.

Yet like Wodehouse and Runyon, he had the run of an artificial language that turned hack's compost to gold. He wasn't that English, of course (I believe he was out of Dulwich in no time), but he had a foreigner's sense of the strangeness of America, and he handled it with a delicacy and wonder that set off its plainness and toughness like rows of precious stones. With this went, I would guess, a timid outsider's sensibility which picked up the American urban horrors louder and brighter than most native receivers. Chandler could not describe a laundromat without freighting it with corruption and menace.

His point of view *was* original—his wish-figure Philip Marlowe is as far from Hammett's Sam Spade as a pretty dream is from a despairing reality—but he has suffered the opposite fate from Wodehouse. Where Wodehouse outlived the competition, the competition only came to life after Chandler, so that he seems more of a hack in retrospect than he was at the time. Sensitive private eyes came snarling out of the nation's libraries, bookish types magically equipped with courage and muscles, and Marlowe was buried.

Which gets us to Ross Macdonald, a gifted post-Chandler mannerist who brings to the form so much calculation and knowingness that it no longer seems hacking, but more like studies in hacking. In his early period *To Find a Victim* he seemed willfully to make himself the perfect trap for hack-snobs—those merry-andrews like the late Evelyn Waugh, who gurgle over such nonentities as Erle Stanley Gardner, like philosophers crowning the village idiot with bay leaves. It was as if Macdonald embodied his own slumming readers and knew exactly what they wanted. His man Lew Archer felt guilty and rotten about his work (as don't we all?) but rather smugly superior to the middle-class sellouts around him. And even these perennially trendy sentiments were not artistically developed, but slapped on like name tags—Nero Wolfe's fatness, Holmes's pipe, Archer's awareness. Only in a detective story could this seem impressive.

Yet as artifice, Macdonald's variations on the Chandler myth were interesting even then. The narrator's similes were more farfetched and stylized, the hero's sensitiveness more laborious and ill-suited to action. Macdonald was nudging the form into pure fiction, where the metaphysical possibilities of private-eyeness could float loose from police radio naturalism. Unfortunately, he was still stuck with a mess of tired conventions. As an L. A. shamus, Archer passed his days and nights climbing in and out of name-brand cars or moseying over sun-dappled patios. It was hard to see how a first-rate writer could willingly trudge through this liturgy in book after book, or keep on drumming up enough whacked-out babes and tough cops to confront—as crippling a ground rule as having to make up, say, a different train conductor for every story.

The next Macdonald I read, *The Zebra-Striped Hearse,* written ten years later, showed that most reassuring of sights, a writer who seemed to know what he was doing. Macdonald had learned to finesse the conventions, so that I didn't feel I was watching a General Motors commercial or a bungalow prospectus. Archer's personality seemed better synthesized with events, and there was less need to take out little ads in the text to describe its features. Macdonald rode looser on the form, introducing scenes and characters for their own sakes, and barely justifying them in terms of plot.

In short, he appeared to be easing out from the safe shallow waters where the hacks paddle in circles and into the gloomy depths of the Novel. The detective-story genre makes a skimpy life belt out there. And indeed, the detection in this later book seemed perfunctory, hardly enough to sustain interest. The hack's first duty, whatever the highbrows may think he's up to, is to his middlebrow client: to do the job he was paid for, tie up the loose ends and wipe off his own fingerprints. Macdonald, like his alter ego Archer, increasingly takes the risk of offering the client something sloppier and more complicated.

Serious detective writers ideally should be read in sequence, like any other writer, and I haven't crept up on the latest Macdonald yet. But at this stage, his autopsy of the American middle class was still a bit too smooth and familiar—failed parents and rebellious children, routinely arrived at—for the best fiction. Like Graham Greene, trying to turn his "entertainments" into novels by laying a heavy theme on them, the result at times was just an entertainment staggering around under a heavy theme. But Macdonald seems to have a Scotchman's caution about this: he hangs tightly onto his genre, and if the Big Novel doesn't come, as it never quite would for Greene, he will still be afloat.

As for Greene himself: I believe he muddied his own definition by dividing his fiction into those categories. The entertainments such as *The Confidential Agent* and *Ministry of Fear* are really much better novels than the novels are. His memoir, *A Sort of Life,* suggests that he has always thought he had a touch of the hack about him. He admits that he learned more technique from Robert Louis Stevenson than from Flaubert, and he knows that great novels don't come from that.

Yet I have no doubt which of his books Flaubert would have preferred. Hackwork is in the soul of the performer, and the half-insane fear and pain conveyed by the entertainments would place Jeeves himself in a different class. It was only when Greene tried, in *The Heart of the Matter,* to identify the pain and talk about it, that he trivialized it, and one felt for a treacherous moment that he might be a hack overextending himself after all.

1971

9 / *Writer as Something Else*

Just to put a little suspense in this thing: What do you suppose the following people would have been if they hadn't been writers—Philip Roth, Jean Stafford, John Updike, Kurt Vonnegut, Murray Kempton, and Norman Mailer? Is there some shadow career that lopes alongside their prose and occasionally sticks its disappointed bloodhound face into their dreams?

Mull on that for a moment, while I futz around with some artless patter. Some writers could probably not have been anything but writers—the stoop, the little watery eyes, the dirty mind; it was all there in Doctors Hospital. And *all* writers, once the bug has landed squarely, tend instantly to become unemployable. "Dammit, Thurber, stop writing," his wife used to say at dinner parties. But the rascals can't stop, even after lights out. So you can hardly imagine them checking invoices, or whatever the hell people do in offices.

The above list was chosen because the writers involved all look as if they might have been something else, without being downright laughable. Philip Roth, for instance, wanted to be a breast. I don't know when he decided he wasn't going to make it, but I'm sure he would not have been as laughable at it as some.

Miss Stafford, that most agile and graceful of authors—but you'll have guessed it by now—writes:

"I'm not in the least shy about admitting that until I was thirteen or so it was my ambition—indeed, my *intention*—to be an acrobatic dancer. I was a whiz at cartwheels, a degree less accomplished at handsprings and I could do a sensational backbend—the fact that I couldn't get up didn't seem important to me because I was sure I could learn that with proper instruction. My toe-dancing which, of course, was essential to the act, left a good deal to be desired but I blamed (blame) that on the fact that I never had any toe-dancing slippers and had to make do with my brother's basketball shoes, stuffed with socks in the toes.

"I was about ten when we moved to Boulder and in that university town I very quickly realized that I had another calling: I wanted to be a PhD, and my most engrossing daydream was of being driven in an open car through the streets of Oxford while the crowds cheered and threw roses to me. I am vague, I'm sorry to say, about how I planned to combine my talents in a universally newsworthy debut.

"When I was *very* young I longed to have buckteeth."

Murray Kempton, who sees good in the worst of men, and grounds for hanging in the best, reports: "It was always my dream to be a bishop, but I suppose I would never have been summoned [demure sigh here, very hard to transcribe]. Instead I would have been left to be a curate in some parish on the Eastern Shore, awaiting a gift of hoecake from the Faithful and giving an occasional warning against temptations to incense." So Mr. Kempton gives us instead the finest Episcopal-type prose since Bishop Andrewes.

People who think of Kurt Vonnegut as Captain Space have obviously missed the pastoral earthman side of this eerily gentle writer. As you shall see:

"Listen: As for what I would like to be right now, rather than a writer —I would like to have my age legally changed to twenty-two, and I would like to be a nut-brown Austrian ski instructor at Sugarbush.

"As for what I might have been and sort of wish I had been instead of a writer: some part of my mind has insisted for years and insists right now that I would have been an able and serene horticulturalist, puttering around in greenhouses. I have no friends or relatives who ever did that, so I am mystified. But there it is. I must have walked into a greenhouse when I was a little kid one time, and nearly swooned with joy. Maybe that was in another life. It's a dream of having dignity and beauty, maybe, without working very hard. It's a dream, too, of having my creations somewhat sheltered from acts of God. It's a dream, too, of being in command of a sort of ship which isn't really a ship. I wouldn't have to navigate dangerous passages or dock neatly or any of that. Still —people would have to do what I told them to do, and promptly. And they would call me 'the old man.'

"I have said on occasion that I would endure the agonies of van Gogh in order to paint the paintings of van Gogh. I would not endure them in order to paint the paintings of Gauguin. I have endured the agonies of being Vonnegut in order to write what Vonnegut has written. In retrospect, it seems to me to have been a straightforward and rather uninteresting business deal." Some of us would take it like a shot anyway.

Norman Mailer, former mathematics prodigy, appears to be keeping his big secret under his hat, while toying with his latest victim-oppressors —but who can tell with Mailer? ("Do not understand me too quickly," he says. Good grief, little danger of that.):

"I hate to be the meatball in your symposiastical stew, but it's possible I can't think of what I would have been if not a writer. Could say doctor, lawyer, actor, thief, movie director, bum boxer, pol or insane chief—not one rings true. Let us say that I would not necessarily care to keep hard-working and sweet but rather be a lazy lover with women working for me. Print this, you Papist."

Consider it done, Meatball. Women with any thoughts on the above should address their replies directly to Mr. Mailer—someplace in Saskatchewan, I believe.

Another question, while we're down among the trivia, is—which writers are drawn to music and which to painting? John Updike, with his uncanny, eye-aching vividness and his not particularly compelling rhythms, would seem like a clear case of a visual arts man. But then, I already know the answer.

"My true and passionate ambition—though as a badly hooked moviegoer I did have yearnings toward being a private detective, a test pilot, or Errol Flynn—was to be a cartoonist, first for Walt Disney, then for the syndicates, lastly for *The New Yorker.* What I have become is a sorry shadow of those high hopes. The unqualifiable *dasein* of a black line on white paper still fills me with joyful witness and (since years have gone by since my fingers have known the smudge of India ink) wistful envy; in comparison, words strung together to make a sentence are mere cumulous clouds, into which each reader, lost in his own subjective and semantic haze, can read what he will."

Hard-core Roth fans will have to wait till next month, while his reply works its way cautiously down from Connecticut by U.S. Mail. It should be interesting because Mr. Roth confides that he really wanted to be a writer all along but will make something up anyway. I'd like to thank him and everyone else, for graciously filling that most tiresome of writers' functions—the answering of silly questions.

Nobody asked me, but . . . (as the great Jimmy Cannon used to say), my own dream was ballplayer all the way. I listed "lawyer" in our eighth-grade paper, because my classmates had *seen* me play baseball; and I guess the idea of being paid to argue had at least the charm of a Glasgow whore, as Mr. Mailer might argue. But the real lowdown dirty one, so good it was sinful, was the dream of rounding the bases gravely, as the horticulturists, acrobatic dancers and lazy lovers rose in a body and chanted my praises in Latin. . . .

Ah well, scribble scribble.

1973

10 / GEORGE ORWELL
Artist

The English are determined to get George Orwell straight if it takes all night. An excellent new collection, called *The World of George Orwell* (editor, Miriam Gross), devotes itself to this slippery task—which turns out, as usual, to be like catching a greased pig at a fair. In the end, Orwell trots off into the woods, still a bit more equal than we are.

There is much fine stuff, though, down among the trivia. William Empson breaks the news that Orwell actually did stink, as he had feared since schooldays. Then again, another friend says he didn't smell bad at all. One Jacintha Buddicom claims that George really had a happy childhood (someone always claims that), and someone else says he was a happy policeman in Burma, too.

Malcolm Muggeridge reports that Orwell once beat up a friend in a drunken rage, and this I believe. His letters and reviews are a mixture of scrupulous politeness and wild squalls of spleen. His famous decency seems to have been a series of victories over a wanton murderous temperament. He spent a lot of time apologizing to people.

He was called the "conscience of his generation," but if so, he was a traditionally English one, unsystematic and gorgeously inconsistent. As

D. A. N. Jones points out in a first-rate essay, "Arguments Against Orwell," a young radical following Orwell's advice would wind up doing nothing, because writing poems for the workers is effete, serving on committees is ludicrous, and changing classes is impossible—except, of course, that doing nothing is unforgivable.

One can only answer that there *is* something wrong with all these activities and that it is good to know what this is before going ahead and doing them. A conscience is a style of thinking, not a rule book. Orwell's politics would be impossible to adhere to literally, because he felt that "to succeed is a species of bullying" and that policemen are always wrong: so your side is not to be allowed either policemen or success. And if you agree with that you are probably wrong anyway, being some kind of damn saint or holy willy, too good for smelly old mankind.

Even Calvin never loaded the dice more conclusively. Good people by definition cannot win, because winners are no good. Power is evil and must prevail. One imagines the kind of smug preacher whom Orwell loathed nodding to this. "*1984* is what I've been warning the flock about all along." Orwell was quick to spot displaced religious belief in other political forms (notably Communism) but never located it in his own.

However, do not imagine we have captured our pig. For Orwell also despised despair. In numerous other writings, he lashed the chic pessimists ("people with empty bellies never despair of the universe") and even himself for being a pessimist. His reaction was always impulsive, intuitive—any other reaction smacked of "attitude"—and, Englishly, he trusted a feeling over an opinion any day. It is worth remembering that he never set up to be a Conscience but did set up to be an Artist, and he brought to politics a basically artistic temperament, complete with death wish, life wish, and amusement at both. For instance, he thought that *1984* was a parody.

His truth, as Muggeridge says, is artist's truth—and no more so than in his version of himself, which we have swallowed too easily, not bargaining on artist's cunning. This new collection finds him out in several places, though in no spirit of cackling revisionism. For instance, it seems he went to Burma because his father sent him, not because he wanted to taste "real life." (Miss Buddicom says he really wanted to go to Oxford.) His hatred of oppression surely began with his father, wherever else he places it.

And he did not go down and out in Paris and London just to assuage his guilt. He went to Paris to write novels and he lived there for eighteen months in comparative comfort before a combination of illness and a stolen wallet laid him low. At some point, he may have seen this as a chance to work off guilt—but even that was an artistic experience. Because he had stumbled upon his best material: squalor and his own reaction to squalor.

This was important because, for all his passion to write, he had a limited imagination, and material could have been a problem. Reading Orwell's collected essays and letters, one is startled by the narrowness of his interests. Certain obsessions—a little-Englander's hatred of Catholic converts and the Scot's mystique tiresomely restated, a genuine love of animals and country life, but no music or painting, precious little of the popular arts (he used all he knew), and, surprisingly, precious little politics. Even when he got to Spain in 1937, the political side of the war frankly bored him. And, in 1939, he suggests that maybe writers should keep out of politics altogether.

The only things vivid enough for him to write about were things that happened directly to himself—and, of these, only certain things. I used to think that Orwell had the most sensitive nose in history, since he went to a smelly school and fought in a smelly war, etc., and was even conscious of his own smell. But I believe now that smell was one of his "properties," something he jotted down while thinking of something to say. After that there is often a reference to tobacco and sitting on his bum and spotting a stray turd. (English public-school writers are often fascinated with the fecal.)

His evocations of scene thus have a certain similarity, but they are still immensely powerful. Because he clearly hated squalor, he shrank from it; but he needed it if he was to survive as a writer, and as he plunged in again and again he must have felt like Winston Smith in *1984* with his head in the rats' cage, facing the thing he feared the most. In fact, the worst side of *1984*, if my nerves record correctly, is precisely the physical shabbiness of it, so close, as critics have said, to the shabbiness of England in 1947.

The necessary element of perversity in Orwell's work was that he wrote best about the things he hated. When he tried to write lyrically it came out stilted and anonymous, and his poetry is flat and schoolboyish with a touch of E. M. Forster's "undeveloped heart" or at least undeveloped language of the heart. Like a great many writers (Graham Greene is a spectacular example), he could not use part of his character in his work, and we need other people's memoirs to fill him out.

Although he had found his material with the nonfiction of *Down and Out,* he did not abandon fiction itself, then or ever. In spite of all he had seen in Spain and Wigan, he praised Henry Miller in 1939 for his "irresponsibility" and his rejection of politics. He still wanted to write such novels himself, recording the actuality of middle- and lower-class life with absolute aesthetic fidelity, using politics only insofar as they affect that consciousness and precisely *as* they affect that consciousness (i.e., if lads at pub think socialism means a fair shake, that's what it means and that's all it means).

He did not quite have the gifts to bring it off completely in fiction, but it would be a mistake to think he was trying something different in his nonfiction. *The Road to Wigan Pier* and *Homage to Catalonia* are superb expressions of this same aesthetic, an attempt to render ideas as pure experience. Poverty and Communism are only what their victims think they are. Therefore it is the business of literature to dump conceptual baggage and find out, like Miller, Zola, Joyce (his heroes), what actually happens down there. Orwell's tantrums toward the pansy Left and his attempts to talk cockney are thus not affectations but a furious creative effort (well, perhaps that's what affectations are) to enter his subject.

His passion for literature was far greater than his passion for politics if indeed, hatred isn't a better word for the latter. But politics had been thrust up his nose by circumstance. The people he wanted to write about were fenced in by politics, you couldn't get *at* them now the way Joyce and Miller did. Part of the dirge in *1984* is over the sheer suffocating presence of politics, and his nostalgia is for a time when people lived on something else as well.

Of course, he had lived in that world and hated it—and hated it for its political indifference, too. He knew you couldn't have the old public school virtues of courage and loyalty without the bullying and brainwashing and the layer of fat safety around it all, and you couldn't have the working class virtues of decency and good humor without the blinkered vision and unthinking hopelessness of the old workhorse in *Animal Farm.*

Since his imagination only worked on things he already knew, his vision of the future had to be made of exaggerated bits and pieces of the past. But his head did not necessarily go along with that. In reviewing T. S. Eliot's cultural theories, he says that we simply don't know what a classless society would be like. We may take him for a prophet, but he didn't himself and he went on believing in a new socialist society in spite of his fears of it. (Incidentally, although *1984* became a Cold War scripture and Orwell seems now a prototype of the CIA intellectual, I cannot see his cantankerousness settling for those particular bedfellows for long, although I do think it possible he would have devoted himself more to fiction, less to politics, in the drowsy fifties.)

What he most feared was the blind spot between us and the future, the space between identities where we could get lost forever. For that reason, he wanted people to remember who they were and what they had been before jumping. His own darkest moment seems to have come at the age of eight when his Blimpish father sent him off to boarding school and he was caned for wetting his bed and made to understand that he was really too poor to be there at all. Typically, he shifted the blame to the System from where it belonged. For there is no suggestion that his cool parents ever warned or explained or comforted. He only says, sparely, that he didn't like his father. For once, his candor fails him.

He came out of this, according to his friend Cyril Connolly, a very knowing boy with a supercilious voice, one who was born old—his classmates call him Cynicus, and one sees all the makings of a pretty insufferable adult. The chilly letters he wrote years later to both his wives show how close he came.

Yet finally he handled his "givens" heroically and became an extraordinary adult. He obliterated his father by changing his name from Blair to Orwell; but some of old Blair's Blimpishness settled in him, giving his nature an exquisite tension. His opinion-feelings would not be half so interesting or useful if he'd killed his father altogether.

He also found that by returning to that first black moment of loss and abandonment, by letting himself be deserted and helpless all over again in Paris and London and Catalonia, he could discover art. I believe he would at times have preferred to be a dandy like Connolly, a pure aesthete, but that way was closed to him. His art could be found in only one place. And he had the guts to go and get it.

1972

11 / CYRIL CONNOLLY

A while back, John Leonard the Agitator suggested that Malcolm Muggeridge was the best writer of English since Evelyn Waugh. This had the intended effect. Within moments, I was scratching down names feverishly: Cheever, Hardwick, Stafford, Cyclops—there *had* to be someone better than the Mugger.

Not that Muggeridge isn't good, mind you. Like the hedgehog, he knows his one thing well. His style is to jab your head off with basically the same kind of sentence, in combinations so fast and stinging that you can't get your hands up. Bernard Shaw, the peerless Irish lightweight, is the prototype: Zap, zap, hey, you're cheating, zap. It is an ideal prose for clobbering bishops and other slow-moving targets; but it allows no time for music and barely time for consecutive thought.

The trouble with my own list, though, was that it turned out to be packed with hedgehog. For instance, while Cheever's atmospheres are golden, I doubt if he could write a tract about birth control; likewise, E. B. White might have trouble covering the roller derby (or perhaps not). In general, the short-sentence boys cannot lengthen the line to stillness, and the mandarins can't jab worth their hats. The only writer I came up with who can do it all, from garbage collection to star gazing, is V. S. Pritchett; yet even he lacks the poetry of my ultimate favorite, Cyril Connolly—who, alas, died a few weeks ago, throwing the contest open once again.

Connolly was (so much for theory) a king among hedgehogs. The *New Left Review* once accused him of being "all suggestion and no assertion" (which I find infinitely preferable to their own style of all assertion and no suggestion) and in fact he could only do short tone poems and epigrams. His models were Latin lyric poets and French aphorists, and these cannot be sustained for long. " 'Dry again?' said the crab to the rock-pool. 'So would you be,' replied the rock-pool, 'if you had to feed, twice a day, the insatiable sea.' " Only a Latinist could have written that last line, and Latinists are denied certain harsh but useful effects in English. So to hell with versatility. We'll change the rules.

Despite his unearthly elegance, Connolly was emphatically not the kind of author you want to call up and say "hi" to after you finish his books. There is something to be said for such authors. Connolly did want to be liked, and said so; but he also warned the reader that this would be impossible. Here is his calling card: "A fat, slothful, querulous, greedy, impotent carcass; a stump, a decaying belly washed up on the shore . . . always tired, always bored, always hurt, always hating."

Connolly followed the Cavett principle that putting yourself down is better than not talking about yourself at all. But unlike the likable Dick, he really meant it and left an image of such physical and moral repulsiveness that one flinched, as at a three-day corpse. "Gin, whiskey, sloth, fear, guilt, tobacco had made themselves my inquilines; alcohol sloshed about within, while the tendrils of melon and vine grew out of ears and nostrils; my mind was a worn gramophone record, my true self was such a ruin as to seem non-existent."

This was how he appeared to himself in a dream, and the image is, by Connolly's standards, comparatively ingratiating. Waking, he is his old charming self, "a ham actor, moth-eaten with self-pity . . . approaching forty, I am about to heave my carcass of vanity, boredom and guilt into the next decade."

All these lines came from his masterpiece, *The Unquiet Grave* of Palinurus, and there is a thematic point to them: he was recovering from a cuckolding and was writing word-pictures of this state, cartoons with horns on. The strategy is not unlike Scott Fitzgerald's in *The Crack-Up.* By an exuberance of melancholy, these two Celts hoped to blow it out of their systems. And each tried, by overstatement, to edge it into humor, their home grounds. "Others merely live; I vegetate," crows Connolly, and he is cured, for a time. "That's very funny, Scott," says Zelda, and a murderous fight is averted.

In later years, Connolly was still flogging himself, but mechanically and without artistic point. In *The Evening Colonnade* he goes over his sins one last time, dissecting his sado-masochism or whatever he thought he had, but the melancholy is a routine, a shtick, by now. The sorrow may be more serious (one hears he was painfully ill for the last years), but the art is less so, a distinction he would appreciate. So, out of respect one slips away, while the clown is still flailing himself with his old banana.

It is a pity to judge writers by their last years, and in Connolly's case it would be fatal. He had never been a good critic, because among other things, he could not pan a friend. (I know this seems a barbarous test, but without it, everything comes unstuck; and nonfriends suffer disproportionately.) One felt that, with Connolly, everything had been settled at the club. The judgments were arty-establishment: Huxley, Maugham, dear Hemingway, when all that was correct. For a man with his taste in Latin verse, this is impossible; and one begins to see the point of Connolly's self-loathing. "Vanity, sloth, cowardice." He could attack anyone in parody, even a fellow clubman; but for all his surly independence, he could not make the *assertions* that criticism requires.

Thus, for him to have made book reviewing his final career seems a culminating act of self-degradation. And we watched him gradually becoming one of those gloomy effigies who sit above the English book pages (as I sit here), too lazy to move and too bored to look around, keeping out anyone under fifty. While the young novelists are herded into the caboose of the Sunday *Times* and *Observer,* five or six at a time, the Connollys and Mortimers apply themselves with Edwardian languor to the twelfth volume of Margot Asquith's memoirs, or some picture book of Georgian houses. This would be no time to bring up these grievances from the caboose, where they often treated one jolly decently, except that they bear on Connolly's immortality, which he cared so much about. This dandy who did so much to help young writers in the forties, with his magazine, *Horizon,* has few young mourners now and may not even get the ten years' immortality he craved.

Yet of all those "posh paper" Druids, Connolly most reliably gave you your money's worth. And he wrote so vigorously and well, even about Lord Puffball's years at the embassy, that readers may still be persuaded to turn to the early books—where they will find surprises.

I recently returned to *The Unquiet Grave* with misgivings, because no book ever excited me more in the possibilities of writing, and an author must pay for doing that, as Connolly himself might observe. I needn't have worried. The book gets off to a shaky start, as often happens when the English compete with the French. Also the hero, Palinurus-Connolly, is looking for God, and P.-C., like Edmund Wilson, is an earth creature, and his thoughts on religion are either facetious or earnestly superficial. He finds it significant that dogs don't have monasteries (how does he know?). Abstract thinking ruffles his prose, and in a pinch he chooses sound over meaning.

But then he settles upon a multiple theme that suits his style perfectly —and that's where your masterpiece lies, if your hands are steady. It seems that Palinurus is crawling back to life after a broken love affair and is trying to reset his pulse to the rhythms of the universe. Once upon a time he had identified with the animal world, skimming joyously four feet above the ground, but now as a twitching outcast he finds even that too violent and threatening.

So he turns to plants, which also drum with activity: the grape demanding to be made into wine, so it can keep its status on the vine; the last strawberry clamoring to be picked; strange drugs whispering "eat me" to early man, like the mushroom to Alice. Of Connolly's nature writing, I can only say that its sheer sound moves me even when I don't know what he's talking about. Nature lives and schemes in every pore. The roses threaten to take over at any moment.

Connolly is a pantheist, and his gods are knee-high. But nature at a certain point turns brackish and ugly: it doesn't want him after all. He must return to Art and the City. But here he finds desolation. England is at war and civilization is boarded up. Connolly's political thinking is not far ahead of his religious, and thank God there isn't much of it. He had gone to Spain, presumably to please his pal Orwell, and wrote suitably grimly about the Aragon front; but within a year, he is back in the south of France with his peaches and Vichy water, happily at war with his own flesh, his natural enemy.

Now Palinurus squats among the ruins and debates the good life, if there still can be any. His hero Pascal leads him this way, memory leads him that. Prewar Europe is an aching tooth to a wartime Englishman, and he evokes it with an economy of brilliance, one diamond in a picture window, that no other writer can match—because no other writer has the prose for it. Yet Europe too has rotted like a ripe quince. Palinurus seems to hold it in his hands as a Beckett character might—Palinurus is at bottom a Mick, loving the senses and hating them, lusting and scourging—while the storm boots of Group Man bang closer. There is no resolution to this. What will Palinurus do with the postwar world? Will he be just a melon, or a ferret sashaying around Paris? We shall see.

In a piece written years later, he gave the answer he liked best: he would dance on the table like a Greek clown, declaiming "Connolly no care." If only he had done so! But his heart was too heavy by then, and his act, like so many prewar acts, didn't play in Austerity Britain. Palinurus became the slightly unsatisfactory figure noted above: a collector, a bit of a crab, a good friend if you could stand him. His English obituaries strain for praise, like nuns asked to write about the Mother Foundress. "Her fiery temper was an inspiration to us all"—that kind of thing.

But Connolly's early work is quite sufficient justification for him, lightly though he regarded it. *Enemies of Promise* is like a set of firecrackers illuminating the literary life in sudden bangs and flashes. Here's a minor one that I have found especially useful. "A writer's health should not be too good," intones Connolly, because his readers, if English, are probably "slightly mad sufferers from indigestion" and will resent him. He was still dancing on the table in those days (1938) and having a fine time of it. *The Condemned Playground* is an exquisite miniature of his school days and is notable for making the prep school that Orwell pilloried sound like a garden of wonders. Connolly, fighting sentimentality as only an Irishman can, found a nice dry compromise with wistfulness.

Connolly wasn't really Irish—except on both sides. He played down his Irishness in later years, a vice the English encourage. But his role in English letters is particularly Irish, or at least Celtic: his pure dedication to Art, his rambunctious melancholia, his rhythm of indulgence and remorse come from outside the Anglo-Saxon conglomerate. However he may have tried to dull himself down, his reflex for self-dramatization was overpowering to the end. He still wrote endlessly about how little he wrote.

I myself believe he wrote exactly enough. Some of his masters, La Fontaine, Tibullus, etc., could all be fitted into one volume apiece, as he himself remarked, and so could the best of Connolly. He fretted that this was no longer enough in an age of mass production: but some instinct (call it sloth, call it book reviewing) kept him down to size. He left us, like Jane Austen and E. M. Forster, wanting just one more. And who is to say the old literary strategist didn't plan it exactly that way?

"It is no use getting angry with Cyril Connolly," wrote Edmund Wilson. Although I never wanted to meet him, I salute his memory as of a friend.

1975

12 / EVELYN WAUGH

No Snob Like a Snubbed Snob

If you ever got the boot from the classic English cad, the rubber-faced bully whose hands crawled on the social ladder while his feet kicked, Evelyn Waugh was your natural enemy. Waugh wasn't just a harmless class-romantic like Wilde or Fitzgerald, pressing his velvet suit and his epigrams for a desperate assault on the capital. He was the real belching, sneering thing, with all the foul manners of the world's great Power Centers.

Yet somehow one never minded him. Even now in his diaries (recently excerpted in the *Observer*), where vile thoughts are shown to have lurked behind the repulsive exterior, he seems like one of us (whoever *we* are). Why? The prose, of course, with its simplicity and lack of display, not a cad's prose at all. And then, the self-loathing, strong and dolorous, with the force of genius behind it. (E.g., when he met his mirror-cad, Randolph Churchill, he flinched in horror: before resuming his own imitation, worse than ever.)

But, finally, I suppose one likes him because, in a crucial sense (the record book, where it counts), he was not the real thing at all. The first time I heard him discussed by his social betters, one of them said, "Wasn't he that little pink chap who used to show off on the hunting field?" End of literary discussion. Waugh mastered the trick himself and could talk like any bottle-nosed squire about "an undistinguished Yank called Edmund Wilson." But dishing it out to Americans and interviewers is child's play, the minor leagues of arrogance. The gallery he played to still talked about him like this: "Who should Evelyn marry? Honestly who cares? The son of a butcher in Stepney . . ." (overheard by my parents). He was actually the son of a publisher, but it made no odds to the gang he was trying to court—the illiterate county families of England, who found this national jewel no more than "a delicious little snob" to the end.

Since he could have picked up glory to burn elsewhere, his pursuit of these savages has a certain grandeur about it. A writer who would rather be dined by Lord Chowderhead than praised by Wilson is a genius or he's nothing. Also, Waugh must have known that snobs are funny; yet he plunged on with it, blinded by his obsessions. And he never had a chance to win. His public school was a byword in mediocrity—it's a marvel he could ever bring himself to use the word "undistinguished" again. And his college at Oxford (Hertford) was a social climber's disaster.

His diary omits the Oxford years, for whatever reasons of shame or alcoholic delirium, but out of them a rather prudish censorious schoolboy emerged as a Jazz Age dandy with his wing collar askew and one dance shoe missing. His family was alarmed by his change of character. Yet if we bear in mind his rather peculiar grail he had not changed so much. As a scholarship boy with a middle-class allowance, the only aristocrats he was likely to meet were dissolute ones. The rest were sealed off from him in Christ Church and the better clubs. But a drunk with his pants down didn't care who you were or where you came from. Much has been made about hints of homosexuality in the diaries. But as Evelyn Waugh later wrote in his famous reply to Nancy Mitford, "Sodomy is U." If buggery was *comme il faut,* so be it. It was part of one's class apprenticeship, like learning to hunt or to insult a waiter or other gentlemanly attainments.

At Oxford there are usually enough of the best people around to cultivate an amusing little fellow like Waugh, and one imagines him adopted as entertainer, *tumler,* outdoing them all in sporting the teddy bear and other neo-Wildean frou-frou. But they can't do much for you after you've gone down, old boy. The party ended abruptly for Waugh, and he found himself suddenly back with his middle-class income and prospects, teaching at a school minor to the point of farce or beyond (see *Decline and Fall*). His remaining lifeline to the all-night party was a neurotic girl called Olivia Plunkett-Greene who led him a cruel dance (the yes, no, you bore me Percy shuffle) at the end of his rope. Waugh doesn't apologize or explain even in his diary, but somewhere around then he tried to drown himself—only to be stung by a jellyfish, named Marmaduke, no doubt.

The Ruling Class was not quite through playing with their gifted slave. The Hon. Evelyn Gardner married him and was almost immediately unfaithful to him. Waugh's delicate pride was smashed. Physically short, financially nowhere (how he must have bluffed at Oxford to hide that), unsure with women—well, take that, little man. Triumphantly, he got a masterpiece out of it. *A Handful of Dust.* Still, what's a masterpiece if you wanted to be a duke? Waugh hit the road and wrote about Abyssinia and points south (real savages, boy) and came back with a carapace that could ward off anything, and an income to maintain it. In World War II, he added the military style, an officer *is* a gentleman, sir, and that kind of gentleman he could do as well as anybody. But to the best people he remained a plaything (brilliant, of course. *Oh* yes, brilliant) because he *tried* too hard, old man—the one thing one mustn't do.

Why did he put up with it? Partly because he seems to have thought he was doing fine (there is one surprised entry, where he learns that some people he assumed he had charmed were actually bored spitless) and partly because it suited his comic genius to. But there is always an exciting sense with Waugh's fiction that resentment is about to break out in hot streams. In *Vile Bodies* he lashes the kind of Best People who had let him into their playground—like Groucho spurning any club that would take him as a member. Waugh admires the aristocrats he can't reach, a mythical people as simple and unmannered as his prose, a class that is really too good for him—even if he has to invent it, as he did in *Brideshead Revisited.*

This gives his work a strange power, so long as his crazy vision is implied and not stated. The potty peers and dim dowagers of Wodehouse are suddenly made to carry some portentous secret of grace that even they have forgotten. When he tries to tell the secret in *Brideshead,* it disappears—leaving a dry rustle of drapes. The reception of that book made Waugh meaner and nastier; he'd tried to be serious and he'd made a fool of himself. Wilson the insignificant Yank accused him of bowing the knee to the county families, and Cyril Connolly did a popular imitation of Lord Marchmain's deathbed conversion. (Waugh had actually witnessed such a scene and was seduced by the truth.) O.K., catch him trying to explain anything again: instead he burrowed further into eccentricity, where his real beliefs could not be laughed at.

It wasn't just touchiness—although it was always that, too. His religion was unwaveringly important to him, and it must have hurt him deeply that he explained it so badly. (Later he blamed it on Spam and blackouts, but he really wasn't much of an analytic thinker.) Snobbery for him was never more than a handmaiden of religion. If God had died in the blare of the twentieth century and in houses too new and cheap to be haunted, one must seek him in the old quiet places, where he might still live on in retirement. Waugh's ruling passion was architecture, and it probably meant more to him to get into those great houses than to meet their owners. They were temples, quiet and pure enough for someone of God's taste. How not to make this sound silly? Waugh loved order and beauty, he was cursed with perfect taste, and modern life was a jangling torment to him. He found God where he could, in the sum of what was left when you subtract the twentieth century; but he shouldn't have tried to name Him.

At first glance his diaries may seem disappointing. For long stretches you would never guess Waugh was a writer at all—maybe something in wine, or a minor gossip columnist. Artists are always doing this to the culture vultures, as when Proust and Joyce debated the red vs. white wine question before their agitated claques. But still—during the years of the great satires, not one word on technique, on plot or character, or even a stray grunt of satisfaction—it's almost too much amateur gentleman to take. One notes the emergence of the famous quick cut. "Poor Mr. McGregor turned up after having lain with a woman but almost immediately fell backwards downstairs. I think he was killed." Cut. A crude early example, but it gets better. Unfortunately, this method works against a diary's nature. "Billy and I unearthed a strap and whipped Tony———." Cut. Eh? What was that? Any special reason for whipping the chap? It works wonderfully in the books, where the anecdotes are better and the heartlessness has a context. Here it simply hangs up there. Waugh is just a camera going about his business, and we feel we can wait for the finished photographs, the books.

Yet there is much that fascinates beyond the abiding question of how anyone could write so elegantly without affectation. Why was he keeping a diary at all? The first entries arc strange little bursts of spleen, written age twelve, aimed at "vile Southend trippers" and "an atrocity of about seven who spoilt our badminton game." So the first impulse seems to have been rage, and that would always be part of it. Then, having announced itself, the diary falls silent for three years, to resume as adolescent soul searching (not bloody much of that for Waugh) and regular diary stuff. Later it becomes a record of hangovers and vomiting and idle ruttings, and here it seems to find itself. The diary becomes his confessional. Waugh despises the orgies of the bright young things ("too sick-making") and is horrified, upon sorting the bodies, to find his own at the bottom. Writing a novel down there, but still—.

There is not one word here to make you like or admire him. Not even the crow of the breastbeater—Oh, what a sinner am I! He cuts away from his own remorse. "Never apologize, never explain"—even in the confessional. There are no theatrics of repentance, and no luxuries of self-analysis, only a mumbled resolve to do better. Otherwise, state your sin clearly, omitting nothing, and take your punishment like a gent.

You can't really hate a man like that.

1973

13 / *Honoring Ezra Pound*

Of Ezra Pound, as of Bobby Fischer, all that can decently be said is that his colleagues admire him. There is no special reason for anyone else to. Pound belongs to an all-but-extinct priesthood which believes that Art is God, that kindness to other artists exhausts Charity, and that the outside world is slightly unreal. "Does one honor him?" Daniel Bell asked recently in a letter to *The New York Times.* But what kind of honor could he possibly want from us, who are not of his faith? A heathen's blessings are wasted on a priest.

In 1949, the Bollingen committee voted its prize to Pound anyway —for the sake of the prize. "To permit other considerations than that of poetic achievement to sway the decision would destroy the significance of the award." In other words, if you take away Muhammad Ali's championship, you hurt the championship, not Ali. His replacement will be getting nothing but a nice-guy award. Even a judge can't argue with the scoreboard.

The poet Karl Shapiro dissented from that decision on grounds that he couldn't vote for an anti-Semite, prize or no prize. Fair enough. Literary anti-Semitism has to be condemned within the profession itself, even if it means calling off prize day occasionally. For what it's worth, Pound also abused my own native country, England, while it was fighting for its life in 1941; and I might, had I been a judge, have felt inclined to tell him to collect his damn trophy from somebody else. But now the American Academy of Arts and Sciences has refused Pound its Emerson-Thoreau award; and Daniel Bell has given an explanation from outside the kingdom of Art altogether, which looks to me like a full-scale assault on that kingdom for the sake of nailing one man.

According to Bell, the Academy's decision was not political but moral. Yet surely political would have been better. Politics deals adequately with one's public accountability, however grossly the case is arrived at. Morals tends to more delicate inquisitions. The American Academy was apparently soon awash in psychiatric testimony—surely a strange approach to a literary prize. Was Pound finally judged not insane enough to win? And what other moral judgments might the Academy feel empowered to make in future? Private cruelties, abandoned children—do these come into it? Or are we just out to get Pound?

Unfortunately, it seems unfashionable to discuss Pound's treason to his own country, so anti-Semitism has become his only offense, and this lays an unfair weight on Jewish judges. Professor Bell, in his tortured efforts to sound fair and impersonal, arrives at an aesthetic principle too edifying for Art to bear. He says in effect that you can explore evil, drawing "on the tap roots of the demonic," but you may not approve it. But when you draw on those tap roots, who knows what you will find? Writers just back from their season in hell are likely to be covered in goat hair and blood and tend to rave. The moralists can sort out the evidence later. But the writer with the correct attitude could not have entered hell in the first place.

I far prefer Shapiro's simple formulation—in especial because I believe Pound's anti-Semitism was partly an anti-Semitism of convenience and not a deluded passion. The peculiar stench of it has not, I think, been analyzed. (In what follows, I draw heavily on Noel Stock's comprehensive *Life.*)

Professor Bell places Pound among "those who have allied themselves with" the murderers of the Jews, which has the labored and weakening sense of legal language. In literal fact, the Final Solution had not commenced when Pound gave his famous broadcasts, and indeed he spoke explicitly against pogroms. Maybe "the sixty kikes who started this war [*sic*] might be sent to St. Helena . . . and some hyper-Kikes and non-

Jewish Kikes along with them." The repulsive note with Pound as always is the frivolity: the sense that he doesn't really mean it.

His sin against the Holy Ghost, literary and otherwise, was precisely this forcing of his emotions. Nature had blessed him with all the equipment for a great poet except (like the Tin Man in *The Wizard of Oz*) a functioning heart. His early work reads like something poured out of a high-strung computer, into which has been fed nine languages and every verse technique known to man. "What do you believe?" T. S. Eliot asked him, and he knew he ought to believe in something, for the sake of Art. So he flung himself wantonly into his hatreds and resentments hoping to generate some warmth, but achieving more often only that tinny profanity and big-mouthing of his letters. Pound's raging sounds oddly ineffectual even in the broadcasts, with a Fascist army at his back.

He did care about Art, though, and he cared about money, and he swarmed over these two subjects with the full force of his sensibility, producing some of the finest poetic theory ever written, as well as the most fatuous economics.

Ezra's father had been an assistant assayer at the Philadelphia Mint, and the very name Pound has a financial ring. So it is not surprising that a poet who believed in the connectedness of words and things became bemused by coinage. As an overripe, struggling artist, he had never had enough of it himself and had been receiving scraps from home like a child. His funny money theories boil down originally to the cheerful proposition that he and everybody else should be given unlimited spending power.

As a medievalist, he naturally blamed the usurers, but not necessarily Jewish ones. Note the concept non-Jewish Kikes, even at the height of his delirium. Back in 1935, he had written: "Usurers have no race. How long the whole Jewish people is to be sacrificial goat for the usurer, I know not." And in 1938, "international usury contains more Calvinist, Protestant sectarianism than Judaism." The anti-Semitism crept in with horrible casualness. The artist's usual mixed desire to please and to offend was tilted by the war. The Italians gave him a microphone, and he was theirs.

Maybe the Italians know more about how to handle artists than we. When Pound visited Mussolini, the Duce allowed that the *Cantos* (which he had just been handed) were "entertaining," and Pound considered this a most profound criticism, cutting through the foggy ruminations of the critics. It takes so little to please. Had Roosevelt written a kind word for Pound's metrics, we might have had him on NBC.

As it was, Pound paid a poorly timed visit to the United States in 1939, expecting to be of service in Washington, and even hinting a willingness to serve on President Roosevelt's brain trust if requested. He was snubbed and his confidence shaken. On the way back, according to Stock, he heard of an actual live international Jewish banker, an Englishman called Wiseman, who carried some weight in America, more weight than he did anyway. Old Ez, who'd been running America from abroad for years, may have flipped then and there.

Pound is such a model of the romantic poet, the spoiled boy child made arrogant by his admirers and bitter by his ignorers, a god wheedling favors from pigs, finally going willfully insane (if that's what it was) to find a more perfect solitude, that it is easy to overlook how often one hears goofy theories like his among veteran expatriates. It's rare to meet one who hasn't at least cracked the riddle of the universe or the secret of money or the truth about sex. It comes from talking to oneself while watering the ferns.

To get back to the prize. Pound's contribution to letters is towering; he gave his soul for it; and, if he is to live out his long life dishonored, I believe he deserves an explanation with some passion in it like Shapiro's, not a rap on the knuckles. If I were Jewish, I would hate his guts, and I don't love them as it is. But I think it would be the right kind of honor to say so.

1972

14 / *Writers' Politics*

How long would it have taken Lord Byron to become as stuffy as Wordsworth? How much gestation to allow before the Grand Old Man steps stiff-legged from the young poet, cracking the mask and throwing off the curly wig?

These are questions that never lose their staleness. The English press, at least, always enjoys a cackle over the latest crop of radicals turned posh. Precisely how much does the new house cost, Mr. Kingsley Osborne?—Never mind. I'm behind on me payments as it *is.* And that was a new Rolls, wasn't it, Mr. Brainsley?—Get stoofed. Yes, I quite understand. And so, year after grudging year, we trace the laureate in embryo. "Angry young man mellows. Interviewed yesterday in his 23-room Georgian mansion, Viscount Pettigrew (formerly Mr. Barnsley Fang). . . ." The dirty old public eats this stuff up faster than royal weddings.

Actually, there is nothing so very sensational about a man's changing politics as his economic and class interests change. But writers tend to make a scene about it. They are, of course, paid to make scenes and can make them out of practically anything. But there is a special shrillness about writers gone Right. For one thing, they know that conservatism is supposed to be a sign of old age, and they can still hear, clearer than most people, those adult voices saying, "Wait till you're older." So they rant, screaming at some dead granny, "It isn't like that, not in my case." And since granny's face doesn't change—dead, you know—they shout all the louder at us, the suffering public, overdoing even the normal grumpiness that seems to attend most conversions to the Right.

They have, it goes without saying, an excellent case against the Left. There is, in fact, an excellent case to be made against everything, as every Catholic child knows. If you wish to satirize the other side for a change, you just turn your guns around: targets just as juicy await you.

Considering the possibilities, surprisingly little top-quality Scorn has come from the neo-reactionaries. Mr. Amis's recent efforts in *The New York Times Magazine* seem heavy going indeed, not as loutish as Al Capp, but almost as leadenly ironic. One imagines a wheezing Blimpish snigger greeting each line. "Give it to those frightful pink chaps, Kingsley!" But perhaps I caricature his audience as much as he does his enemies. A writer like Amis, with a beagle nose for folly, is expected to be unfair. (Who needs an impartial satirist?) But rage has temporarily thickened his touch as well—the rage to be a real, knockdown convert and not just a turncoat. *The National Review* used to be littered with samples, from Morrie Ryskind the gagman to Max Eastman the sage.

The generally poor quality of converts' ridicule is puzzling, unless one understands that a convert *must* overdo it, must find his former position abnormally ludicrous, in order to justify leaving it. Since, repeat, *all* large organizations and groupings are packed to bursting with absurdity, second-drawer satire is objectively worthless. When an Al Capp functions at half-speed, giving lectures roughly on the level of the cartoons in *Krokodil,* it tells us nothing about the New Left, but plenty about his anxiety to dissociate himself from it: to the point where he will lay down his art if necessary.

Amis sounds echoes of another sort when he says that, anyway, *he* hasn't changed, it's everybody else that has—a line I seem to remember from John Dos Passos and, further back in the echo chamber, G. K. Chesterton. Since the Left and Right do switch places constantly in their weird dance, this is quite a possible position (though the dance has its reasons for changing). But since writers like Amis and Dos Passos manifestly *had* changed, their insistence that they hadn't takes on its own interest.

Well, one thing: obviously, if you haven't changed, you've outfoxed grandpa: you haven't grown older after all. Not to change is to stay young forever. But you have an appointment with grandpa in Samarra: not changing was precisely what he was talking about too. This is what you learn when you get older—that none of the old men have changed. They are all young men from the twenties or thirties in heavy disguise.

Here a distinction might be made between writer-ideologues and writer-writers. The former stop along the wayside because their feet hurt or because they feel silly haring after the young—or because they have come to a good place. (I'm not suggesting that all positions are alike: my subject is only the blind lunges of temperament.) The interesting thing is that these footsore veterans often go on calling themselves Democratic Socialists or anti-Stalinist-leftists or whatever, long after the category has been closed down, and even though on all questions of the moment they line up squarely to the Right. To surrender one's name tag, fought for through the long CCNY night, is to surrender Youth for sure.

The ideologue is commonly content to squat down with his group and wait for winter. Members of a family never grow old to each other. Writer-writers are in trickier case. Their game is personal immortality and they are not about to be buried in the bobby socks of their generation. They will, by God, speak in the new styles so long as they can: their ear for that being their greatness. When they can no longer turn the trick, they round on the present with Job-ean wrath. Saul Bellow, who made us what we are today, has just issued a fine blast of rage in *Modern Occasions,* a masterpiece for the smaller fry to study, which, by an irony, should appeal to precisely the sensibility he attacks. American writers are always thinking the parade has passed them by when it has simply stopped to browse by some stream. Bellow suggests one extreme possibility: a writer who thinks he *must* be on the Right by now, when he's plumb in the middle. (Incidentally, the whole game may have to be abandoned in this country until somebody can locate the Left.)

The writer-writer, however sedulously avant-garde, knows that the world must hold still for a moment, if his own best work is to be understood. Sensing that others, young devils like his own old self, are pushing, he can only splutter, "You're not avant-garde at all. We did all that years ago." Grandpa, now, himself.

Cultural conservatism is becoming in an older writer: anything else is cosmetics anyway. If he whores after the new thing, he will only get it wrong and wind up praising the latest charlatans, the floozies of the New. His business is keeping his own tradition alive and extending it into its own future: an old writer can grow indefinitely, what he cannot do is keep up. If he enjoys in his spare time swiping at the culture fads of his day, O.K.—God knows, we've always got some silly ones—but his blame is likely to be as wild as his praise, and a cleaner job can usually be done by people closer in time (e.g., Robert Brustein's *Revolution as Theater*). Old men's complaints of the New sound as if they all came from the same old man—the kids all dress alike, no individuality (as opposed to the wild motley and adventurous phrasing of the old).

Cultural conservatism and political are some distance apart and connected only by the finest of tightropes. The lowering of artistic standards can be traced, I suppose, to egalitarianism, and that can be traced to the Left. Low standards in Greece or Turkey would have to be traced to something else, and low standards in our own Gilded Age to something else again. "There are nine and sixty ways of constructing tribal lays and every single one of them is right," said Kipling. And so it goes with explaining low standards.

A couple of years ago, the incomparable Dwight Macdonald was touting Aristocracy as the keeper of standards—not the Spanish aristocracy, mind you, but a fine tweed one like the English. Yet the English aristocracy never did much for its Amises and Osbornes, except make sure that any muffin-headed peer got a better education than they did. Aristocracy considered Evelyn Waugh "a dreadful little climber"—and that's about what a writer can expect who claws his way up the drainpipe and into the castle.

Yet there comes a time, as there always has, when a writer would rather be insulted by a duke than have to go back to his old neighborhood. The delights of snobbery haven't changed essentially. Success still de-classes you, burns your old clothes like Eliza Doolittle's, and boils the dirt off. And the mob that seemed so friendly while you were in it sounds threatening the moment you leave it, a dull roar beating on the study window.

Much nonsense has been talked about the lonely road of the writer (there is no more brainlessly gregarious life in the world, especially if you like the company of publishers), but it is just lonely and different enough to cut you off from any sense of working-class solidarity. Your verbal intelligence, swollen like a tennis player's forearm, can barely endure the conversation at the pub any more, old friends are dropped regretfully, just the way they were by H. G. Wells's Mr. Kipps. At first you blame the system for making them all so dull. But then, after all—*you're* not dull, bless you. So perhaps it isn't the system at all. Every ape who has "made it" knows in his heart that Darwin was right.

If they lower the standards, all kinds of people will achieve eminence, and your own will be washed away. The British Angries are especially severe about keeping up those standards, presumably at precisely the height they cleared themselves. Yet that was also precisely the stage of English social history whose awfulness they have immortalized for us: so the irony clangs like a leper's bell every time they speak.

Still and all, the new snobbery may be of better quality than the old, and the new aristocrats may do more for those perishing standards. In Dickens's *Great Expectations,* young Pip not only flinches from his family after he has gone up in the world, but also from his benefactor, Magwitch, the convict. So too, a successful writer of those days might have been embarrassed by his vulgar old talent, the hairy thing chained in the closet, which bought his way into Society in the first place. Better to be a fox-hunting gentleman like Siegfried Sassoon. Right now, it would take several generations of talentless Amis grandchildren to reproduce such oafish aristocracy as that. (Incidentally, for England read America throughout: Wasp philistinism is all of a piece, and Scott Fitzgerald received the same fish eye from it as Dickens and Waugh.)

Since most every writer has a good ear and a knack for imitations, the urge to be one's own Pygmalion and pass oneself off as a duchess is always strong—especially now that duchesses have come down in the world and first-generation celebrities can look them straight in the eye. A writer-aristocrat is not just a role-player now, but as close to the real thing as anybody else.

Coupled with that: the desire not to destroy the palace but to move into it oneself is the occupational curse of revolutionaries. In the case of writers, and especially the English ones, there is the further sense that the Revolution has failed them and that they owe it nothing. Writers like Amis who romanticized the postwar Labor Governments must have hoped for some favor in return, for their own profession: what they got is the most brutal tax situation imaginable, enough to drive anyone to the Right, or at least to Switzerland. The Golden Age of the Common Man didn't give a damn about writers; one still had to grub for oneself; one had no union, no lobby worth the name. And so, like Middle Americans, the writer was driven to resenting the help that everyone else seemed to be getting, the largesse heaped on less enterprising members of his own old class; even the bonuses paid (by arts councils and such) to rookie writers who hadn't played in the minors.

All understandable enough. You start out as one of a group, but end as a solitary sniper, living off your wits. Apparently you have a better chance if everyone is in the same boat, in a fragmented laissez-faire situation. Even the generous-minded, Leftish Graham Greene is on record against government aid to the arts—proud, perhaps, of having gone it alone so well, and as jealous of his own freedom as Ayn Rand.

Yet this has little to do with what, in the long run, makes a better society and a better climate for the arts. My own prejudices, to dispose of those quickly, run the other way—I believe that aristocrats are fairly good at hanging onto their own old houses, but that's about it. They can also commission worse junk than a foundation can, and there's no arguing with them. I believe that big business is the most radically irresponsible agent of change we have, and that Jerry Rubin has even less sense of humor than Bob Hope.

But that kind of opinion is in the nature of a hobby: it is not what writing is all about. As soon as writers become partisans they become something other than writers. Americans especially are all too willing to drop what they do well and take up preaching—even a Bernadine Dohrn, whose only established skill is eluding the FBI, turns up on the Op Ed page of *The New York Times.* Preaching is easier than writing, easier than thinking. I recently saw the talented reporter Gloria Steinem shilling for women's lib (a cause I generally favor) on TV and I thought, you used to work harder than this on your articles and do more for truth and justice besides. In a world where good writers are always in much shorter supply than pontificating windbags, I hate to see even one of them mounting the pulpit in any cause whatever.

In fact, they probably shouldn't even be writing essays like this one.

1971

15/A. ALVAREZ
The Savage God

Books about suicide make lousy gifts, and many people think it's unlucky to have them around the house as well: so A. Alvarez's excellent *The Savage God* may wind up being more talked about than bought. A pity, because the book is also about life, just as suicide itself is about life, being in fact the sincerest form of criticism life gets.

Anyway, of talk there has been plenty, with everyone quite rightly an expert. The book has already caused some of the uneasy excitement of an actual suicide. The first reviews from England suggested something between a public nuisance and a noble gesture, and American critics have been poking at it almost as suspiciously, attracting, one hopes, a crowd.

It seems that the reflex for survival (and perhaps the reflex to be rid of this reflex) stirs at the very mention of the word, and few books have had a *tenser* reception. It is also to the author's advantage that suicide, literary and otherwise, has its own advertising department, working full time. John Berryman, one of Alvarez's representative poets of the Age of Suicide, recently took his life in grim confirmation. Within the same solstice, two equably urbane American writers, Rex Stout and Brendan

Gill,* caused a tremor by declaring that they would like to kill themselves when the sand runs out. And now, Yasunari Kawabata has followed his disciple Yukio Mishima into the inner darkness.

All these cases are in the domain of *The Savage God.* The two Americans come under the heading late Roman: the cool decision to die, made on a fair morning, a sad smile, and a few well-chosen last words. Alvarez finds this "unreal," and so do I. There is a suspicious neatness about so many Roman anecdotes: they all seem to have been rubbed smooth in the interests of moral propaganda. No doubt if a Stoic emperor wanted serene suicide stories there was always someone to rustle up a batch.

Much more real are the twin tragedies from Japan. Mishima, whose first novel, like Hemingway's, featured an impotent hero, spent years methodically turning himself into a fascist he-man and wound up slashing his stomach like a samurai. "I have long since thought I wanted to die not as a literary but as a military man," he told Donald Keene. This is the way a writer dies: impaled on his own imagination.

And Kawabata, who had reached the age for a graceful departure, went out of his way to denounce suicide in his Nobel acceptance speech and to make clear that no departures are graceful—possibly (who knows?) to ward off his own impulse. There would be precedents for that. Alvarez figures that Dante was passing through the slough of despond when he placed suicide in the most squalid circle of hell. So too, Kawabata was careful to rob the act of glamor or even wisdom. There were no fine last words, but only an empty whiskey bottle.

Our new Western stoics would rather dispense with this fuss, and I wish them luck. Certainly sleeping pills or a shrewd swerve of the wheel make it easier all the time. But Alvarez suggests that the Savage God does not like to be sneaked up on. You must first pay your dues in pain and frenzy. The rational man may talk a good game about suicide, but reason must give way to obsession and finally squalor before he can actually do it. Otherwise he will postpone it until the next Nobel Prize announcement and the next. The phone will ring or he'll misread the label. His plans will reveal some laughable flaw he wasn't aware of. The will to live is smarter and tougher than he is.

If he is really serious, he must surrender his fine cool and enter the

**Mr. Gill denies he said this so perhaps we can substitute John Cheever, who has talked of walking out to sea on a fine morning, like Leander Wapshot, and not returning.*

closed crazy world of suicide, where no phones ring, and where outer events have no meaning: where children sleeping in the next room make no case for life. This, I learned incidentally, is why suicide cannot be used as a fictional device. Suicide is not the logical conclusion of anything. Cesare Pavese committed it at the height of his powers, like Mishima, and left us with this message: "No one ever lacks a good reason for committing suicide." The excuses we find for it are no more than triggering devices and probably the wrong ones at that.

I oversimplify Alvarez's point, but so does he. I'm sure he would allow the obvious exceptions, the people who did sneak by the god in spite of everything. But even in terms of his hard-core obsessives, he seems inconsistent about how closed their closed world is. Because, having disposed of all social and exterior reasons for suicide, he finds himself returning to them, bringing in the atom bomb and the general unrest, and other items of coroner's reasoning. His case histories of Sylvia Plath, Cowper, and Chatterton suggest that a lost parent, buried in the child like a rotting tooth-stump, is usually the root of self-destruction, and this could happen in any age. But when he falls to generalizing, we find the Spirit of the Times nudging the lost parent out of the picture. He has an ax to grind about the Spirit of the Times, and his first butterfly escapes as he goes after this second one.

I believe he can have them both, but the matter needs restating—for this reader at least. Suicide seems to be a cancer that does indeed grow on its own without direct reference to outside events, a presence in the system that can be cut back but not removed. But it may lie dormant a long time, depending on luck and the health of the other cells. A poet's brooding might encourage it—we just don't know. Sylvia Plath might have gone the same way without poetry: many do.

Alvarez has aesthetic reasons for admiring those who take the chance. He believes that the cancer of self-destruction is now at large and raging in society (hence, the Bomb, etc.), so it follows that those who recognize it in themselves must witness to it if it kills them. He also believes that there is nothing much else to witness to—but this could just be his own muse dictating orders within his own closed world. He had the disease himself at one time: and like some ex-alcoholics, continues to overestimate the significance of his experience.

For all that, *The Savage God* is a healthy book—come to think of it, a little like an AA meeting, supposing people as bright as the French Academy ever held one. I believe that a potential suicide would be calmed by it (though please don't take my word for it if you know one). There is, as Alvarez says, no way of talking someone out of suicide, and like many compulsions it seems beyond the help of psychiatry. But this book might leech out some of the intensity: as a sort of Suicide's Home Companion, it sweats it out with the patient and even flips into occasional ghoulish high spirits ("if you can't stand a giggle you shouldn't have joined the club"), which might distract the fever briefly.

The reason for this quite unique effect is the author's own on and off vigil with Sylvia Plath, the poet of suicide. His general survey of the subject would at times be only so much superior pop history and pop psychology if it were not for the "held note" of this first chapter, which imposes the face of an actual suicide on all those Greeks and Romans. He seems to have understood and re-created Plath down to the smallest pinwheels of despair. Her husband, Ted Hughes, sent up a howl of outrage and pain when he read that first chapter, which led to some aimless gossip around London; but one imagines he would have to howl whether Alvarez was right or wrong. Fortunately literature doesn't need the details. Alvarez is onto some kind of truth. He is one of the few critics good enough to use a stethoscope on the poems themselves and get the story from that. And he could almost afford to make up the rest.

Perhaps one fully assimilated suicide is the only clue anyone is ever going to get. From the account he gives here, Alvarez got much less out of his own suicide attempt than he got from Plath's—suggesting that one's own despair may be the most unfathomable of all. Nature arranges that the closest witness be blinded. Alvarez stumbled in and out of his attempt like a man looking for his hat, and only from observing Plath (perhaps he was even drawn to her for this) did he learn what had happened to him.

One thing he learned, or guessed, was that Plath's last attempt was closer to a ritual exorcism than a serious killing. Many people would like to root out the cancer, dead parent or whatever, without actually killing themselves. Even the gun in the mouth could be probing for the Evil One, even the knife across the offending throat. The subconscious, according to Freud, does not believe in its own death and can urge the conscious on to these zany operations like a Weatherman putting a bomb in his own house in order to get the landlord.

There are many cases of attempted self-slaughter where the victim is satisfied with a mutilation and is never troubled again. "If thine eye offend thee, pluck it out." I know of someone who blinded himself with a shotgun and has been happy ever since. In Plath's case, she seems to have felt that just going through the motions of suicide would do it. But, for the operation to succeed, it must be serious. A game won't do. So Sylvia Plath took some risk, only a little, of its working—and, by horrible chance, it did.

In proposing this theory, Alvarez may be doing what he accuses society of doing—of robbing a suicide of her gesture, and of trivializing her death. When presented with a real case, he does what we all do: denies it, covers up. But an ambiguous response to suicide is surely the correct one. For instance, on a larger scale, Alvarez seems to applaud the growing enlightenment on the subject and yet to miss the days when it was cursed. When the Church called it a mortal sin, it really stood for something. An outcast is better than a statistic.

Perhaps, too, religion or sorcery, a calling to spirits real or fancied, could pierce the closed world of suicide in a way that enlightened chat cannot. Dante may have thought that, when he put a curse on himself if he took that path. A Divine prohibition might stop a suicide like a lightning bolt, where sensible advice slides off like mist; or it might, contrariwise, give one a last chance to show off before God and show him, in one stroke, precisely what He could do with Himself and His so-called Creation. Or perhaps none of the above. If Alvarez found a solution, I believe he would make sure to lose it again. He likes his question, finds it fruitful, too much to want to see it disposed of.

1972

16 / *On Keeping Closets Closed*

If you like to think of fictional art as a branch of magic, authors' jacket photos have to be a terrible disappointment. André Gide called fiction a collaboration between the Holy Ghost and the devil: yet here you have this florid mountebank in his turtleneck gazing out to sea, or this road company Blanche DuBois and no one else in sight. Is that all there is to an author? It's almost as disappointing as meeting one.

Books in general seem more powerful if they come from no one in particular: manuscripts found in a bottle or brought down from Sinai. Everything you learn about their origin is downhill after that. The author's writing habits, his little bursts of melancholy and laughable taste in women—all serve to stuff the genie back in the can: not written on the wind at all, but on Remington four-ply extra-fluffy by a wizened little anxiety case.

So be it. The author wants to be famous and the public wants to skip the book and hear about him, and there's no keeping these two apart.

Still, an author should probably try to keep one veil on for reasons of box office. TV interviews featuring the stammer and the fluttery wattles don't help him in the long run. Once the oglers have seen it all and

Norman Sallyrand stands shivering obligingly in the buff, they're off to look for Salinger. "Take it off, take it all off," they moan. But Thomas Pynchon buttoned to the chin is their favorite this season.

In this spirit, and this spirit alone, I question the wisdom of writers coming all the way out of the closet—any closet. Having been recently accused of closet Christianity myself, I speak with feeling about closets. Graham Greene and Evelyn Waugh stuck their heads briefly out of the Christian one and had to fight their way back in. Because, in an instant, the scavengers had their number—they were *Catholic* novelists, which explained everything: every plot twist, every two-bit *aperçu.* The uncreative are grateful for these skeleton keys. Originality is promptly flattened like tinfoil. Catholic novelist, Catholic *woman* novelist: the more words you can pile up front, the less remains to be done.

Thus I was mildly sorry when my old hero E. M. Forster's homosexuality was announced as if it were the debut of the year. I had always assumed that Forster was homosexual—of which I imagine there are at least as many varieties as there are of Englishmen. But with the italicized disclosure, a universal writer contracted sharply to a sectarian totem: Forster became a propaganda counter in a winless war. "We've got Whitman, and I'm pretty sure we've got Byron, and we're still working on the big case, Shakespeare," say the Gays. And the Straights reply by hanging on to Shakespeare's Dark Lady for dear life and giving up Whitman altogether.

But who can read any of them intelligently with all this gabble going on? In the big game of is he or isn't he, the author is the one sure loser. I remember how we used to jump for joy when an author converted to Rome, and how we'd automatically promote him two literary notches; and, in no time, we had him all to ourselves. G. K. Chesterton has barely recovered yet from the stuffing and mounting the Catholics gave him.

In a case like Forster's, there is not only homosexual glee but heterosexual revisionism to contend with. The old canard that homosexual writers don't understand women and can write only about men in disguise will probably be trotted out again with the force of fresh discovery. Yet nobody knew women better than Forster, or wrote a more authentic woman's book (if there is such a thing) than *Howards End.* Forster finally gave up fiction because he was tired of writing about "the love of men for women and vice versa." Yet his trumped-up heterosexual contexts are at least as convincing as anything in his private homosexual writings—which proves either that he was latently heterosexual behind his false heterosexual facade, or that he had absorbed the oppressor and was his own worst censor, or that he wasn't very good at love-writing, any way he sliced it.

I am not proposing that writers lie about their religious, sexual, or political bents, but that they insist on keeping their writing selves free to cross borders at will—carrying only such beliefs as are tattooed on their psyches. Their nonwriting selves are, of course, on their own, to assert whatever solidarity their cause seems to require (my old Catholic chums would have paid many a famous convert not to mention it at all). But in most novels and plays there should be some doubt where the voice is coming from.

This can be a simple matter of degree. When *The Glass Menagerie* first appeared, nobody knew much about Tennessee Williams. Clearly, he wasn't the Elks Club Father of the Year—but nobody questioned his credentials for writing about women. Now that Williams has been pushed to the front lines of the sex war, matters are different. His women are seen as a fag's projections or a fag's revenge. Or so runs the current balderdash.

In fact, male homosexuals have always ranged along a wide arc of woman-hating and woman-accepting (maybe the tired question of who's truly mature around here could be settled *de facto* on this line) and the accepters have written brilliantly and irreplaceably about the other sex. If Henry James was indeed a homosexual—which to me is this year's least burning question—he still created a raft of far more convincing literary women than, say, Iris Murdoch put together.

Unfortunately, where we need them the most—i.e., in descriptions of their own turf—sectarian writers sometimes disappoint, partly owing to their own loyalty (why give *them* ammunition?) and partly to the vigilance of their own OGPUs. Mr. Greene couldn't say the word Catholic without a frog chorus of it-isn't-like-that's from down in the swamp, where they know so much more than novelists. Philip Roth has had the same trouble with Jewish material. And the authors of *The Boys in the Band* and *The Faggot* must wonder from their gay reviews if they ever met a real homosexual. Partisans want their writers out of the closet all right, but on a very short leash. Just say that you're happy, Ivan, in spite of the mistreatment, and we'll handle the publicity.

Which is another good reason for staying inside and being your own master. The only alternative is to be a Solzhenitsyn to your own group. The thought-police will never be satisfied anyway. Your stories will never be "representative" enough; you will always have left out too many positive aspects of Presbyterian life, or whatever. To hell with them. There are plenty of party hacks to take care of the guided tours. Your boss is in the streams and the burning bush, not the Chamber of Commerce. Besides, if I know my causes, they'd rather have your royalties anyway.

For now, I'm supposing that all movements are equal, which they're not, except in this respect: that none of them gives a damn about artists beyond their immediate utility. Good movements will use a writer just as ruthlessly as bad ones; since they all fancy they have better things to do than worry about one man's artistic survival. Whether you're Virgil or Steinem, they will praise your junk embarrassingly when it's ideologically pure and find obscure artistic flaws when it isn't. They'll also use you to promote less talented brethren: viz., "Typical members of the Presbyterian school of writers would be Bernard Shaw, Shamus Smedley, and Amy McGregor. In many ways, McGregor is the most interesting."

The desire to level the talented spans all movements and causes and may be stronger than any of them. When the women's libbers began to mutter "cult of personality" about their new stars, they were doing no more or less than a Jesuit provincial sending his only saint to the outback to learn humility. Half the time the provincial may be right, but an artist has to bet the other way.

And mind you, while hacking him down to size, movements will ride an artist's or saint's coattails as far as they'll go. His or her name will be used to endorse an emerging vegetarian literature or a New Jersey revival (as if we had gifts enough for more than one literature among all of us) or, as in the case of Thomas Merton, to promote a Trappist monastery, which had done for him approximately what Wheaties did for Willie Mays. But the genius will finally fly too high for them (unless he intentionally grounds himself) and all the little Amy McGregors and Shamus Smedleys will drop off and he will become a voice on the wind, without passport. Who now cares that Pascal was a Jansenist or Shaw a Fabian? They belong to anyone who has the wit to catch them.

After that, the only thing that can cut a writer down to size is his jacket photo or ten long minutes on the Johnny Carson Show.

1973

17/ *Watergate as Literature*

For Watergate freaks there is much good wallowing to be had this season. Sources close to sources have asked us not to wallow, but alas this is like telling the crowd at a burlesque show what to feel. Wallow we must: not from malice anymore (normal spleens were strip-mined months ago) or fear for the Republic (a pretty emotion more talked about than experienced) but sheer gibbering curiosity. What happened next? The trivialities of party strife are suspended when human nature goes into such an act as this.

I don't know what all this does for the dollar, which apparently bursts into tears at a frown, or for foreign affairs. (It could be that other nations will eventually grow testy because they can't follow the plot.) But, for the average citizen, such living political fiction undeniably quickens the spirit. A nation needs a novel to follow, a story to bring us crowding round the bulletin board, be it a war, a scandal, or a humble moonshot (this is one of the big problems with nations: the next major novel could kill us), and Watergate is a dilly: deeply flawed, as the boys say, but a hell of a read—or rather, a hell of a wallow.

Because this word, chosen with genius, describes precisely the right approach to the subject: namely that one go back and forth cheerfully over the same mud. No new book is going to tell us much we don't already know about the Watergate; even with the most harum-scarum publishing, the author is going to be several months behind the reader. Besides, the latter is gorged and wheezing by now from sheer information. My own psyche has still scarcely gagged down the decline of John Mitchell. As the Irish say, "My jaws still work, but I can't swallow"; one has to get rid of Mitchell to make room for the next mouthful.

All the more reason to wallow. The new books will be denounced as quickie operations, and most of them will be. But the solid unoriginal texts, such as *Watergate: Chronology of a Crisis* and *The Watergate Hearings: Break-in and Cover-Up,* edited by the staff of *The New York Times,* should be read—in fact, the less original the better. The need to write about subjects millions of people already know is one of the seedier pretexts for the New Journalism: so expect two-bit character analyses based on eyebrow readings and doodle-ology, fresh collections of leaks from a cauldron that's already boiled over, and sleazy breaches of trust à la (nonpolitical example) *The Marx Brothers Scrapbook* wherein the great Groucho is revealed to have grown a dirty mouth in his old age—to whose benefit revealed I know not. Better, if one must have a fringe wallow, the Watergate coloring book or Frank Mankiewicz's urbane gloss on the public record, *Perfectly Clear: Nixon from Whittier to Watergate.*

The Watergate should be approached, like Madame Bovary, with a minimum of interpretation and extraneous blather. Just let it happen to you. Mull the marvelous language, not just the familiar examples but the whole cunningly flaccid tone of it: "I am hopeful that" for "I hope"; "he is supportive of, dependent on, cognizant that." The bureaucratic mind recoils from active verbs because they fix responsibility. So, too, "I was wrong" becomes "my judgment was incorrect." The petty official abandoning ship becomes passive in every pore, barely breathing: perhaps we'll take him for a passenger.

The master who gave us this novel moves with ease from the twittering of minor functionaries to the brutal swagger of the high command. Suddenly all is bully-boy overstatement: deep-sixing and wasting and shredding, White House Horrors and Saturday Night Massacres. It could be a gang of kids with a skull and crossbones on the door and real blood oaths; the childishness of evil is one of our author's more chilling themes. "Let him twist slowly, slowly in the wind" is worthy of one of

Shakespeare's child-men, Iago or Richard III, an exuberance of gloating rarely found outside of English nurseries.

For backstairs comedy to please the groundlings, our author has chosen the Senate Select Committee itself. The essence of the joke as I see it was to take a committee that didn't really want to find out anything and confront these monkeys with witnesses who insisted on telling anyway. James McCord persisted in the teeth of the most inane questioning ever flung together. The President's man, old Fly-Me-to-Florida, tried to bore us to sleep with minutiae about the door handle; the other fellow, the junior statesman, did it with philosophy (what-is-your-concept-of-the-role-of snooze); the Falstaff of the outfit couldn't seem to follow anything that took place after lunch and blustered in proportion, but this might have been the most fiendish ruse of all for avoiding fresh information. And so it went, each man a marvelous specimen of political comedy, which occurs whenever the need to show off is combined with the imperative of doing nothing; i.e., all the time. Thus the firm jaw and the empty sentence. Any good comic writer can do you a Sam Ervin, but Howard Baker is a work of art.

For dramatic irony, this group of reluctant hangmen, this klatch of Ko-Kos, was accused of being out for Mr. Nixon's blood. Except that there wasn't any Mr. Nixon, only a sinister character called the White House, whose face came off in one's hands. When a statement didn't work we were told it wasn't really the White House at all, and that Mr. Nixon had no knowledge of it. One imagined at night a vent opening in this Kafkaesque creature and a spokesman flying out with a footprint on his pants.

This character—a house, my God—gives the novel a unity it desperately needs. Otherwise it would sprawl with characters like the Ganges. But these random folk are given a theme to twitch to by the bleak house with the curtains drawn, the fairy-tale house where the trouble comes from. And then another house and another, magically transformed into White Houses by the lonesome man and his dog, on spectral visitations.

The novel also packs a full class system, from the earthy Sancho Panzas like Tony Ulasewicz in the kitchen to the knight of the raddled countenance aloft. And the story is set in rollicking motion by the night of the red wigs, and by something more tender: the concern of Martha Mitchell for a humble plumber. I hope it's not trespassing to say that

James McCord reminded me of a younger John Mitchell, and that a woman who loved the one might at least sympathize with the other. Anyway, it gives us the kicker we need. When Martha saw that McCord was taking the fall, she alerted the nation as no investigative reporter could have, with a real yell for help, blood-curdlingly cut off as in the movies. She may also have given McCord the determination to fight back—she'd do that for most men. She also gave the White House the worst single enemy it could possibly have, namely herself.

It would be just like the zombies who run the fairy-tale house not to appreciate the human value of a Martha Mitchell. The Right loves her, of course, but they may be a little embarrassed by her; but a lot of the Left loves her too, without embarrassment. What the hell, they've got Bella Abzug; they're not afraid of a little eccentricity. So when the boys stuck a needle in Martha's backside, the whole nation jumped. After that, it availed little to attack the liberal press for hounding our President. We'd heard a human voice from the nest of grotesques; and, when in doubt, trust the human.

This is one story to be coaxed from the limpid text, and there are many others. I do not agree that they add up to a searing indictment of America in the seventies. That would be playing into Billy Graham's hands. It is a searing indictment of those particular people. I don't trust novels that say much more than that. The motivation was money and power as viewed from a foxhole: abstract and distorted as a hermit's temptations. The Nixon gang came back from World War II talking dollars the way others talked God or sex. As for the moral: How about "everybody prating 'bout honor ain't got any"?

To find out what this tells us about America today, you go to the next booth. My concern here is solely with the Watergate as literature. And I can't leave it without a few mean-spirited quibbles. The author is much too anxious to shock. The pornography of surprise wears us out eventually; we want more, we are hooked, but we feel slightly sick. At times, I also found the melodrama a touch unbelievable. The bit with the tapes seemed particularly farfetched. Couldn't the White House have said, "Mr. Graham tells us it's wrong so we did the difficult thing and destroyed the tapes even though they would have proved our innocence. That is, if we could have heard them at all, with the President kicking the desk and all."

Well, one must fling a few mudpies at the big raw talent who wrote Watergate and who threatens to put the rest of us out of business for a long, long time. The last novel I read, about murder, incest, and rape, seemed like a nice little thing; but I went slavering back to the set in search of really major fiction. I only hope to God the author decides to take a rest after this one.

1973

18 / *Dirty Business*

"I fancy I can handle that, Miss Phipps." "No, me me!" "I'm the one, dearie." The subject of pornography has been assigned, and all the columnists are busting their buttons to have a go at it. The reader will just have to put up with this for a while, although, truth to tell, he would probably rather be writing about this fundamentally dull subject himself.

Little remains to be said about the new Supreme Court ruling (concerning local option in matters of skin), which never stopped a columnist yet. What we adore is a vacuum and pornography is nothing if not that. The voyeur will never speak for himself: long after the last sado-masochist has dragged his chains down the avenue demanding more lib, the voyeur will still be in the closet, because the closet is his natural habitat. This good gray man resists even scientific analysis or Presidential Commission, because if cornered he will rend his binoculars and deny that pornography turns him on at all—he's in the wrong theater or thought the film was about tracheotomies or something. Mild of countenance, neutral of clothing, he goes out of existence completely a few feet from the exit and becomes you and me. If he is a columnist, he naturally goes home and writes about how dull pornography is.

Fringe questions abound concerning the ruling: e.g., which of the Founding Fathers would have listed sexual intercourse under free speech and which ones emphatically would not have? (After reading Gore Vidal's excellent *Burr,* I have my hunches.) Or again: could a busload of Frenchmen alter a community's standards overnight? and what if the other side ran up a convent to counter this? Imagine Spencer Tracy rushing into court with news of a new Jesuit rest home. Chaos.

Anyway, presuming that the censors will try to censor a little bit more each year (because, like editors and other officious people, censors don't feel they are getting anywhere unless they are up and doing) and that each case will produce at least five letters to *The New York Times,* we may find ourselves spending more person-hours just talking about pornography than any society in history. I wouldn't put it past us. In time, the reading of pornography-trial transcripts may replace the real thing, unless these, too, come to be censored (see *Nevada* v. *Wiggins:* are porno trials predominantly prurient in intent? And what do you do when a judge talks dirty?).

Since movies and disposable paperbacks will certainly feel the first heat, serious book writers can observe all this with a measure of calm for now. Nobody reads a good book for the sexy parts if he can find a bad one (artistic merit is damnably distracting)—or reads either if he can see a movie without being seen seeing it. Skin houses, approached underground in black masks, through tunnels clogged like the catacombs, would put the cheapie books out of business in no time; so would cassettes, if the cleaning lady doesn't pry.

But for now, dirty books that incinerate or hide easily seem to have a purpose in this strange childlike world of buried treasure and censorious adults. The voyeur's closet and the lonely child's tree-house are both marked: "Keep out—this means *you.*"

All this has given serious writers a freedom they should value. They have been allowed to advance under the skunk spray toward a potentially richer treatment of sex. Writers as orthodoxly Christian as Dickens and Evelyn Waugh have chafed under the old inhibitions. Dickens couldn't track a man's perversions to their lair; Waugh, trying to write about love in *Brideshead Revisited,* stammered into a phrase that even embarrassed him in retrospect: "he made free of her loins." Trying to locate the loins wasted a lot of valuable time for young readers in those days, and even then an overwhelming vision of pork chops ruined it for many.

It has been much argued lately that novelists used to be all the better for having to work a little harder and more obliquely for their effects. Dickens, for instance, conveyed an infinity of perversions, including sexual, without naming them; and maybe Waugh should have been steered off sex anyway, if that's the best he could do with it even under the old code. I agree that restraint is an essential literary tactic. But good writers can usually select their own chains without the cops being called in. For all the Communist permissiveness that is raging right now, scores of masterful understaters, like Jean Stafford, John Cheever, Louis Auchincloss, are still functioning pretty much under Victorian ground rules, self-imposed: and sensibilities as oblique as any Victorian are probably sidling around the nation's writing workshops at this very moment. The problem, such as it is, is not with the writers but with the public. And if you don't think so, check the sales of *Lolita* against *Pale Fire.*

The question is, where are people to turn for their weed of titillation? In Dickens's day, the theater was locked up even tighter than the novel. So if Dickens had written about sex, be it ever so mildly, it would automatically have become pornography, because it would have been the hottest thing around. Balzac and Maupassant used to be corseted in cellophane as late as the fifties and placed on the Wilt Chamberlain shelf. "Looking for something, kid?" (Yeah, you got any new Aristophanes?) So long as novels could go a little further than movies, generations of maddened schoolboys and mature audiences, too, tore at the pages to extract the hidden ounce of honey. It wasn't much, but God knows not much was expected. Semi-serious, semi-commercial authors took to planting one or two sex scenes per book to meet the need, in about the same proportion you now find in R movies. As the furthest extreme of respectable titillation, middle-brow novels carried this foolish burden for years, before movies stepped up and relieved them of it.

As not even the third hottest thing around anymore, the serious novel can now treat sex in some depth, without fear (or hope) of arousing the skittish reader. The titillation ante has been raised way above the novelist's head, and he must now bring to sex standards of art and intelligence he hasn't needed before. Hard-core pornography can be as good or bad as it likes; the excitement is brief and undiscriminating. But that doesn't go when you're fourth hottest. To describe physical love to an unresponsive reader requires literary skill. This jaded fellow, as I see him, knows the basic mechanics backwards and sideways by now and has finally tired of hearing them one more time. He knows how the jaws work; now he needs the taste of the fruit, and art can begin.

What makes this particular coition different from a million others? These people at this moment: everything around the moment: the whole world of this particular novel. And if that's not enough, the thoughts of the performers. The mechanics needn't be excluded anymore—though, like other standardized procedures, eating, walking, etc., they don't illuminate every character that practices them, or every occasion. But when they do, when physicality is the point, as in Mailer's *The Time of Her Time* or Bertrand Russell's autobiography, the writer can let fly with no danger of selling 10,000 extra copies. Sears, Roebuck assembly instructions are no longer necessary, because we've seen the movie.

Thus from a literary point of view, I'm happy to see movies out front, absorbing the finest energies of the voyeurs and semi-voyeurs. If X movies and R movies are peeled away, the boys will be back at the bookstall, baying for frippet (see Supplement to the *Oxford English Dictionary* for definition and nifty surprise). A few years back I wrote that pornography was robbing me blind because I don't write it. That excuse is gone. Can anyone who hasn't read it say whether *Gravity's Rainbow* is sexy? Does anyone care?

As a movie fancier, though, I'm not sure I wouldn't like to see some other form out in front—maybe ballet. I understand it's becoming so hard to blast Western Man out of his house and away from his set that X movies may soon be the only way to do it. Still, it's tough to see good directors out of work and good films going undistributed, while films that don't even pretend to be good grind on oafishly, taking up valuable midtown space. It would be nice if mankind's need for pornography could somehow be met without commandeering whole art forms like this. Meanwhile, though, books seem to be relatively safe both from obligatory pornography and from pornography-sniffers—until, that is, the movies topple.

1973

19 / *A Moral Problem*

And I said to him Dickie Bird,
why do you sit,
Singing wallow, tit wallow tit wallow?

This will not be a Watergate column, nor yet—our latest affliction—a column denouncing Watergate columns, but a meditation on the difficulty of resolving novels these days to anyone's moral pleasure.

The author of the fictional classic *Watergate* (sounds like a George Eliot title to me) has had the audacity to give us an old-fashioned ending, with Papa wasting away in embarrassment while his family wrings its hands. The irony is that our boy might still save an inch or two of face if he could only say "take the money and do something nice with it." He is too sick to enjoy it—looks, indeed, as if he has never enjoyed it—yet spends his blank days asking for more.

Mr. Ford, an old-fashioned reader, tells us that this man has suffered enough. But we of the Pepsi now-generation cannot be so sure. Can someone with all that bread really be suffering? Most of us would take killer doses of disgrace at those prices. And besides, what kind of disgrace compares even dimly with being poor?

In the 1900s Chesterton argued that millionaires would *not* do anything for money; they would not, for instance, wear their evening clothes backwards for money, or drink directly from the soup tureen. But this is clearly because nobody had asked them to. Nowadays with Joe Namath simpering in pantyhose and a President playing with his yo-yo in public, one has to wonder in what embarrassment might still consist —let alone sufficient embarrassment to run a novel.

Would General de Gaulle do it? The question itself brings a blush. The General would have suffered enough if one ungrammatical or infelicitous tape had appeared. The difficulty for the novelist is in getting anyone to believe in a character like de Gaulle anymore.

Of course, Aristotle would be the first to agree that you don't have to believe in de Gaulle to enjoy him. The skeptical Greeks probably watched plays of honor mainly to get it out of their systems. They knew that in real life Oedipus would have copped a plea and hightailed it to Corinth; but they liked the idea of a man who goes blind from embarrassment. It makes a better story than group therapy or even finding Jesus.

Jules Feiffer once drew a cartoon of Oedipus talking out his hang-ups, concluding, if I remember, with the thought, "You should see my daughter Antigone"; but the joke is that in our stunningly prosy epoch the cartoon would make an acceptable novel and the original wouldn't. If everything is a hang-up, there is nothing left to write about but the contemplation of hang-ups. Hence the low-budget couch novel, featuring one mouth and a cast of shadows.

The idea of a disgrace too great to live with doesn't really speak to us now. Our lawyers, like William Calley's, wouldn't permit it. And the idea of someone's being brought low by mere embarrassment seems downright unhealthy. Ajax, in my favorite Sophocles play, is deluded into killing a flock of sheep whom he takes for enemies. Not his fault, but it is a *professional* gaffe and cannot be borne. Conversely, in the movie M*A*S*H, when a girl loses her dignity publicly, it is considered good for her. "Hot Lips" naked becomes one of the boys, as de Tocqueville or somebody warned us.

What is good for life is not necessarily good for the novel. One wouldn't really want anyone to suffer like Captain Ashburnham in *The Good Soldier* for even contemplating adultery with a young girl in his charge. But it makes more dramatic reading than Bruce Jay Friedman's

About Harry Towns, in which the hero "gets laid" at will until there are no faces, no issues, no point.

Towns is the ultimate *Playboy* man, and his path through life is so smooth that he can no longer make stories out of it. Leaving his wife is no story, rejoining her is no story, sniffing cocaine, not sniffing, it's all the same on this *tabula rasa* of a soul. Friedman is a measure of the distance we've come in moral comedy. His early book, *Stern,* quivered with moral complications: Harry Towns cannot even invent any—except, significantly, with his son: children are the last frontier of moral sensibility. Otherwise, trouble is for nebbishes: there is no need for an intelligent man to persecute himself with stories anymore. A kid wading through the anguished tremors of Henry James can only ask, "Why don't they get divorced? Why don't they get laid?"

Friedman is a fine, golden-eared (not literally, of course) writer who has shrewdly elected to stay just below "literature," unlike his fellow temptee Roth, and I believe he has elegantly traced this kind of novel, in semi-parody, to its present resting place. Where it goes from here, I can't imagine. Since these books give us nothing we don't already have, but are just another tour of the living room, they can only end with the hero-person resolving to live, to endure, to carry on. This is bracing to know; but since it could be tacked onto every novel ever written, it lacks specific artistic satisfaction.

Hence today's novelist is not only limited by the thin subject matter of personal experience, but by the pinched clinical conventions of the Health generation. Faced with Othello, say, he would have to divide the man into departments, like a liberal arts course. Race relations—that's still a subject, although of course whites can't write about blacks and vice versa; sexual politics (somehow); Othello's ultimate therapy and decision to endure. Since jealousy is now curable, like TB, we can't have people dying of it anymore. A few rap sessions, some fearless touching, and a new sense of self-worth would have Othello and Iago and Hamlet and Juliet back on their feet in no time; and Fiction struggling.

In real life, some (but which?) people must suffer from personal dishonor as much as ever. But the convention is that they don't or shouldn't, and novelists are bound by convention. A suffering hero is no good for you if the public won't buy him. Lord Jim, expiating one act of cowardice over a lifetime, seems as spaced-out as Lord Profumo devoting himself to good works in atonement for some trifle with call girls. Have they no lecture circuit over there?

Instead, we get Jeb Magruder sobbing his instant repentance into a best seller and whining in the same breath that he and his family have suffered too much for one mistake. It's wonderful how public men love their families at such times.

The naturalist writer has no choice but to follow this graph, from the pagan rubric whereby you simply killed yourself to end the book, through the Christian life sentence spent in seclusion and worse, anonymity, to the suspended sentence and ghost-written memoir of today. Can one really write a tragedy about a lowered credit rating and six months of low-security tennis?

At the moment, it's all we've got. Blame the mushy psychologizing of forties' liberals if you like, but the hard-noses of the Right have since gone gallumphing down the primrose path on a borrowed ass, chirping of compassion and understanding as bright as any Franzblau. So there's nobody left out there to tell sad stories to. "Repentance is bull—" says Ron Ziegler, completing the daisy chain that began more toughly in Vienna. Contrition, like honor, is a Victorian melodrama that the Magruder generation cannot play, except as pastiche.

Or is this, too, a convention?

The French, who like to think of themselves as the wickedest people on earth, would tell you that Americans are in fact childishly obsessed with honor. These things happen, my friend. We are men of the world, no? Yet any stuffed shirt on horseback can get the French prating about "la gloire" and beating their toy drums again. French cynicism is a great comic resource, but its inaccuracy as a gauge of human affairs should be a warning to all of us. Our own cynicism, which sometimes sounds like a bad imitation, may cause us to overlook many quixotic extravaganzas ripe for fiction, e.g., Watergate's one preposterously genuine man of honor—G. Gordon Liddy—whose stoic silence would have met the highest Athenian standards for Promethean dignity.

Even if democracy and its handy club, behavioral science, have finally flattened out honor for the snotty class-conscious virtue it is, they have not quite eliminated embarrassment, either in morals or manners (next month). It is the novelist's business to find what might still embarrass Joe Namath or in what posture Mr. Ford would not allow his picture to be taken. Gay Talese reports that Masters and Johnson were speechless when asked about their own sex lives—not out of prudery surely. But then what? Embarrassment may not seem like much, but in its full magnificence it can almost be the stuff of tragedy.

Concerning which, a last absolutely non-Watergate-related word. In real tragedy, official punishment is strictly pro forma. The protagonist has already judged and punished himself, and five to ten in the pokey is not going to make a Medea or Othello feel any worse, or a ticker-tape parade any better. Compassion is wasted on such, and we are free to indulge it. It tastes like gall to the beneficiary anyway.

If we go through with the punishment, it is on the off chance that just this once we may not be dealing with a genuine tragic hero.

1974

20 / *Spock Mugged*

A New Year's toast, in decaffeinated tea, to the vanishing liberal. Under heavy fire from absolutely everybody, the liberal craftily went out of existence some time ago, and the only people who still claim the title are conservative politicians, labor leaders for Nixon, and Americans overseas.

Although I myself have not met a self-confessed liberal since the late fifties (and even then it was a tacky thing to admit, like coming from the middle class or the Middle West, those two gloomy seedbeds of talent), yet hardly a day passes that I don't read another attack on the "typical liberal"—as it might be announcing a pest of dinosaurs or a plague of unicorns.

Some of these attacks are pretty dubious. It's perfectly all right when Dwight Macdonald fires away from his anarchist position—if anyone can still remember what anarchist means. But when Garry Wills does it, for instance, I'm not sure what I'm agreeing to. Wills seems to be writing from somewhere out in the vague left, where all the best people are gathered. But when he writes, say, about the liberal Catholics of the fifties it is with the knowing smirk of the old conservative, the man who sneers at this year's fashions *this year,* knowing that they'll appear ridiculous sooner or later. How chic and silly we were to discover French Catholicism and German liturgy that year; how much wiser to have passed through the whole period with a small smile.

There's a lot more to Wills, of course, and I hope sometime to consider this gifted writer at greater length. Wills has a tone of such eerie authority that he has staked out a turf (in *Nixon Agonistes* and *Bare Ruined Choirs*) where he is barely challenged. But the subject now is merely the contempt for popular enthusiasms *as such* that Wills carries over, if only in his voice, from his conservative days.

Which brings us to that venerable liberal-baiter Malcolm Muggeridge and his recent remark that Dr. Benjamin Spock is the great buffoon of his era. Even allowing for the Edwardian ground rules—chap has no sense of humor, you know, he's so *earnest* about everything, too priceless—I still find this judgment puzzling. And being called a buffoon by Malcolm Muggeridge smarts.

Spock's chief claim to recent attention has been in making a holy fool of himself over the Vietnamese war—something I would have expected a stand-up Christian like Muggeridge to appreciate. Getting arrested, marching, signing things—these have their silly side after a while. But as Angus Wilson has said of a similar situation, what else is one to do? One knows that the Muggeridges are tittering, but one keeps going. Christians call this "Witness" and expect to be laughed at for it.

Tastes differ, but I would have expected a major buffoon to sidestep the war completely—after all, *every*body's talking about it—and perhaps, who knows, to emphasize personal salvation instead: as Billy Graham has or, indeed, Mr. Muggeridge himself. To some of us, this war is the greatest sin we ever expect to find ourselves involved in, and our private spiritual lives are comparatively trivial next to the task of stopping it.* In fact it's not clear what a spiritual life would consist of after you'd left out this imperative. As a baby doctor, Spock felt a certain additional responsibility for a generation he had cared for, by book, and didn't want it to kill or be killed. Funny?

*William F. Buckley raised the Eyebrow high over this one. But the New Testament frequently emphasizes the simple moral test beside which all else shrivels. 'Lord, when did we see thee hungry or thirsty . . . sick or in prison, and did not minister to thee?' Then he will answer them, 'Truly, I say to you, as you did it not to one of the least of these, you did it not to me.' And they will go away into eternal punishment, but the righteous into eternal life."

What else is buffoonish about Spock? Well, running for the presidency almost makes it—though this particular American aberration might strike a foreigner as funnier than it does us. Doomed minority candidacies have a value as rallying points, and some good people have thought them worthwhile. Spock presumably wanted the kids to put down their bombs and try a little politics. He assuredly didn't expect to win—just to give dissidents someone to vote for.

By stepping so far out of his special competence he ran his greatest risk of ridicule. And, yes, I agree he was a bit silly. His natural constituency of gay libbers, women's libbers, and whatnot clashed aesthetically with the courtly gray-haired Yankee, producing a certain Gilbert and Sullivan effect. And in the end it turned out he knew almost as little about American politics as Senator McGovern, although he'd been exposed to it for several months.

Still, this couldn't be what Muggeridge means. Else why not pick on, say, Dick Gregory with his hunger strikes and equally improbable campaigns? Mr. Muggeridge wouldn't do anything so radically chic as to forgive in a black man what he scorns in a white, would he? No, the major charge against Spock must be in his book, *Baby and Child Care.* And here I must register a personal protest. A book on pediatrics is rather a blank document to somebody out of the child-raising battleground, and I can see why, to switch buffoons a moment, Vice President Agnew doesn't bother to refresh himself with the text before passing on the current cant about it. But when you need it, this book is a blooming marvel. It reads your mind for you, strokes it, and does everything but shut up the baby for you itself. I myself owe Spock a considerable debt and am glad to have a chance to acknowledge it here.

To anyone with a historical memory at all (and what would a Vice President want with one of those?), it must have come as news that Spock invented permissiveness. When I first came to this country as a bootless refugee in 1940, it was generally breathed about in the foreign colony that American children were spoiled rotten, with their progressive schools and their over-Freuded parents and their jumbo malteds; and whether this was true then, it certainly became so in the theorizing of the forties, with names like Aldrich, Powers, and Gesell, leading the charge.

If anything, Dr. Spock's book came as a mild corrective to this. It nodded politely to the going wisdom of permissiveness. But its real message was, throw away this book; you've probably read too much already. Get to know your baby instead, and yourself. It was, in a sense, an "end of ideology" book in child psychology. As Lynne Z. Bloom points out in her useful book, *Doctor Spock: Biography of a Conservative Radical,* even the brief permissive sections were toned down considerably in subsequent editions, until by the time Spock had emerged as a leader of rebellious youth, his advice had become quite stately. "Firmness keeps them lovable," he said, hardly the secret of Abbie Hoffman.

Far from being the dogmatic crank that words like "buffoon" suggest, Spock understood that child-raising was a question that had to be revisited from generation to generation, as the life around the question changed. E.g., if you were raised too strictly yourself, you might want to raise your child too loosely; but, says Spock, this will go against your grain, your instinct for how the job is done, and you will rage inwardly at your kids for getting away with things you couldn't have. "I think that good parents who naturally lean toward strictness should stick to their guns." And so on. Is this the funny part?

It should be stressed that only a tiny portion of *Baby and Child Care* is taken up with such matters at all. Other chapters have names like Various Milks and Various Sugars and Common Kinds of Indigestion. Maybe the joke is in there someplace. Under Croup or Breathing Troubles. I just give up on that. What interests me particularly is that the very mild permissiveness of Spock and the others is now considered such a proven disaster. Having marched in my share of peace marches, I'm sorry to learn that my companions were all hopelessly warped by demand feeding. (That war again. Tiresome little thing.) But I am also puzzled by the fact that administration spokesmen declare this to be a basically fine generation anyway, with only a few rotten apples. So why not a note of thanks for Dr. Spock? Or are we still to blame him for the junkies in the ghetto, whose mothers read Spock under 25-watt bulbs and decided then and there to give their kids everything?

And what is offered in place of Spock? Not, I trust, the bleeding bottoms of old England, the hired nannies, and tender loving schoolmasters. I don't know whether anyone has found a way of raising children that works across the board. Even Dr. Spock can only say, like St. Augustine, "love God and do as you will." Without love, strictness and permissiveness wind up in the same dismalness. Meantime, Dr. Spock at least offers you something for your croup. Also meantime, Mr. Muggeridge might think more carefully about whom he calls a buffoon around here. Some Americans have no sense of humor.

1973

21 / *A Great Place for Bad Writers*

Last year Eire did for writers and artists what the United States does for oilmen: made their gushings virtually tax-free. So far, there has been no great invasion to take advantage of this, only a quick dribble of hacks. Good writers presumably move more slowly. Although literary men talk about money as much as anyone alive, there is a touch of the Sam Spade about it. "Don't be too sure that I'm as crooked as I'm supposed to be." What they really believe in is magic and spells; they want to know how their amulets and charms will travel and whether their sacred powers carry across water.

The question of why writers function better in this place than that can gnaw your brain away if you let it. For simple survival they have always tended to cluster around the great trading centers, holding their caps out to strangers, and they seem to sing harder when there's a damp chill in the air; but, beyond that, the writer looking for the great good place, where his hypochondria won't kick up too badly and happiness won't smother him, can only consult the mysterious record: London, Paris, Russia, Mississippi, and this place here—Dublin, good for some writers, a pleasant death to others.

A writer's weather atlas would probably look pre-Ptolemaic, with a swollen temperate zone and great blank spaces to north and south. With all the bravura of someone who has been here for just two weeks, I should like to consider this strangest of developments, The Great Hibernian Ink Swell, from the viewpoint of the scheming carpetbagger who wants to save taxes and his soul at the same time.

To take first things first: the actual Irish weather report is really a recording made in 1922, which no one has had occasion to change. "Scattered showers, periods of sunshine. Ideal writing conditions." That is, wet enough to keep you indoors, but no occasion for suicide. A little sun to illuminate your manuscript, and enough wind and whatnot to circulate the blood in your palm.

The moral weather is curiously mixed too. A writer becomes a personage quickly, with only one big TV channel to worry about and a superb grapevine, and remains one, like a priest, forever. So he is spared the ghostly cakewalk around the rim of oblivion that Americans do in their sleep. Instead, he may be threatened by dense clouds of smug, and you see the occasional portly one-book poet who has succumbed and who waddles the bars like an alderman, nodding and smiling—one appearance on television has stamped his mug on the nation's consciousness. Whatever Ireland is for good writers, it's paradise for bad ones.

To counteract this is the fair certainty that one's back is being bitten briskly around the clock in all the more literate pubs. Irish gossip, to judge from my brief experience, is still of the very finest quality, like the woolens. It is a form of creation that aims, at once, to enlarge its subjects and to belittle them. When the gossip has done with you, you are a giant clown, a Behan or his opposite, a solemn Paddy, with every strain of criminality, piety, thirst immortalized in anecdotes which then proceed to grow on their own. The town is as full as ever of "characters" all created by each other, and how funny this year's Behan seems depends not so much on himself as on the wit of the storyteller.

This requires a good deal of talking and drinking, and these have been known to distract a man from his writing. Yet I think this menace has been exaggerated. The talking has stringent standards that tend to counteract the effects of the alcohol. Anything which smacks of blather, of sentimentality, or of strained facetiousness will be shot down, now or after you leave. The stories may seem to ramble at times, but the best of them can be masterpieces of organization with the subplots strung like pearls. With everyone else wanting to talk, you have to justify your own noise at each turn.

Excellent practice for writing, if you can be bothered to go home and do it. And if you can't, perhaps it's for the best. The talking is not absolutely compulsory—you can become like Joyce, a monstrous legend of silence instead, with marvelous stories told about it. But, generally, this is not the place for strong, silent writers. You don't really have to be that much of a poet—I'm not dead sure they read each other anyway—but you should be able to talk a bit.

In return for the wasted hours, you get not only the exercise of trying to think well through a haze of booze, but the blessings of the language around you. The queer cadences of Gaelic twisting its way reluctantly into English, and the unexpected vocabulary, influence your prose even before they reach your voice. So if you weary of the flat American sentence, or the overtrained English one, Irish will freshen the mixture for you. (It will also, in the interim stage where I now find myself, produce some unholy mongrel effects.)

So far, the balance is pretty good. Your nerves hum quietly, and your character improves immediately. Even the famous drinking exists largely as material for anecdotes. Half the stories you hear hinge on some colossal feat of drinking, and the other half on unspeakable financial roguery: yet Ireland seems honest as countries go, and the famous drunks I have met have been either out of season or grossly misrepresented. The conversation hardly leaves a man time to swallow anything.

The worst thing that can happen to you is a slow leak of ambition, which for Americans would bring them about down to par, and the compensating delusion that your Irish reputation has worldwide repercussions. More than anyone but the French, the Irish tend to go on incessantly about their own boys, and a native writer might need an occasional trip abroad to take a look at the other ostriches.

Resident Americans are in less danger. Cursed for life with exact knowledge of the slippery quotations on "literary reputation," they are more likely to fret about being out of the mainstream. There is no answer for this: they *are* out of the mainstream. Anything they write about the contemporary world will be a work of audacious imagination. Instead you find yourself sliding around in time, backward into a Victorian prosody or forward into postmodern experiment, absolutely unhampered by fashion. The freedom is alarming at first. You must make your own school. Your influences come from books, not from current events or from the weak trickle of pop culture that arrives via England. And you choose the books yourself.

The writer's life seems to me more abstract and "literary" here than in America. Folk legends still make more likely material than the daily paper, and even a Yankee anarchist like J. P. Donleavy seems more bookish than the American black humorists. The classic reverence for literature as such fortifies one and reminds one of what the enterprise is about.

What does an expatriate write about over here? American subject matter changes with such hysterical speed that you cannot stay away from home for long and still hope to write about it. If you need that pulse, you will lose it particularly fast in Ireland. You may find you do better without it—a pleasant risk. What you have instead is those characters, in a turmoil of self-creation, and the world's most astonishing faces to match: faces all taken to extremes, of beauty, plainness, wit, stupidity, and even the latter somehow striking and poetic.

And you have your own memories, more bizarre and unreal with each passing day.

Whether Ireland keeps its present happy distance, just close enough to overhear Anglo-American literature, without having its own voice drowned, is probably more a political than a literary question. The slackening of censorship, for instance, allows domestic Irish writers to compete in the world erotic market for the first time—though a good Catholic boy may still find this hard to do—but it allows alien sounds in, and an alien approach to writing. Bawdiness is hardly new to Ireland, and neither is blasphemy; but they have hidden themselves in allusion and metaphor. Freedom could drive the irony from Irish writing and leave nothing but honest feeling, a less interesting feature.

But this seems some distance away. The Oral Academy still reigns in the pubs, though of course there is more to the literary life than that. The writers who come here with the tax incentive (at the moment busy groping for some other reason to explain their presence) may give as much as they get, if they don't all vanish into country castles. The Irish literary scene, like any other, needs its periodic injections. And the local characters need someone else to perform for and other bards to interpret them if the scene is not to lapse into the staleness that always threatens.

1971

22 / *There Is No (Irish) Mafia*

The Irish drinking season is upon us (as usual) so it might be wise to heed a few words from the Rev. Andrew Greeley before things get completely out of hand.

"The drinking of the Irish is not a particularly amusing phenomenon, which may be why I am not enchanted with the Joe Flaherty, Jimmy Breslin, Pete Hamill style of Irish journalism. I am angry with anyone who assumes that the Irish drunk is a happy and charming person. He is, on the contrary, a deeply unhappy, tragic human being. . . . Finally, I am most angry of all at the thought that many of us can only be Irish when we have had too much to drink."

I absolutely agree with his Reverence about all this—the Irish drunk is a miserable specimen: and if you think tragic is too strong a word for him, *he* certainly doesn't. On any given night he can spot Oedipus 20 pounds and a home-court advantage and beat him to the wailing wall hands down. Other nights, of course, he thinks he's happy and charming, and this can be just plain disastrous, as Father Greeley says. Imitations of James Cagney imitating George M. Cohan just don't make it anymore. (On the other hand, my own Fred Astaire holds up remarkably well.) The only slight quibble I have with Greeley is over the writers he has cited.

Take Breslin. For centuries now, Irishmen have been listening to querulous sermonettes like the above, and all it does is make them thirsty. You can't get to a drinking man that way. But Breslin's accounts of a whiskey-sodden kitchen with its listless stinks and fur-tongued rages, and the mockery of a sex life that waits next door can give a man pause. Or Flaherty. What writer ever conjured a more poignant image than Flaherty's fear of finding the name "Goodyear" printed across his liver? My hands shake with emotion every time I think of it.

As for Hamill, I've somehow missed his celebrations of drunkenness altogether: I thought his subject was festivity, over a few jars, and friendship and sweet nostalgia—which surely even Father Greeley would allow, in moderation.

The classic Irish confrontation between the prude and the wild man does persist over here: the wild man ripping and tearing some joy from his enemy, life, before it cheats him for sure, while Father Prude trims his lamp like a wise virgin and keeps things going. But it's my belief that the best Irish-American writers contain both these souls, fighting like cats in a sack. Since Flaherty and Breslin have each written novels this season, it may be a good time to see how the battle is doing and who's on top in the sack.

First of all, though, talk of an Irish Mafia has to go: the above three probably do as little for each other as friends can do (who would believe them if they logrolled?) and their prose styles are in many ways antithetical. All one can say is that Flaherty's *Fogarty & Co.* and Breslin's *The Greening of Dermott Davey* show certain traces of a common culture, and a common desire both to escape this culture and take it with them, which is perhaps the most enduring of Irish traits.

Each book has a protagonist who likes to dwell on his troubles at generous length. But either the sacrament of penance or the scorn of near relatives has taught them to blame themselves first (it isn't always so, alas). Shamus Fogarty spreads out luxuriantly all the materials for self-pity—but then doesn't indulge it. He has woman trouble with tassels on—but only such as a rat as himself might expect. In fact, each of these writers shows a notable chivalry to women: Flaherty courteously makes Fogarty's troublesome ex-wife the most fascinating character in his book; Patrolman Dermott Davey is almost reclaimed by a Joan of

Arc of an IRA girl but returns to his mean masculine sins without her; and Hamill can even manage a hoarse lullaby for Bella Abzug.

So, whatever cramping effects a lopsided cult of the Virgin Mary may produce (Fogarty has a fine Chaucerian tale to tell about that) it seems to leave the possibility of an enormous respect, a latent belief in female greatness as well as goodness. Otherwise, the Church is mostly bad news for this crowd. They seem to have left it wistfully, with none of the sour anger that used to turn Irish apostates into such inside-out Catholic bores: but they have left it for a more deadly reason. The Church does not impress them anymore.

The last thing one expected to live to see. But there it is. Fogarty's obligatory priest has all the stature of a stage English parson. Davey's practically evaporates on the page. And judging from Hamill's columns, his would probably be a bloodless fop who wipes the poor off his silk slippers at night. Fogarty remembers more respectfully the ear-twisting nuns of school. But those days are gone. Even the old sexual repression, which once brought Catholic rebels gibbering to their knees (see John McGahern's *The Dark,* out of Ireland itself), translates in Flaherty as not much worse than the usual awkwardness of middle-class arrangements.

At any rate, Fogarty has made up for a slow sexual start, playing masterful catch-up ball, as he might say himself. Breslin's Dermott Davey is a generation back. He lives in a neighborhood where the husbands wait outdoors smoking while their wives pretend to go to sleep, to avoid embarrassment; and his own love life is more like loveless death.

But sex for these people died in the kitchen, not the confessional. The new Irish know that priests and cops come from the same stuff as the rest of us and that attacking them is like hitting your big toe. Only their response to this varies. Hamill favors rebirth all round; Flaherty would rather sit back and laugh. Breslin, the most darkly pessimistic of the three (Flaherty's pessimism is incurably sunny in contrast), tells black jokes until you laugh real blood: but in *Dermott Davey* he relents halfway and allows his hero temporary sanity on the barricades of Ulster. A victory of heart over talent, because this part of the book is also the weakest, like the happy endings in Dickens. Breslin doesn't trust happiness; it's a very small entry in the Irish history books.

In each case, the note is the same old Jansenistic gloom about humanity, lit by jokes, memories, and sometimes just plain lit. Drunks are the perfect subject because they are humanity at its ugliest—and they don't care. They have escaped briefly, if only into the broom closet. But our authors don't hide the vomit on the drunk's coat or the anarchic buzzing in his head. The hangover is life's vengeance, the real moment when an Irishman is most completely himself, if I read my Beckett right.

Next best to the drunk is the entertaining scoundrel. He too has venerable roots, and there are definite rules for scoundrels, as John Leo, the wit's wit, might say: (1) They must be funny—paying their dues to society by providing great stories, and (2) they must harass Them rather than Us. In the monstrously unjust arrangements of English rule, scoundrels were needed to redress the balance. When a foreign landlord with buckteeth and a monocle has just bounced you off your farm, the least you can do is poach it and juggle the rent. But you don't create disorder among your own people. On the contrary, the poacher was often as not a force for good in the community, dispensing his rabbits with an even hand—as a Mafioso frequently helps to keep the peace in his own home town.

Over here, this often converts into a fascination with cops and political bosses. Cops are O.K. when they're Us against Them, as some feel they are right now. Hamill, co-founder of the Boss Tweed Society, can even see a scabrous boss like Tweed as Us against Them, which takes some doing. (O.K., I know it's a gag—but still, some gag!) Breslin, the encyclopedist of cops, faces the hard fact that Us can sometimes become Them and that a New York cop has more in common with a British soldier than with an Irish rebel—but he loves the buggers anyway, for their vestigial lawlessness, and his tales of police procedure in *Dermott Davey* are the funniest and best I've read, in this, the Year of the Cop.

Anyway, there is nothing irresponsible about these writers themselves. They expect no help from God—who was misrepresented to them, and an Irishman doesn't forget things like that—and they look for no relief, or escape, in cursing God, the old way. Hamill bellows and burns instead for a better society, a kingdom of heaven like unto a banquet; Flaherty looks to a love of women, children, friends, cleansed of bull and charged with intelligence; Breslin, a more self-conscious artist-performer, doesn't say what he wants: but his novel gives hints that if he let go of his tight, clown's control, he would be the most passionate of the three.

I don't want to suggest that these writers exhaust the spectrum (if you *can* exhaust a spectrum) of Irish-American writers. The latter come in many other shapes and sizes, some released like arrows by the loosening of religious discipline, and others, such as the incomparable J. F. Powers, who would have happened anyway. I drink to them all, moderately.

Let's just call Hamill-Breslin-Flaherty the New York school, shaped by the city as much as by the Faith, primarily journalists, which city life favors, but with the bright-colored imaginations of country storytellers. They love words—although Breslin will squirm twenty minutes before admitting he works on his prose—and they have a healthy Irish reaction to critics, which is to say, to break their legs on sight: so we'll dispense with any more of that.

To return to Father Greeley a moment: he does make one important point. I have a good deal of Irish blood myself and could use some more, but also some Scotch and English, and on behalf of these two-thirds, I was outraged by a recent incident on the Dick Cavett show. Sir Laurence Olivier had just confessed to a weakness for the grape and Cavett asked him if he was Irish. I understand the mistake, since the man is a fine actor and his name begins with an O: but it remains a heavy insult to English drinking, which is among the world's finest, not to mention Scottish, which, despite a patron saint named Andrew, is unlike any drinking I have ever seen anywhere.

It shouldn't be necessary to add (but probably is in our solemn times) that, while alcoholism is a comic property like death which writers can hardly be asked to give up, it is in real life desolate and murderous and has broken the hearts and lives of some of the finest people I know. It also has nothing serious to do with the rich art of Breslin and Flaherty and the tempestuous craft (art is too fancy a word for his recent work, but keep an eye out) of Hamill.

1973

23 / *A Fun-House Mirror*

The worst news to come this way in some time (if you exclude the recent unpleasantness at the polls) is that Tom Wolfe is serious. I don't mean artistically serious—I always assumed that—but, *you* know . . . *serious.* He has been carrying on at some length lately about his baby, the New Journalism, but with none of his old nerve-racking audacity. More like a . . . *grandfather,* for God's sake.

This could have several dire consequences, even beyond the endless panel discussions it has already launched on "Is There a New Journalism," all of which are on Wolfe's head. It has also robbed us of one of our most resourceful literary performers in the middle of his act: rather as if Groucho were to come back at Mrs. Rittenhouse with a lecture on comedy. That sort of thing should be postponed till dotage, at the very earliest.

Wolfe at his best seemed to be impenetrable. No criticism could pierce the white suit or provoke a straight answer. One assumed that the effect was calculated, but one couldn't quite be sure. That is the essence of eccentricity-as-art (see Tiny Tim). He *is* kidding, isn't he? The clown bats his lids, seems not to hear the question. Gooses you, one way or another.

You have to conclude that Wolfe is either tired of acting—we don't have the stamina of the great Englishmen, your Waughs and Sitwells—or wants to try something else (not more essays on the New Journalism, I hope) or, more seriously, that he undervalues what he was doing. N.J. or no N.J. (the initials are ominous), Wolfe was never in the same business as Gay Talese or Dick Schaap—or they with each other. Call A. J. Liebling, Paul Gallico, and Jim Bishop the Old Journalism, and what have you added to any of them? It is surely for desperate graduate students to discover these schools and for writers to keep out of them.

To avoid any further aroma of the panel discussion (which Wolfe is now conducting with himself anyway in *Esquire*) let's allow that the boys he cites are doing something new in close-to-the-skin reporting. But did anyone ever read Wolfe for that? It is actually a quaint feature of his gift that readers assume his reporting to be inaccurate, even when he swears it isn't.

He claims that he and his friends evoke a subject for you as it really is, and maybe that's what his friends do. But in his own case, this is like El Greco boasting about his photographic accuracy. We enjoy Wolfe (or not) precisely for the distortion. We never supposed the Bernsteins were really like that. All the details may have been right in *Radical Chic,* as Wolfe ponderously argues—and as his critics ponderously argue back—but the result was gorgeously unreal. Why? Because the Bernsteins probably don't give a damn about their canapés or what shoes they've got on. Wolfe does and, like the artist he is, makes you share his values. In this sense, Wolfe's Bernsteins are like George Grosz's cartoon Germans, part them and mostly him. The real subject is his imagination, as affected by the Bernsteins.

Wolfe's prose is also a distorting mechanism. He maintains that he finds a language proper to each subject, a special sound to convey its uniqueness; but loyal readers may find that this language is surprisingly similar, whether dealing with stock-car racing or debutantes, and that it obliterates uniqueness and drags everything back to Wolfe's cave. This is what artists do, and it's strange that he refuses to recognize it. In his frenzied assault on the Novel, he allies himself with some quite talented but prosy journalists who don't do any of this, in order to beat up on a form much closer to his own.

Call it subconscious strategy, if you dabble in such superstitions; but his blindness on the point may serve an artistic purpose for himself. By muttering "Reporter, I'm a reporter" over and over, he reminds his nose to stay down near the details where it works best. But upon these truths he imposes his own consciousness, his own selection and rhetoric, and they become Wolfe-truths, and he is halfway over the border into the hated Novel. He ingenuously wonders why no novelist has ever used the reporting he did on the West Coast Beats in *Electric Kool-Aid Acid Test,* but doesn't realize he has already used it himself. That book may well be the best literary work to come out of the Beat Movement, yet the material is quite inaccessible to anyone else. I pity the poor writer following Wolfe to the Coast hoping to find what he found. It is all in Wolfe's skull. The Beats probably weren't like that at all, as far as anyone else could see. In fact, rumor has it that all they wanted to do was splash his white suit. Like everybody.

So let's hear no more social realism out of Wolfe, that supreme fantastist. The Truman Capotes may hold up a tolerably clear glass to nature, but Wolfe holds up a fun-house mirror, and I for one don't give a hoot whether he calls the reflection fact or fiction. But Wolfe seems to feel burdened by his uniqueness and is eager to be one of the boys in the pressroom again, so he has enrolled the Dublin-type storyteller Jimmy Breslin in his raggle-tag school and roaring Pete Hamill, who is not primarily a reporter at all but inspired street lawyer, and just about any writer he can find under forty. All he has done is give literary glamor to some good journeyman reporters, and some journalistic glamor to the essayists, and provide some company for himself.

So, now that we've drummed Wolfe out of his own movement, is there anything left to discuss? At least one good question came out of those lugubrious panel shows—from Pauline Kael, I believe. To wit: Is the New Journalism to be trusted with real history? Or does its natural tendency to personalize issues and to overvalue the reporter's own experience confine its usefulness to smaller units of material?

The best answer we've had to that so far is probably David Halberstam's Vietnam encyclopedia, *The Best and the Brightest,* although Halberstam cheats by adding much erudition to his own experience and by effacing himself almost squeamishly from the text. (When he does have to mention himself, you can practically sense him reddening.) But the personality is there all right and the imperious angle of vision, and Halberstam has dramatized his material into possibly the best novel yet written about the war.

As told to and by David Halberstam, this godforsaken war would seem to be the ideal subject for nonfiction fiction. Unlike most wars, which make rotten fiction in themselves—all plot and no characters, or made-up characters—Vietnam seems to be the perfect mix; the characters make the war, and the war unmakes the characters. The gods, fates, furies had a relatively small hand in it. The mess was man-made, a synthetic, by think tank out of briefing session. At the top sits the boy President in his tree-house, smarting from the Bay of Pigs and even more from Khrushchev's personal put-down in Vienna, badly needing someone to push around for home consumption—and Vietnam was available. Underneath, there's his military guru, Max Taylor, the kind of smoothy the boy President hits it off with, but by ill chance a devotee of brush-fire wars, needing a specimen to prove his point; and Bob McNamara, the chilly systems analyst itching to do for Saigon what he'd done for Ford Motors; and down through murkier quirks—Walt Rostow's mystical faith in bombing; and McGeorge Bundy, "the minister's son in the whorehouse" (LBJ), mesmerized by his first sight of blood at Pleiku.

It sounds dangerously like the Cleopatra's-nose school of history—could we have avoided war if Bundy weren't quite such a prig and Rostow such an excitable little fellow? But Halberstam is smart enough to sidestep this New Journalism trap: he suggests that behind the Bundys there were more Bundys, a whole class was involved. Vietnam was, above all, the effete snobs' war—the Eastern eggheads, who had been painted pink for girls by Joe McCarthy and were out to prove their manhood or bust. It wasn't just Lyndon Johnson who wanted to be John Wayne (though that was the topper); it was McGeorge Bundy, dean of Harvard, and Walt Rostow of MIT, tall in the saddle and heading for the quagmire.

Well, a whole class of manly Bundys may be even harder to accept than one—the sins of the New Journalism are not lessened by these multiplications. But I think reviewers have missed the subtlety of Halberstam's analysis here. He quotes Emerson's saying that "events are in the saddle" several times, which implies that the Bundy-Rostows were only allowed up there to pose with them. They were just the kind of people who like to pose with events. But it didn't matter. There was no stopping the runaway war. Max Taylor saw his brush-fire skirmish combust into a forest fire but was helpless to stop it; McNamara's charts indicated an unmistakable Edsel, but he couldn't pull it off the market. The book ends with Nixon about to set off on his four-year plan to end it. And he may have had one at that. By then the war was devouring plans like a dragon chewing on paper.

The difficulty remains: If a whole class did it, why pick on Rostow? And, if events did it, why pick on a class? Well, because it's interesting, that's why. In respect to Kael's question, I would say that Halberstam's personalizing of issues makes for better reading and, occasionally, more dubious history. Some of the vignettes are wonderfully shrewd (Bundy again), some are blown-up cartoons (LBJ). All the Army officers tend to be stiff and reserved—Halberstam doesn't allow for how much of this is a standard professional mannerism. In each case, we are at the author's mercy, depending on his omniscience, psychological accuracy, and personal honor (did Dean Rusk call him Fred by mistake one day? does this boy carry grudges?), a heavy burden even for a priest.

Because this isn't gossip and opinion anymore or Tom Wolfe zipping along the strip in his outasight Gucci-puccis. Vietnam has reached the war-criminal phase, at least in the public mind; and the reader starts out with blood in his eye. The historian doubles as prosecutor; and a sloppy, spiteful hatchet job goes into the record with the rest. We can thank God the task has fallen this time to someone as scrupulous and informed as Halberstam. Still, the fine malice of his portraits shows what one of the hairier new journalists might do with it.

Not that we need be too concerned with the reputations of Jack Kennedy's whizz kids, who seem to be doing very nicely for alleged war criminals. But, for the delicate task of analyzing how and why we get into wars, one has to doubt the capacity of the new personal journalism as practiced domestically, unless backed, as here, by massive scholarship and impersonal historical sense. Halberstam's dramatization of events is beyond praise, and for that he does need faces. But if the space and skill lavished on these leaves us supposing that the war was caused by faces, we might have been better off without them at that.

1972

24 / *Beat Down and Beatific*

"Did you catch Kerouac tonight? He was wild." "Yeah, well, we had Kerouac last week. Equally wild, man." Columbia forties-fifties, long before *On the Road.* As a neighborhood kibitzer, I kept missing him by five minutes, with the new smell, marijuana, still heavy on the air, like Satan's home-brewed incense. You probably had such a hot dog at your school—the country was starved for hot dogs then. But this one, in the media capital, produced with just one formidable friend and a few assorted spear-carriers, the Beat Generation.

I was reminded, sight and smell, of that period by Bruce Cook's *The Beat Generation.* The Beats belonged to their time and place as firmly as the 1920 flappers to theirs. The streets round Columbia had just been cleared of naval cadets singing "I've Got Sixpence." The veterans were back, of no mind to settle down with Greer Garson, or Philip Wylie's Mom, or the propaganda-sodden homefront. Jewish writers were enrolling at Montana and Iowa to discover the country they'd been fighting for. Kerouac and his pals were pounding the highways—aimlessly, said the old man, who could understand traveling so long as you dropped a bomb when you got there—to find something commensurate with their war-primed excitement. It could have happened anywhere, there were two to six guys like that on every campus; but it happened at Columbia, with San Francisco as matchbox: two places beautifully prepared for it.

At that, what happened was only a happening, never a real generation. The two coasts were away out of sync. The omelet fell apart, as with such eggs it must. Kenneth Patchen didn't like the Easterners from the start. Rexroth approved on principle but wound up slashing Kerouac in *The New York Times* (for *Mexico City Blues*). Kerouac, for his part, thought that Rexroth was "just a crazy old anarchist anyway, who might twist the Beat thing into something political." The Westerners, tracing through Jack London and the Wobblies, always carried the germs of social action; and the Easterners had struck West, as usual, to escape just that. Within a year of *On the Road* word has it that Kerouac was being laughed at in the Bay Area for his drunken, mystagogical caperings: and only Allen Ginsberg, with his superior sense of history and Napoleonic gifts for organization, was able to establish even the appearance of solidarity.

And, in time, even the Eastern half of the omelet proved none too solid. The establishing documents, *On the Road* and Ginsberg's *Howl*, were as unlike as two cries from the depths can be. Kerouac insisted on ecstasy, an imperative that would eventually drain him dry. Jack loved America more than any country deserves, and it was through no inconsistency that he would end up as paranoid about it as a Minute Man. Ginsberg saw mostly woodworm, dry rot, and tears in the same material.

At first, it didn't matter. Ginsberg maintained that his "Howl" was really for hope, a spring canticle. Kerouac allowed that, while Beat stood for beatific, it also meant beat down and furtive. What they were really celebrating was their own brand of open, swinging friendship, as opposed to the stiff sexual arrangements and resolutely loveless male friendship of commercial America, and trifling points of dogma could be overlooked. By the first frost of middle age, though, Kerouac had turned from Ginsberg, manic rejecting depressive; except that by then the parts were reversed. Ginsberg had faced his despair earlier, when he still had the strength to cope with it. Kerouac had postponed his too long.

The last days of Kerouac are enough to strike terror in any writer's heart. I tend to believe he handled his tormented, overloaded temperament as well as it could be handled, squeezing out what joy he could and retiring to his tent when his liver clouded over, trying to write to the end. But let's stick to such of his story as affected the Beat phenomenon.

His most famous contribution, besides the Compulsory Joy, was Automatic Writing—a theory of speed composition calculated, like psychoanalysis (another postwar toy), to surprise the subconscious and shake out the real stuff. It now seems possible that Kerouac wanted to bypass the subconscious by outrunning it. There is little in all those speed books that doesn't confirm his elected persona again and yet again. The words on the top of one's head do not necessarily come from anywhere near the subconscious.

Kerouac's manicness was a necessary strategy for fighting off the forest-dark, French-American glooms. He had been mustered out of the Navy in 1942 as a schizoid personality; and even allowing for the pin-the-tail-on-the-diagnoses of those days, the Navy may have been onto something. But what for him was therapy became for himself and others aesthetic doctrine. Everybody else was buying electric gadgets and pressure cookers, so why not pressure poetry? Charles Olson of the Black Mountain school talked about poems in terms of pure energy discharge. Ginsberg and Burroughs were fascinated with electronics, neural patterns, molecular structures, etc.; and it seemed for a while that the years that gave us IBM would also give us an electromagnetic literature to match, with readers fried and hopping to volts of poetenergy.

Kerouac's type of manicness could also be harnessed by a generation to another preoccupation of the time—the advertising style. Burroughs for one was fascinated by Madison Avenue and talked of a merger between art and selling—of artistic commercials, packed with glittering juxtapositions. Beat euphoria fit beautifully into the spiel of the postwar pitchman. *Howl,* for all its originality, has some of the cadence of advertising slogans. And such Ginsbergian combos as "hydrogen juke box" or "skin of machinery" are just what copywriters still grope for through the Westport night.

There were other things in the air that could use Kerouacian energy for booster fuel. The celebration of the low-life ordinary, after the neurasthenic strangeness of war, was one such; the need to sell, to convert, to make like Bishop Sheen or Arthur Godfrey was another. Poetry could be used for incantation, and Ginsberg worked out a theory of metrics based on breath and body rhythm that would have also been ideal for pop preaching. It suited him, so long as he was there to read the poems himself. But the tyranny of breath had bad effects on less gifted cantors. It meant that poems could be read only one way. It also meant that what the eye, moving faster than the lungs, saw on the page was flat as a song lyric without music. (Traditional metrics also allowed for breath, but gave you a greater choice of tempos.)

The hottest thing on the 1940–1950s' agenda was the urge to defy the Academy, which had grown flabby and remote as academies will, and had made the practice of Art seem a hopelessly difficult penance. But just as the first Reformers spoke excellent Latin, so were the first Beats well-read Ivy Leaguers. Burroughs of Harvard was the teacher, Ginsberg, with straight A's in history, and Kerouac, a bilingual dropout and campus-sniffer, willing to talk literary theory forever, were the pupils. Later they picked their own Villon, Gregory Corso, troubador, boy-criminal, prison, *and* a trace of Harvard, an exquisite literary touch.

But once the walls were down, there were plenty of visi-Goths ready to swarm in. Why shouldn't everyone write poetry? It went with the GI Bill and the open roads. Never mind Ginsberg's breath metrics (a new academy in the making) or the rigors of the best Black Mountaineers. They dug Kerouac's mood and Ginsberg's use of private subject matter and thought that was all there was to it. The air was thick with confessions right then, movie stars becoming nuns, Communists becoming pigeons, everyone cleaning the plate for the New Age, so there was subject matter to burn. And the new open-admissions policy to poetry produced a situation comparable only to the land grab in Oklahoma: Sooners racing each other for the big homosexual admission turf or the junk and jazz concession. Philip Lamantia, reaching far out, was knocked off a park bench by an angel.

The hip Sooners grabbed up the earth in no time and reached for the sky. Kerouac still led the charge, war-whooping through Zen Buddhism, opening up Hinduism for trade, and wheeling back to Christianity. But when there was no sky left for the untalented, a plague fell on his young followers; and the speechless poet, the cool beatnik, with nothing to offer but Attitude, landed among them. The postwar world was over, and all the balloons came down together. Kerouac turned away in disgust. "I don't want any beatniks on my milk route," he muttered and stomped back to his beginnings in Lowell, Massachusetts. He couldn't even stop off at a university as an over-the-hill romantic should. "Success means 5,000 English instructors sneering at you," he said. There was no place to go but home.

I wouldn't propose this is strict chronological history. These things were happening at once, or backward, depending on which coffee house you went to. But the Beautiful Dream of everyone being a poet woke to an awful hangover at some point. Where it might have led to a love of poetry, whether you could write it or not, it led to a lofty, if-I-can't-do-it,-it-can't-be-worth-doing silence. The Beats had always been too clannish, listening to each other in indigestible earfuls, and they wound up bored stiff with poetry. Since they were too loyal to blame each other (only an older man like Rexroth could do that) they, or their young imitators, blamed poetry instead and said that words were just inadequate and even called on the wisdom of the East to bear them out (though no one chatters like an Indian holy man with a head of steam).

LSD completed the route, blasting away the last vestiges of the neurotic perfectionism that even a speed writer needs, only needs faster. Acid-heads may or may not continue to write—their tongues are sometimes loosed to flapping point—but they don't sweat so hard for the word that will make *you* see: because they see it so easily, and you'll never see it.

Writers afflicted with vocation would refuse to enter heaven itself if they couldn't describe it afterwards. They'd rather stay in hell with words. So the Beats dropped out of their own movement. Burroughs, the ex-junkie, shied away from LSD and insists you can't write anything on drugs. Kerouac stuck with his port jug, trying to find the word in a million that would save him; and Corso still plugs along on his own, no part of Timothy Leary's drug spectacular. The Beats were, goddamit, a literary movement, of whatever quality; and whatever Leary's running, it isn't literary. Just talkative.

That leaves the other founding father, Allen Ginsberg, in charge of the old ship, Beat. Ginsberg is quoted in Cook's book trendily pooh-poohing verbal communication and, more dishearteningly, prating about ecology. (Couldn't a poet find another word?) Allen may just be trying something new, his hair-trigger sense of history responding to every feather breath of fashion, or he may be happy to be out of the hell of words at last.

Watching him lately on TV chanting like a beaming choir master to a group of baffled self-conscious-looking kids, I thought how far he'd come from the blind-rat maze of *Howl* and the screaming nightsweats of *Kaddish*. He thought he'd seen the best minds of his generation destroyed even before he'd started and, since then, he'd seen Kerouac's destroyed for real and had wept at his friend's grave and had seen his own very nearly destroyed several times over; and I thought, you've probably earned your chant, even if the audience hasn't.

And there in the background, doing anonymous penance on the guitar, was Bob Dylan. By current change rates, the Beats actually had some staying power. The gelatinous Eisenhower years could have slowed down mercury itself. And the Beats outlasted any pop fashion we are likely to see soon.

1972

25 / *The Beat Movement Concluded*

Bruce Cook's *The Beat Generation* is a brave attempt to find a missing link between the booziferous Beat and the acidophilic hippie. But this question seems to be still in the awkward stage—too stale for journalism and not ready for history—and the specimens he interviewed backed off from it in a body. The Beats are still recovering from old limelight burns, self-inflicted, and are currently in the silent ward with Sontag, Bob Dylan, and other victims.

In fact, as early as Kennedy's inauguration, the original Beats were on the run from their own publicity. In 1961, Norman Mailer said, "When you write about something the way Kerouac wrote about hipsters, it's never the same afterwards. Instead of the actual thing being the model, the writing becomes the model." Bad beatniks had long since driven out good, and the real McCoy was harder to find than a Nazi general. "That all happened 10 years ago," said John Clellon Holmes in 1959, and Holmes had been in on the actual christening and knew his baby backwards. "We've all changed." *On the Road* had been out less than a year at that point.

It is often forgotten that Kerouac used the word Beat nostalgically. The Beat thing *had already happened:* whatever was left of it, he killed with his book, sure as Hemingway killed Pamplona, and as sure as every book kills something or other. The period Cook explores might better be called "The Death of Hip," when people sat around in their Kerouac masks, waiting for new prophets with new instructions. To find live faces one must trace Beatitude back the other way to its beginnings, before self-knowledge and death slithered into the garden in book form.

Although the big explosion took place after World War II, it was, like many postwar items, something of a synthetic. Most of the elements existed already and were bounced together in troop transports, C.O. farms, and other unlikely meeting places of war and postwar. To take just one ingredient: much of the Beat life-style, or at least notes toward it, existed among a small group at Columbia University as early as 1939 and needed only missionaries to take it on the road and blend it. In this sense, Kerouac might loosely be called St. Paul as farce.

The Columbia progenitors were making a conscious retreat from politics, and the dates for this were suggested to me inadvertently by an interesting book of James Wechsler's called *Reflections of an Angry, Middle-aged Editor.* It seems that Wechsler (class of '35) and Kerouac (1940–) had an old-boys' confrontation at Madison Square Garden in 1958. Kerouac read a poem to Harpo Marx, that went in part: "Harpo, I'll always love you/ . . . Oh, when last you powder-puffed your white face with a fish barrel cover/Harpo, who is that lion I saw you with?" Wechsler notes sternly, "I find little rhyme or reason in these reflections." It was American schizophrenia at its finest—political man staring blankly at gypsy moth, each with half of his brain missing. Kerouac tried to patch things up by saying that a tangerine had recently fallen on his head and he had decided on the spot to believe in a personal god. The meeting ended in confusion.

It could have been Abbie Hoffman twitting the good Judge (trivia note: Groucho's real name is Julius), except that these two were only eight years apart in age. Student politics had crested in Wechsler's graduating year (and perhaps one always retains the style of one's graduating year). Had he hung around campuses longer, he might at least have seen the point of the Harpo poem. "I and our various friends must have seen all the movies that were produced, without exception, from 1934 to 1937," wrote Thomas Merton (class of '39). "Most of them were simply awful . . . yet I confess a secret loyalty to the memory of my great heroes: Chaplin, W. C. Fields, Harpo Marx." The Great Escape was on, Harpo to Mrs. Rittenhouse to Zen, and what Wechsler was confronting in 1958 was actually the last exhausted fugitive: Kerouac, who freakishly defended Eisenhower that night, as our last refuge against politics.

The years of Beat gestation fortunately cover the whole undergraduate career of Thomas Merton, and he has left some valuable notes on it in *The Seven Storey Mountain.* In 1935 the political temperament was so ascendant that even a spiritual type like Merton gave the Communist party a whirl. There was a peace strike that year (though Merton wondered who cared whether a student struck or not—only a writers' strike could be less effectual), and Ad Reinhardt, the abstract painter, got into trouble for drawing a political cartoon which featured Nicholas Murray Butler swinging a stick at some helpless children.

Within a year or two Reinhardt had started his move to abstraction, Merton was climbing his lonely mountain, and the stage was set for political delinquents like Kerouac. Merton dropped out of politics in 1936 when the Spanish Civil War started and the Communists decided peace wasn't so great after all. (Pacifism had been almost the whole of Merton's politics.) The juicy disillusionments of Stalinism took care of the rest one by one.

According to Ed Rice's excellent little book on Merton, *The Man in the Sycamore Tree,* Merton and his group proceeded to stage a complete dry-run of the Beat movement. Up at the poet Bob Lax's place in Olean they held novel-writing contests, watching each other narrowly to see who was going fastest. (Later Kerouac would retire the trophy.) They grew beards and shaved their heads, and by 1940 the place had swelled to a regular commune, with people cooking, chopping, writing, and listening to Bix Beiderbeck around the clock. They even built a couple of tree-houses to emphasize their position on adulthood, responsibility, politics. An old friend says that Merton and Lax remained the most childish men he'd ever met, right to the day of Merton's death.

And back at Columbia, the boys kept a guru named Bramachari, a Hindu monk, and dabbled in all the name brands of mysticism. They read a book called *Witchcraft, Magic and Alchemy* and they read Pantanjali's *Yoga* and some of them ate health food. "There is a lot of rushing about in cars and trains and buses," wrote Rice, adding that there were at least twelve different names for marijuana. ("A friend with weed is a friend indeed.")

Of course, these men were all of draft age, and they knew that all the peace strikes in the world would not help them now. The political activism of Wechsler's Columbia looked ludicrous, and all they could do now was play hard and become saints in the time that was left. Merton decided to become a Catholic the day Hitler invaded Poland, and he entered his monastery three days after Pearl Harbor: Not out of cowardice for sure, nobody ever joined the Trappists out of cowardice—but out of an implicit despair with human solutions and a sense that the war was the sum of our sins; the only way not to be a Hitler or a Stalin was to be a saint.

It may be observed that Americans have not greatly changed their ways of reacting to the draft. The Beats and Korea, the hippies and Vietnam—these mystic flights have become as regular as bird migrations. But there is more than some dumb biologic law involved: there are also several genuine traditions of anarchic escape. A class graduates and takes its secrets with it, but something is left on the still air of universities. And the class of '40 left something at Columbia.

For instance, Merton's private letters are written in a speed shorthand distinctly related to Kerouac's bop prosody. Quoting randomly—Merton (from his last days in India): "is everywhere jovial Lamas who acclaim me the chenrezigs and the reincarnation of the Dops of Lompzog or the Mops of Jopsmitch." And Kerouac: "Be crazy dumbsaint of the mind. . . . Writer-director of Earthly movies Sponsored and Angeled in Heaven." If Merton's letters are ever published, closer parallels will certainly be found.

They will also be found in Bob Lax's letters and Reinhardt's and Rice's. This private language, made out of bits and scraps of Henry Miller, Joyce, Groucho, Thomas Wolfe, and other thirties' voices, seems to have been bantered around in various subdialects by all of Merton's friends. (Lax's poems have since refined it to a kind of semaphore.) Literary time then stood still for that weird moment after the war, and Kerouac's version of the class of '40's code language blended with other national sounds to become the voice of postwar youth.

Only a small part of the story (the Bay Area contribution requires less than a bookshelf) and only a small part of Columbia itself. The big men on campus included John Hollander, Jason Epstein, Norman Podhoretz, each a far cry from Beat-pidgen. (Podhoretz later attacked "these young men who can't get out of the morass of self.") And the Trillings, of course, had never seen the like. Still, there *was* a tradition, however vague and subterranean. In later years, Kerouac used to come to the magazine, *Jubilee,* that Rice and Lax had founded, with a pocketful of religious poems, not so far from Merton's. And Merton, for his part, discovered Zen and Hinduism in the same order as Ginsberg, finding in Oriental playfulness the same release from Western psychic pressures as Allen has.

There is a curious similarity in the arcs of these two very different men. Each was jolted toward mysticism by reading Blake in the Columbia bookstore. Each, with gregarious appetite, had swallowed more of the twentieth century than he could handle, and suffered heavy internal bleeding from it, and each came back by way of Indian wisdom to the simple exuberance that builds tree-houses and pulls daisies. Call it coincidence, but it didn't happen at Michigan State.

In the sixties the politicians came back, and a new *kind* of anti-politics, all culminating in the screaming climax of the SDS risings. For a short while the political temperament was ascendant again, and the older mystics had to accommodate themselves to it as best they could. Kerouac fumbled grumpily with public affairs, following his master Céline into a liverish fascism and disowning such heirs apparent as Abbie Hoffman and Jerry Rubin. Burroughs began to concern himself with population control and soil exhaustion, just like a solid citizen. Ginsberg took to re-enrolling in Youth periodically, but his attempts so far to mix political concern with Eastern wisdom have produced a god-awful hybrid. Even Merton, prophet and journalist, returned half-way to politics, writing more and more about peace and civil rights, like the Wechslers of 1935. Those who roll with the times are doomed to just keep on rolling. The Beat era ended, RIP 1936–60; and, although people went on wearing the death mask, the next serious wave of escapists had to start all over again on their own. Right now, to judge from Mr. Cook's interviews, nobody wants to talk about it much.

1972

26 / *Kael vs. Sarris vs. Simon*

On and on they come in murderous waves (they must have a Cause, Captain Sanders): the little grim books about Erich Von Stroheim, the large playful ones about Miss West, Blondie & Dagwood retrospectives, theological studies of Preston Sturges—last year the film books may have outnumbered the films themselves, suggesting at least two points. One, that the true-blue buff really prefers still pictures to moving ones (the passion for movie stills being a paradox G. K. Chesterton might have considered farfetched); and two, that though Film is King it needs its Old Retainer Print to do more and more of the work. Fact is that fewer films are distributed each year of the reign, and more books published.

As one of the last of the shrinking invisible printpeople, I get an extra shiver of pleasure when a pure-cinema man has to grope with prose to express his love. "Draw us a picture, you big boob," we cackle weakly. "Wave your arms or something."

One mustn't deny a corpse its bit of fun. The cineastes will presumably have the last mumble. But meanwhile, they are stuck not only with prose but with its venerable laws of euphony, rhythm, and precision. If they don't write well, it matters not a whit how beautiful their thoughts may be. Even the other cineastes smother a yawn when a lead-tongued brother speaks: it is when faced with, say, Richard Roud on Godard that they remember that they're not supposed to like books anyway.

Like them or not, they, or somebody, seem to be buying them—and not just the picture books. Several of our more literate critics have recently taken to collecting their own reviews—a gauge of the talk-value of a subject, since old reviews are nothing but talk. To juice things up a touch and to fend off the book reviewers who say, as by rote, that journalism doesn't keep overnight (tell that to Dr. Johnson, Addison, and whomever you like) one or two of these critics have contrived running feuds with each other, on the order of Jack Benny and Fred Allen, which help to organize their pieces into those new entities, books.

To your average vague layman, the Wars of the Movie Critics must look like a cross between a thirteenth-century theological squabble and a fixed wrestling match. Thus Andrew Sarris and the *auteurists* believe in salvation through election: once a director has been appointed to the Pantheon, he can never be damned again. Faith triumphs over any number of bad works (see, Hitchcock, *passim*).

Miss Kael and the Paulines are said to believe that the last shall be first. Only the unpretentious can enter the Kingdom: the non-arty real folk (see, or rather don't see, Bergman). John Simon (Johannus Malus) thunders back that both heresies lead through the same wide gate: the condoning of mediocrity, goats in the holy places.

So much for Sunday morning chitchat. The resemblance to a wrestling match comes from the ferocious snarls of the competitors and the swooshing roundhouses they wheel at each other's kidneys. Those aren't real punches, are they? whispers son of layman. Yes they are, and they hurt like hell.

The notion that warring critics all go off and play polo together over the weekend, like parliamentary debaters in England, is only half true. The above trio are, or were, nominally friends—at least they never in my day followed the tacky method of feuding known as not speaking to each other—but they cannot get together for five minutes without whaling away at each other like long-lost relatives. Movie critics are more theatrical than bookpeople and they can put on a gorgeous show, howling, giggling, and hissing, from left to right; but the fights are basically serious, they are *about* something, however petty the detail work; and I believe a constantly improving movie aesthetic is the result of them. (Incidentally, Simon's famous nastiness is the most theatrical thing since Bela Lugosi: Simon must be understood primarily as a man of the stage.)

Recently, a skirmish broke out in *The New York Times.* Sarris, aiming at Simon, managed to pepper the whole landscape with buckshot and grapes vinaigrette and I caught a piece in my hat, though I have long since retired from film reviewing. It seems that Simon, in a rare moment of muddled generosity, had listed me among the film critics he admired (I believe he was thinking about some play reviews I'd once done) and Sarris darkly accused me and the others of being friends of John's—a charge so startling as to leave forked tongue temporarily tied.

I'm not sure what point Andy was making. Most critics get on better with people whose work they like. But since, clearly, one isn't safe even on the sidelines, I am tempted to fire off some random volleys of my own, starting with the book that began the trouble: John Simon's *Movies Into Film*—a haymaking bombscare (consulting my metaphors to now) in an unfixed theological war game.

Simon's brief for insisting on "films" instead of "movies" reminds one of two monks chaffering over the word "consubstantiation"—no mean issue in its day. Movies means popcorn, double features, and coming in in the middle: democracy. Film means, well, at least chewing quietly, no talking (a rule Mr. Simon has been known to break in person), the seriousness one brings to the other arts: aristocracy.

Mr. Simon's case against Miss Kael and the "movie fans" is that their enthusiasm for honest trash and their chronic suspicion of artiness argue a deep unease with Art as such, and a democrat's urge to level the best and exalt the Procaccinos of this world. His case against Sarris and "the film buffs" is that they want to be intellectuals without the equipment for it and, as such folk will, have devised a jargon so elusive and standards so arbitrary that there is no way of being found out. Thus, one can talk of the stylization of, say, Jerry Lewis, so vivid in its precise *absence* of style, or of so-and-so's sheer badness, which transcends goodness, and wind up making all manner of atrocious judgments in terms that are virtually unanswerable. Style can be good, style can be bad, depending on how Mr. Dumpty feels today.

Sarris's case against Simon is not so easy to make out, since Andy tends to scream and pull hair when he fights: but it seems, like most Simonology, to take off from Simon's Transylvanian accent, and the remoteness from American reality which that implies. Simon is, to be sure, not your typical American boy. He staggers under a formidable load of cultural baggage, gathered at a time and place (middle-century Central Europe) when and where it did seem possible to grasp *all* that Art was doing; to make, as Mr. Simon can, a good fist at criticizing music, painting, sculpture, theater, the works.

Film, or movie, his critics might say, simply does not fit into that kind of portfolio. As a fur-bearing, duck-billed moneymaker, which occasionally stumbles into Art and out again as if it were Mr. Magoo, movie requires either a totally new language and cataloguing system, such as Aristotle Sarris desires, or a critic who can at least see whether it serves its folklore functions honestly, as Miss Kael does. A Sarrisite might say that Simon makes films sound indistinguishable from plays and is really more at home with a simple turn-of-the-century romance like *Elvira Madigan* or a filmed stage comedy like *Alfie* than with a real spanking film-film. A Kaelite might say that Simon is all at sea with American folk legends like *Bonnie and Clyde* or *The Hustler* and masks his bewilderment with lofty abuse and clever-foreigner puns—nothing changing the subject like a pun.

Far from me to play the mealy-mouthed compromiser among three gifted friends, but I think all these characterizations are wrong, though some wronger than others. Without sinking into fens of cinemology, one can say for openers that all three critics cross lines continuously in practice. Sarris often forgets his *auteur* (or hunt the director) theory for weeks on end and poaches Miss Kael's social honesty territory heavily, frisking for moral cop-outs a lot more energetically than he does for directorial brushstrokes. His review of *The Great White Hope,* for instance, was a fascinating disquisition on racism and prizefighting and —peace to his solemn fans—I could hardly tell whether he was describing a film or a play.

Meanwhile, the anti-arty Miss Kael can come the old aesthete as hard as Simon ever did, as for instance when she defends *Reflections in a Golden Eye*—a movie that breaks every rule of honesty in filmmaking that she ever held dear. Simon for his part is too easily typecast as the pan-Slavic curmudgeon. As a graduate of Horace Mann, Harvard and the U.S. Army, he can hardly be a complete stranger to our ways. In fact, if he'd got here a year sooner he'd probably sound as American as Henry

Kissinger. There are notes he doesn't catch, but these are as much temperamental or cultural; and he mightn't catch them in Budapest either. His distaste for *Bonnie and Clyde* is not dissimilar to his loathing of *8½*; both are too flashy, both are tainted with (ach!) sentimentality and disguised self-pity. In this respect, Simon crosses lines too, although to him these lines seem to be nonexistent; he talks a big game about Art but he is first and foremost all unrelenting, unforgiving moralist. And yet even that line can be crossed. He rather liked *Easy Rider*, the *summa* of self-pity.

Anyway, the three caricatures are useful in the public forum. Simon can hit, through Sarris, at the really silly "buffs," who echo the master's occasional vapidities without his saving film sense, and through Kael, at the really soft-headed "fans." I hope they will continue to hit him back —they'll catch somebody back there.

Simon accuses his enemies of drawing ever closer to each other: presumably, like Russia and the United States, from glaring at each other too long. But, to repeat, I find that even the China of the outfit (Mr. Simon) differs more in ideology than he does in practice. One might expect three such irreconcilable philosophies to produce a stream of irreconcilable opinions; yet Kael's review of Fellini's *Satyricon* might have been endorsed word for word by Simon; and each of these two is capable of sounding just as *auteurist* as Sarris, without ever calling it that. Once the quarry is sighted, the philosophies tend to get left at the post, only to catch up again when the three friends meet.

I don't mean to suggest, by the by, that these three are the only critics around: it is just that they all have books out at the moment. Besides Mr. Simon's, there are Miss Kael's *Going Steady* and Andrew Sarris's *Confessions of a Cultist;* and all three must be read by anyone who wants to know what our best film writing is up to these days. Miss Kael's book was roasted in *The New York Times Book Review* by an ideological enemy, Mr. Sarris's praised by an ally. Some people affect to be bored by all this professional infighting: not I. Criticism is a contact sport; and besides, who will criticize the critics, if they don't jump each other? All the same, when their armies clash, or cuddle, by night, I believe they should hold their flags up where we can see them.

1971

NOTE: *The reader may have to strain a bit to believe that these three actually are my friends. But indeed it is so. This essay is part of the phenomenon it describes. I had just come off a stint of reviewing movies myself, and it was the convention in our set to spring at each other's throats, in public and private, without worrying too much about hurt feelings. Perhaps a measure of childishness goes with an obsession with movies. Looking back from the senility of the book world, I feel as if I'd just stumbled upon an old high school yearbook: pleased but puzzled.*

27/ *Walker Percy Redivivus*

Walker Percy's fine novel *Love in the Ruins* opens with the hero seated in a pine grove with a gun on his lap awaiting the end of the world. The gun looks Confederate, the waiting is Catholic: these are the positions from which Mr. Percy does his own sniping, at what Mortimer Adler might call the *Three Great Tenses.*

It is a risky thing for a satirist to blow his cover like this. The moment he reveals his own philosophy, he can be demoted instantly to comedian. Consider the parade of yesterday's Society's Scourges, shrunk to the size of sideshow midgets. Parson Muggeridge, Viscount Waugh, Mahatma Huxley, even that finest of Catholic satirists, Marshall McLuhan—all show how you lose divinity and become as crazy as the rest of us the moment you leak an affirmation. (It turns out that McLuhan's global village and Waugh's Brideshead are just two ways of saying Vatican, while Huxley's waxworks were simply oriental propaganda in the making. Andy Warhol may be next—I hear he's a regular churchgoer.)

Percy labors under not just the one, standard-issue stereotype, but two, and these the very worst. A Southern satirist is free to join the crowd mocking dehumanization and the other popular Northern vices, but he had better keep his own Golden Age to himself; likewise a Catholic can fun himself with Masters and Johnson, but let's leave canon law out of this. Edmund Wilson dismissed Waugh's *The Loved One* by asking in what way California funeral practices were sillier than lighting candles for the dead. Percy must not only anticipate questions like that, but also the kind Tom Wolfe gets: what do you *really* feel about Panthers and such.

Impossible odds. And Percy has only made them worse by setting his fable in the future. There are solid reasons for doing this in a novel of public events—the past has hardened to stone, you can't mess with it much, and the present is journalism—but even solider ones against. Because if you make your future too different from the present it becomes a thin exercise in ingenuity. (How can you satirize a hypothesis?) And if you make it too similar, you are a dull clod, clumsily twisting the present to your own shallow purposes.

Percy has been lightly scolded on each of these lines. Yet it is amazing how much he has gotten away with. He has written a blatantly theological novel, with a Southern agrarian bias, set in a future so close it's already happened. Nobody, not even a clergyman over forty, would buy a theological novel if you called it that. But readers have become so vague in this respect that you can leave theology lying about and they'll only think it's something else. At a symposium I attended some years back for Beckett's *Waiting for Godot,* every speaker, including the trendy minister, insisted that the play had no religious overtones whatever, even though it is honeycombed with New Testament references. So, Christian fiction may creep back undetected.

I would hate to threaten Percy's sales by suggesting he has written such a book (the only thing deadlier would be to praise an author's "beautifully understated treatment of sex"). But the themes of fall, atonement, resurrection should be in the public domain by now, like the themes of Greek tragedy. And while Percy's wit and style have been properly noted, there is a danger his book may seem frothy and aimlessly crotchety if the heavy religious motif is overlooked.

Thomas More, Percy's hero, is descended from the saint who was preeminently a martyr to Fashion, the perennial heresy. Sir Thomas More had a mischievous modern mind and his *Utopia* has never been recommended by the official Church for spiritual reading. Yet he opposed his king precisely in the role of Supreme Fashion-setter and Official Wave of the Future, and lost his head for it.

So, too, Percy's More is a Catholic scientist seeking an unfashionable Utopia. He is dispirited because the old heresies, in their new styles, look in a lot better shape than he does. He has also invented a machine called a lapsometer, which records man's fallen, or lapsed, nature, but which can't do any more about it than the Church can. Thus the Christian's oldest dilemma: what to do with the patient until the Second Coming of the doctor?

Enter the devil with his little black bag, as the Good Book says he will. Before Christ returns He will be preceded by all manner of quacks, swamis or, in this case, a CIA man bearing foundation trinkets (in exchange for the lapsometer, which he promises to use for human betterment). More is grievously tempted. He is as tired as an old priest of diagnosing sin and not being able to do anything for it—especially since all the diagnosed sinners round on him with a snarl. The devil also offers him a Nobel Prize, the closest thing to canonization going.

But the devil can't cure anyone, because he is only ourselves taken to extremes and can merely urge us faster along the same groove. What he prescribes as health is a liberation into more disease, a burst of vitality as we burn the motor. A little more of such devil's medicine and the world could die of apoplexy or apocalypse.

More expects the end of the world, as Christians have since St. Paul, trembling yet eager for it, but it is only another false alarm. Anti-Christs come and go. The devil vanishes in a puff of sulfur and deodorant, and More is left with his diagnosing instrument. What to do now? Wait. Watch. Keep awake until the Master cometh. Only *really* keep awake this time.

People have felt that *Love in the Ruins* ends weakly, but it is the same ending in spirit as the fadeout in Graham Greene's *The Power and the Glory* and even the coda to *Brideshead Revisited*. After beating off the false gods, there is nothing for it but to wait—in despair, like Beckett, or hope, like Dr. More. The characteristic scene is the dawn Mass, in a small chapel with a ragtag collection of vigilants: the promise of morning, of resurrection. Not today? All right, Godot, we'll be back tomorrow.

Percy's own gloom seems oddly to lift with this fiasco apocalypse. As an American medical scientist, his Thomas More will continue to work on his lapsometer and cut down on his drinking: no endgames or garbage cans for him. Yet, as a Southerner, he is half in love with defeat too. He ends up helping fat Bantu ladies to reduce and gratefully accepting their Christmas tips (why be half humiliated?), but there is no Swiftian horror about this. More is a better man on the bottom than he was on the top. And these political shifts do not matter much in the eye of God.

Percy's greatest technical problem is that he does want his Christian allegory to show: which means he has to point and wave at his symbols from time to time. His devil arrives in a thunderstorm while Don Giovanni's descent into hell is playing; flinches when More says "goddamn," and, as the end of the world looms, tells More not to go back for his coat—the same flight instructions the Gospel gives. Yet readers I have consulted say they didn't spot Old Nick even then.

It's the old case against symbols: if you get them, they seem obvious and artificial, and if you don't, you miss the whole point. I believe that Percy pumped his symbols so big and fat partly because he enjoyed planting outrageous clues and partly because they have a lot of work to do. For instance, the Don Giovanni theme resonates in Dr. More's relations with his three girlfriends. More's Catholicism is pagan, carnal, incarnate; he espoused it to "get away from the world of spirits." But loving the body and keeping your hands off it is a problem to tax the keenest neo-Thomist.

It could be that Catholicism in its current dither strikes even some of its own members as a harmless aberration and can for the time being raise its head safely in books. (When it redefines itself, back to the trenches.) Southernness is something else, and reviewers have expressed a vague unease with what they take to be Percy's sly conservatism. He deals out his blows with scrupulous evenness, but to the Northern liberal temper they will seem inherently uneven. When More tells a Bantu revolutionary, "I don't think you [people] can make it," it wipes the slate of all the white man's folly we have seen: this is what he *really* believes, the other stuff was put in for fake balance.

But Percy's mind is not simple on this point, any more than the South's is. The Bantus may not make it, but then, nobody else has made it either. Alternately tempted by too much flesh and too much mind, fallen white man lurches like a drunk between shining gutters. The Bantu must get "at least as far as we have"—but when he does, he will have only the same large bowel movements and morning terrors to show for it. However, the lapsometer does not work on blacks, it does not pick up their fallen natures as it does whites'. They remain a mystery to More, and his words read more like a question than a judgment. When the

Bantus take over his district at the end, he is happy to stay there and see how they make out. America's original sin, he firmly believes, is its treatment of the Negro. As a Southerner and a Christian, he sees no future life until this is atoned for.

1971

28 / *More Light on Luce*

It looks as if Henry Luce is going to go down in history as a mythical beast. And serve him right. His own magazine manufactured enough of them, magically transforming bubble-headed tycoons and party hacks into steel-jawed dynamos prowling the corridors of power, for weal or woe. Several employees, such as Ralph Ingersoll and Charles Wertenbaker, learned the trick well enough to write novels applying it to the boss himself, and thus was launched Harry the Titan, the Big Fellow, Mr. Power. And now a biography has come along clinching the myth: Luce as the ultimate *Time* cover story.

Time used its Bad Magic on villains, inflating them hideously, on a field of pygmies, making their smallest mannerisms seem like deformities, and editorializing every inch of the way, just in case you missed the point. W. A. Swanberg has now alchemized Luce in his own juice, a punishment fitting the crime; in fact, he has done everything but paint a false mustache on him.

Swanberg's Luce is portrayed as having a mind like a steel trap, but the manners and human sensitivity of a warthog. From which it follows, as sure as Dean Acheson's mustache, that his foreign policy must have been inhuman, too. *Time* at its worst could make bad table manners as ominous as World War II. So the first caveat must be registered over the soup. I would maintain in this case that Luce's mind was nothing like a steel trap and that his manners were no worse than your average Cambridge don's—bad enough, you might say.

Manners first. Swanberg harps and harps again on how Luce used to ignore his food at restaurants and waved waiters away from other guests as well. Can this really have happened so often? The only time I ever dined out with Luce, he got sore because I ordered leg of lamb, and "you don't order leg of lamb in restaurants." Swanberg said he had no sense of humor, but I'm not sure he wasn't being funny that night. Anyway, he was attending closely to his food, and mine.

As to the steel trap, Luce asked me another time what the Dred Scott case was all about, and no steel trap ever asked that. Luce did fill the air with questions—I guessed because he thought at one time that that's what journalists did (he wasn't a natural) and because he was stuttery and deaf and found it easier to talk in rapid set-pieces; but he played with facts like a cat with a ball of wool, doing everything but digest them. His memory span was just great for a weekly newsmagazine.

Such fluff would not be worth going into, except for what Swanberg, *Time*style, makes of it: in this case, the picture of an icy, flawed intelligence drawing up scenarios for Armageddon, as lightly as he might insult a waiter. I happen to find Luce's politics pretty disgusting myself, but can't quite see them as the rantings of an emotional cripple. There were too many others in it with him. (This is where the field of pygmies is important. By shrinking everybody else, Swanberg makes Luce the sole Frankenstein of American foreign policy.) The Cold War made horribly good sense for America, whatever it made for anyone else, and Luce, under the rhetoric, was as pragmatic about it as the Rand Corporation.

Swanberg sees him, more entertainingly, as irrevocably scarred by the Boxer Rebellion, which drove his missionary family out of China, and by a later trip to Russia on which everybody smelled bad; but there was nothing irrevocable about Luce. Anyone who could embrace Mussolini, Nasser, Tito, and LSD could embrace just about anything. If he was a fanatic, he was a mercurial one, a Presbyterian who could bend the trouser in a Catholic church and could carry his liquor advertising. True, he romanticized his Chinese background, partly because he saw himself as a *Time* cover story; and, if you couldn't have royal blood and be raised by gypsies, you did the best you could. But his China policy was not just a dream of old pagodas. He wanted a client state to service American power—the most benign power he could envisage in a world of brutal power mergers and takeovers. Really, quite a practical fellow, as Swanberg might have deduced from his business dealings.

Swanberg also makes much of the "two Presbyterians," Luce and Dulles, who engineered our Holy War policy (very warlike people, these Presbyterians); but surely these two old salesmen would have kissed the Blarney stone in yarmulkes in exchange for an airbase or two. Luce in particular understood that the other great modern power blocs were animated by ideology and he reached for the only one America has in bulk, Christianity—unsuitable for warmaking, but people never stop trying.

Presbyterian? Even in Kick-a-Protestant Week, I don't quite see it. Call it coincidence—but immigrant Catholics make much likelier anti-Communists than Presbyterians do, not to mention better picture stories, and Luce's interests became scandalously papist. Call it chivalry, but he also stood buffer between his Catholic wife and his chilly Protestant relatives, and a good biographer should have looked into this further. It was pretty rough in there. Luce was personally devout and even prayed in the elevator (of which Swanberg makes heavy capital—though has anyone thought of anything better to do in elevators?); but his theology in conversation was nothing like the primitive, me-and-God thing that Swanberg derides. He rather ponderously pursued theological questions, as he pursued cultural ones, seeking the top thoughts from the absolutely top people, believing, tragically, that they could be popularized and still be the top thoughts.

Luce also knew it would take a miracle to get America to go international, and he was willing to give it a try, using every trick he knew. His use of his magazines for Cold War propaganda was unconscionable. And again Swanberg thoughtfully demonstrates the method himself: by inserting a grisly passage of Mickey Spillane's in which Mike Hammer mows down some Comsymps, presumably having been inspired by the Lucepress; by equipping Luce himself with a bowie knife, six-shooter and machine gun in various metaphors; by winging in a paragraph by Richard Hofstadter about religion being a possible "outlet for animosities," again reducing Luce's thinking to sunspots and hot flashes. No *Time* hatchet ever did more.

Fortunately, there is enough material in the book to make your own Luce out of the leftovers, and some of it is sympathetically presented. Luce's "American Century" is touchingly Kiplingesque—the boy raised in the colonies dreaming of home, and getting it all wrong. Similarly, his early admiration for businessmen had some of the romanticism of a young Gatsby—*Fortune* is just the magazine Gatsby might have founded; and his belief that he could have been a tip-top intellectual, if he'd had the time, completes the cycle of American yearning.

It also explains his extraordinary success at journalism. Luce dreamed all the American dreams in turn and was trendily alert to the latest myths of his time. Thus, he did not invent the Cold War, but heard it coming on his transmitter and helped to make it a hit. He turned heavily to God just when the nation did. "Names make news"—perhaps that was his overriding weakness: he thought that names make politics, too, and Chiang Kai-shek was the name he knew best in Asia. At that I'm sure he would have dumped him like a worn-out editor if he'd found something better.

Beyond that, he was a boss and nobody loves a boss. Too much of the poop on him comes from underneath, in either sycophancy or resentment. Knowing him only casually in my late teens, I found him no larger than life, in equal parts thoughtless and domestically sweet-tempered and curiously vulnerable. His deafness made him seem more opinionated than he probably was. He had just discovered sports that year and monologued me at length about why baseball was so popular (ingenious balderdash, like many of his theories): but the point was, he couldn't have heard a word I said anyway. And his "whut-whut? very innerressing —very innerressing" froze one's responses rigid. But he did read a lot and tried most solemnly to improve himself. "Man is a puzzle-solving animal" (he really said things like that) was his excuse for the nightly jigsaw—busting a gut to be a sage, like the ones he read about in *Time.*

What made his newsmagazine so excruciating in the old days (fortunately since then *Time* its ways has mended) was the clash between tone and intention. The style seems to have been largely the doing of co-founder Britt Hadden (although Clare maintained it read like a Chinese translation), an incorrigible wise-guy, in pursuit of the totally smart-aleck magazine. The intention was Luce's and it was, as Swanberg truly describes, earnest and missionary. Piped through Hadden's facetiousness, it came out as leering sanctimony, more hideous as the world became more hideous.

Otherwise, Luce's right-wing opinions were about what you'd expect from any big publisher, whether the Boxers had kicked him out of China or whether he'd lost his sled. If he was abnormally powerful, that was the fault of power—magazines had it in ungovernable quantities for that brief period, and if we hadn't got Luce, we'd have got another Hearst, or worse.

But was he that powerful? Readers snowed by Swanberg's grandiosity may be puzzled to find no mention of Luce in the Pentagon Papers or other state documents; surprised to find that he backed more losers than winners politically and that he could never wipe that grin off Roosevelt's face. Reading *Luce and His Empire* is like growing up with *Time* magazine and finally realizing that that tiger on that week's cover had not altered the course of history or possibly the real life of a single reader, and that names don't make news, they only make newspapers. Luce did leave that legacy, and it is still going strong, in advocacy journalism and advocacy biography, producing strange history but occasionally passable entertainment, as in Swanberg's book: and as I say, it is only fitting that Luce should get his lumps from it, too.

1972

29 / *Men's Women Women's Men*

The basic women's lib letter seems to have subsided slightly—the one that used to turn up even in the sports pages, embroidered round the line "You wouldn't say that about a black man." Maybe someone over at Womentern realized at last that the worse we treat people in this country, the more delicately we talk about them; and that if we ever talk as nicely about women as we do about blacks, women are in trouble indeed.

By the same token, the basic-black letter writer may learn something from the female experience. "How dare a white man criticize black art," says the letter, taking the words out of the white critic's mouth. But what's the alternative? Women's novels used to be sent invariably to women reviewers, and it was no mark of respect. Reviews by blacks of blacks could set up a similar closed circuit—O.K., if that's what you want, a self-sufficient folk literature. But such literatures lead a lonely life. After the Gaelic poets of Ireland had fought their way bravely into a corner, they found that Uncle Toms like Yeats and Shaw were considered the voice of Ireland. And to be a Yeats, you have to abide with boneheaded foreign critics.

At present, most reviews of books by blacks are critically worthless.

White reviewers tend to babble ingratiatingly, as if they'd just received a death threat. They know they're going to get that letter whatever they do. Many of us, I suspect, hesitate to review such books at all, unless they're written by a James Baldwin, who has truly abolished the race barrier and can be kicked as hard as a Wasp.

Black reviewers certainly do much better by black authors, but too often they seem either to be promoting a large Cause or working out of some interior political position, like poets from different schools gunning for each other. There are conceivably more important things in the world than honest book reviewing, and if black self-confidence were really served by nervous flattery on the one hand, from white men with watermelon grins, or by logrolling brothers on the other, it might be a fair bargain. But what actually happens is that truly excellent books like Toni Morrison's *The Bluest Eye* get drowned in the overall gush. Nobody trusts the reviews, because the small boy who writes them has shouted "genius" once too often; and eventually nobody reads the books.

On the same general principle, only played as farce this time, I believe that Joe Colombo and his merry men have taken a step backward by insisting on underdog touchiness privileges. Italians had seemed so firmly established in our society that one could twit their gangsters at will, like Protestant bankers or Irish cops. Nobody seems to understand that this is the empyrean we strive for. If you want to be written about as daintily as black people or even women, you must give up an awful lot and preferably live like a dog.

Mr. Colombo does at least grasp that no one was ever ruined by a book and he sticks to film censorship. Never mind. Most writers are more than willing to censor themselves. Nearly everyone is prepared to go along with the routine diplomatic ground rules, based on a delicate scale of ethnic vulnerabilities (dumb Swede? maybe; dumb Pole? better not), figuring that a pinch of censorship is better than a pound of pain. We are so tactful about it that we don't even let on that we do it, and this may be carrying self-censorship too far: because we purport to be giving a true record of life and we're not quite.

On the whole, I accept the ground rules for fiction. Like pornography, a racial slur has a nonliterary kick to it which often works against your real intention. You may need that dumb Pole for your story, and you don't have occasion to match him with a bright one: so you just do without and call the fellow Foster as usual. As with all artistic restraints, it can be turned to good effect—like the satires-in-code written by oppressed peoples. But let us have no cant about artistic freedom. When James Gould Cozzens wrote a book, *By Love Possessed*, recording what small-town Wasps think of other groups, he was considered a howling bigot. And Philip Roth has been called an anti-Semite by at least one Gentile critic; imagine what he'd be called if he swung his knife at Catholics.

Nonfiction is harder to write in code. Tom Wolfe does it with his language of shoes and cocktail spreads and is called a fop for his pains, instead of the heartless moralist he is. Jimmy Breslin does it with comic license; by exaggerating his effects, he can slip in much straight abuse. Public discussion is so unwaveringly cautious in a pluralist society that one learns to dance out one's message. Most readers will get it wrong, but enjoy the dance anyway. So art profits again, even if truth doesn't; and we have a slew of fine ironists at the moment.

One problem about discussing the Sisterhood is that they would seem to want the ice of politeness broken and to have a nice honest brawl and at the same time to be treated as gingerly as Negroes, around whom this ice is thickest. Male response is predictably uncertain. The David Susskind type thinks that a woman stamping her foot is cute; and it only makes him more outrageous, like an oafish brother-in-law. Sympathetic males, on the other hand, waste precious time protesting their sympathy, and then find themselves in a box: Is it chauvinist to pull one's punches with a lady? Am I supposed to *hit* her? Would I hit a black man? When he finally does swing, it is as awkward as two men fighting in their overcoats.

The reviews of such as Kate Millett or *Sisterhood Is Powerful* seemed to fall into the second camp, while much of the word of mouth landed in the first. Miss Millett's persona didn't help: that dry, facetious type that used to turn up a lot in groups with names like Catholic Families United could always jangle the sexual protocol, even when that kind of thing seemed straightforward.

There's no profit in reviewing Miss Millett yet again—her book having been reviewed very nearly to death—but perhaps the endless American problem of manners and tone can be resolved by adopting hers for now and doing a mirror-opposite study on men in women's fiction.

Here are some random notes to be going on with: Millett's three authors—Mailer, Miller, and Lawrence—had one thing in common which Millett, being Irish-hence-family-hence-Freud-prone, slighted.

Each was born in a position of social inferiority and their sexuality must be contrasted not with average female passivity but with their real opposite numbers: those gifted women who use sex to get on in the world. These movers and shakers must conquer the opposite sex at each stage of their advance: for information, for confidence, for a social leg up. Lawrence married upwards as much as any scheming heroine, and Mailer has been admirably frank about a dynastic marriage of his own. Miller, a cut-up and harder to pin down, used sex as an alternative to society.

Taking three women authors who have always made me feel pretty small—Doris Lessing, Mary McCarthy, and Nancy Mitford—I find similar social complications, at least in their literary selves. Misses Lessing and McCarthy write from a perspective of bright girls from the provinces conquering the capital, and I don't see how Miss Mitford could object to being called a snob. In *Love in a Cold Climate,* all Miss Mitford's males were unspeakably drippy until she met Mr. Right (or Monsieur Droit), a French gentleman.

The net effect of reading these and other women was to grow up feeling like a heavy-breathing clod who made inept lunges after supper prior to snoring smugly. Such ladies might yield to one out of economic necessity, but they would register each fatuous move with a scorn deeper than Mailer's ego. (I might add, since this kind of confession seems to be in season, that some of us were so careful *not* to conform to this model that we frequently lost out to the clods with the lunges. The trouble with being the kind of deeply sensitive fellow that women writers seem to favor is that you keep getting beaten to the draw by sexist pigs.)

I suppose that on this level of competition, the mumbo jumbo about clitoral orgasm and penis envy has some kind of significance. But among the quieter female writers, and making all allowance for reticence, there seems to be no great concern about genitals or even flesh. They may go on about curly hair and humorous eyes, but even those as symbols of the spirit. *Their* counterparts, the less aggressive male writers, are a touch more anatomical in the early going but liable to melt into vagueness and metaphor as they approach their goal. This sounds like real life, where you never met a man who cared a fig about the clitoral orgasm until he'd read about it; and as to penis envy, the great castrations of history have all been performed by males on each other.

If you're going to discuss sex through literature (which is a bit like fighting an enemy by the reflection on your shield), you have to sample a lot more of it than Miss Millett did. Outside of that steamy cockpit where the social strivers have at it, one's impression is one of vast misunderstanding, usually kindly intended. The men's characters in most women's fiction are pretty much like the men's faces drawn by small girls: cute as a button, with a cigar and a mustache struggling to hide the fact. Superficial accuracy may be greater in this age of the tape recorder, but an Iris Murdoch man remains spiritual cousin to one of those Victorian concoctions.

As to men describing women—most everyone is onto Proust's little game, but some male writers have gotten away with murder. When Arnold Bennett was asked how he drew women so well he said he wrote the stories first and chose up sexes afterward, as it might be an Iron Curtain track team. If such things are still possible, it would bear out the Women's Lib contention that femininity is artificial, based on a shifting intuition of men's wishes. (Machismo may be artificial too, but it's a lot easier to imitate Hemingway than the Eternal Feminine.)

Anyway, if fiction tells us what the sexes think of each other—the Albee woman and the Murdoch man, the Hemingway dream girl and the basic Charlotte Brontë—one might expect much confusion in the world. And looking around from one's shield, one sees that it is so. Homosexuals rage at a caricature, heterosexuals moon over God knows what—a collage of images fashioned by their own sex. With a different feed-in of myths, they might well reverse roles.

Ironically, the competitive women describe men much better than the passive ones: partly perhaps because they share the temperament, partly because it is their business to be watchful. Writers who like and trust the opposite sex are all at sea with it. The hard lessons which may yet help to sort out the confusions seem to come from writers like Lessing on a good day or Scott Fitzgerald after he'd been burned, who like the opposite sex but don't trust it an inch.

1971

30 / *The Subject of Ethnics*

Somebody had to pay for the Polish jokes and the Agnew watches, and it might as well be the White Anglo-Saxon Protestants. Not necessarily because they started them (as we shall see, there is some question whether Wasps ever have any fun at all) but because it is their turn to pay for something. Also, Wasps are the only group in the United States guaranteed not to fight back, being either too arrogant to notice or too sick with guilt to defend themselves, and in either case, quite extinct, poor chaps.

Two recent books, *The Rise of the Unmeltable Ethnics* by Michael Novak and *The Decline of the Wasp* by Peter Schrag, suggest that white Protestants are so stiff with inner discipline ("robots," says Novak) that it's a wonder they can still croak out their dismal hymns of a Sunday. This would not apply to my friend Charlie W. from Memphis, who almost drove through my front window last summer howling like a banshee (and you should see him when he's drunk), or to State Attorney Percy R., last seen hijacking a bicycle outside the Princeton Club and riding off cackling. The Wasps I know lack not only inner discipline but plain good sense; and I wouldn't bring them up at all except that there don't seem to be any actual people in Schrag and Novak, only an old bust of McKinley, so I thought I'd mention a couple.

Before reading these books I had assumed that the height of reserve and inner discipline was a Sicilian under oath, or any other time. Or else it was my Polish friend Tom D., who could drink anyone under the table so long as you didn't ask him to speak or express any emotion whatever. But it seems they had simply absorbed the attitudes of their Wasp masters. Even the three legendary Italian ballplayers who once drove coast to coast without speaking (DiMaggio, Crosetti, and Lazzeri, if you're interested) were just trying to behave like English gentlemen.

So the new pluralism gets off to a rousing start by flattening out our largest and most varied group, all the white Protestants from W. C. Fields to Huey Long. Novak senses that this could be a difficulty. "I do not want to assert that *all* Wasps show the characteristics I am going to mention," he says. "I do not even wish to assert that *any* Wasp allows these characteristics to dominate his conduct." Before finding out what, if anything, there is left to assert, mightn't we just drop the whole thing and talk about what *does* dominate our conduct?

It seems it is still necessary to invent the Wasp. The liberal fallacy was that people could define themselves without reference to an enemy. The new pluralists know better, but they hope they can at least boil the enemy down to one. The Poles, for instance, used to define themselves opulently by not being Irish, Italian, German, etc. Now they are asked to do so only by not being Wasp. Is this enough for a definition—only one bigotry? Mr. Novak's Poles, Italians, and Greeks suddenly begin to look ominously alike. They are all simply un-Wasp—that is, earthy, passionate, spontaneous, all that great stuff. Thus the new pluralism, barreling on its way and reveling in our differences, has just flattened out another group, the ethnics themselves.

According to Schrag, the Wasps have just about had it anyway, even as bogeymen (though one last kick in the kidneys can't hurt), and are by now barely distinguishable from other technocrats around the globe. This is the real subject, of course, the bourgeoisification of us all. But ethnicity may still have something to say about that. Novak, along with Andrew Greeley and others, argues also for an ethnicity based not only on Rage (which is this year's glibbest emotion) but on certain stubborn qualities that have survived miraculously like flowers in city streets, preserved in the kind of family enclaves that writers used to curse, but now admire, though usually at a distance. This seems more promising

—it might at least make a possible last line of defense before we all just surrender to B. F. Skinner.

But can it really be more than a holding action? The Scotch are as pugnacious as the Irish ever were; but the American-Scotch don't march on St. Andrew's Day, because there's no one to march against anymore, even in dreams; and the cult of Scotland has died for want of an enemy. Similarly, the Irish in the South have forgotten the English penal laws sufficiently to produce numerous Protestant ministers.

The two strongest types of social cement, common hatred and common worship, are under constant stress in this fluid, flooding country. Novak uses both cements lavishly, somehow suggesting a situation where suspenders and a belt are needed to keep the pants up. Greeley emphasizes worship and the continued health of the Catholic Church (and I hope he's right). But healthy or no, the Church seems less and less likely to go on shoring up ethnic cultures for long, as it becomes more American every day.

Without war or religion to sustain him the ethnic must be himself from memory, and memory is elusive. Even a scholarly man like Greeley has been known to come on as a brawling Celt, and Novak has recently discovered dark Polish passions in himself, and maybe both impulses are genuine. But they are suspiciously like stage characteristics. Expatriate ethnics tend to forget the many varieties and nuances of their national character and to cultivate the ones everybody recognizes. (This, incidentally, could be what Novak means by listening to the blood which on its little trips to and from the brain comes back with exactly the messages it left with that morning.)

So if the ethnic revival catches fire, watch for a host of flamboyant Italians, carefree Greeks, etc., who would shock the natives of those countries out of their Snoopy T-shirts. A cultural style suitable to raising sheep on a hillside begins to go funny in a city apartment—like carrying a pitchfork downtown on the subway. But as a fad, it has at least more good juice to it than astrology. If you happen to have a lousy temper, it's good to know it's an *Irish* temper. And you can walk a little taller if that rotten disposition is Slavic soul. It certainly beats "you know how sensitive we Scorpios are."

This is emphatically not what the new pluralists want—though Novak's blood-thinking might encourage it. To pretend to have a second national identity is like claiming to be descended from the Bourbons, pure escapism. Nationality is not comparison shopping—choosing between the Greek name you got from your father and the Irish name you *didn't* get from your mother—but the weather and smell and talk of your own region. If you don't like it—well that's all you're going to get out of nationality. Try something else. Skinnerism will finally have to be beaten by something in our own system and not by calling in the Mounties.

But what the pluralists are after is not little dead sanctuaries of Old World custom, but an alternative way of being American right now, based on immigrant experience and issuing in a living culture as sturdy and weatherproof as Judaism and Catholicism. A tall order. And they might, I would tentatively suggest, begin by taking a more, let's say, pluralistic view of immigrant experience itself.

Take the question of spontaneity, allegedly damped down by those prune-faced Wasps. Novak talks approvingly of the volatile motorists of Rome—as compared, I suppose, with our own reserved taxi drivers. But most of our immigrants did not come from Rome. There is some distance between a North Italian who can afford a motorcar and a Sicilian trudging the dirt roads in back of a donkey. Joe Bonanno (and would he lie to you?) was largely raised in Sicily and has only one cheerful memory of it—a group of *Americani* yokking it up at a bar. The local crowd simply went round in permanent mourning, black as a Pilgrim's outfit.

Such people did not need lessons in discipline and perseverence from the Whiffenpoofs or Hasty Puddings or whatever the devil they call themselves. They practiced the so-called Protestant ethic before they knew what it was just to survive. So I would like to propose a portrait slightly different from Novak's, though still only part of the story: namely, that the ethnics also brought a welcome grimness and toughness to the Wasp playground and are still doing so, now that the Wasp kids are trying to turn it back into a playground.

Just consider the history of American sports. The Ivy League, to some small extent, still believes in playing at least some games for fun. But for a man working eighteen hours in a mill, playing games at all was strange enough and playing them for fun was meaningless. One played for blood or money, goals commensurate with real life. So the Ivy League became a joke and Vince Lombardi became a representative American. And who had converted whom?

The ethnics of Novak and Schrag are too much the saintly patsies. (Their emotions about blacks are "delicate" according to Novak. I'll bet they are.) One pictures them being dragooned onto boats and forced by sadistic, masterful Wasps into acting like Gregory Peck on arrival. Yet anyone raised as a Catholic in this country knows very well that we weren't supposed to attend those Wasp indoctrination centers, or schools. We learned how to be Americans all right, but nobody thought that we were learning how to be Protestants. Our mistake, no doubt, but what the hell, Gregory Peck was a Catholic himself.

Our authors too easily equate ethnic with primitive. So any display of dignity becomes a betrayal. In fact, each of the mother countries has its own tradition of aristocratic behavior, of reticence and stoicism and, if you prefer, uptightness. The Kennedys and Scott Fitzgerald were not imitation Wasps but genuine Irish dandies (pedants note: the Norman name Fitzgerald, in both cases). Likewise, most European rabbis would be as surprised by Lenny Bruce as you were. If anything, this country liberated more styles than it crushed.

Schrag also carries on at length about the inevitable Wasp movie heroes and ethnic villains that assisted in our brainwashing. But my impression was that the true-blue mainline movie-Wasp was invariably a chump who lost his girl to a neutral American type we could all identify with. And we always knew that Bing Crosby would beat out Fred Astaire. As to villains, Wasp bankers and businessmen outnumbered Peter Lorre by plenty, and their names were usually Miller and Sanders.

The worst sin that Novak lays on the Wasps is their missionary complex and their mania for social management. I sometimes wish that it were so—we might have some decent social services to compare with Western Europe if so. In fact, the Wasps may talk a good deed but they are not particularly missionary either at home or abroad. If they were the latter, we might also have a reputable foreign service in Vietnam and some flourishing neighbors in Latin America.

The true Wasp vice is indifference—or, as they would put it, respect for other people's freedom. This must surely be the most disorganized major country in the West—real missionaries would at least see to it that the courts worked and the schools had money—and minimalist Republicans and Southern Wasps can take most of the credit for it. Open door. Benign neglect. Outside of robbing you blind (as you would rob them) nobody leaves you alone like a Wasp. Even on a private scale Protestants tend to think it's a nasty Papist habit to try to convert people. And when a Catholic like Novak complains of the Protestant censors of television, one has to wonder what religion he's talking about.

What does all this imply for ethnic consciousness? For one thing, that if the ethnics have survived as such so far, it may not be a miracle after all. The Wasps didn't really care what they were so long as they showed up for work. If contrariwise, the ethnics Americanized, it was largely their own doing—fault them for bad taste if you like. They could still be doing their peasant dances as far as the folks on the hill are concerned. When I asked Joe Flaherty if he'd ever been oppressed by Wasps, he said he didn't know, he'd never met any in Flatbush.

As to the future—maybe the machine will get us all, but as Schrag understands so well, the Wasp can't harm you. No one's going to help you and no one's going to take the blame for you either. You're on your own. You always were.

1972

31 / *Unnecessary Roughness*

The literature of nausea has come to professional football: the "I Was a Vampire for the Chicago Bears" school for one crowd, and "I Was a Rich Owner's Plaything" for the other. On the constitutional principle that anything we enjoy that much must be evil, we have begun gobbling up exposés like health food—book upon relentless book proving the essential rottenness of coaches, players, hot-dog purveyors, and even us fans. It is a brand-new chapter in the history of meaningless outrage.

Because if we took the exposés seriously, we would simply have to stop watching the game altogether and cease tax-supporting new stadiums. And nobody seriously expects that, not from one reader in a million. So we are just reading the books for fun. In fact, if I may expose the essential dinginess of the football reader, I suspect we buy the books for the football parts—as the authors will discover when they write that next book about the Esalen Institute or the power of prayer. We listen to the sermon for the dirty bits, as we always have.

As literary entertainments, these books depend heavily on the unfathomable innocence of the old yellow-press client, who never ceases to be shocked that businessmen like money or that athletes have sex lives.

When it comes to more specialized information, the exposers fall to babbling in tongues. For instance, where does the sickening violence come from in football? Hear Bernie Parrish in *They Call It a Game:*

"I think a lot of the more evil problems of pro football might be cured if the owners were forced to cover one kickoff—and to repeat until they made one tackle, however long that took." In other words, the violence comes from effete owners sending young men to their deaths, like Lord Cardigan. (Unfortunately, the one owner who *has* played, George Halas of Chicago, is known as one of the meanest men in the game.)

Yet a few pages later, Parrish is denouncing coaches as pussycats because they're not violent enough. "When an opposing runner goes down they don't have that urge to stomp him into the turf so he won't get up again." Coaches have no feelings. Parrish himself has the urge to stomp in spades. "I relished hitting people, I could hardly wait for the next collision. I even enjoyed being hit," says he; and this was in high school, before he'd met his first rascally owner.

Turning to Dave Meggyesy, the pioneer malcontent, we learn that the violence and sadism were "not so much on the part of the players or in the game itself, but very much in the minds of the beholders—the millions of Americans who watch football every weekend in something approaching a sexual frenzy." So that is where the trouble lies—not in the owners or the players, but the fans. How he knows how we watch I don't know—at my place, aphasic torpor would be closer to it. Yet Meggyesy admits that he, too, likes to hit. In fact, he played the game more ferociously than anyone asked him to; and it seems possible that he quit the game because he actually frightened himself.

One is reminded, on a miniature scale, of Lieutenant Calley's confessional style: the system may be evil, but you don't have to embrace it quite that ardently. If we are all guilty for Meggyesy and his pals, it would mainly be for tolerating a game that feeds and clothes the beast in them. What would happen to this beast if we took away its ball none of our philosophers quite gets around to analyzing. Chip Oliver in *High for the Game* says that football players behave like animals because they are expected to. But Oliver, like Meggyesy, so exceeded beastly requirements that his own teammates called him Rudeness. Both authors stress how football indoctrinates you. But no one seems quite as indoctrinated as they were.

Does pro football tear down character faster than it builds it? It depends on what you're trying to prove. On one page, Parrish calls the players "overgrown, self-conscious children," on another he says they are "even more sophisticated" than the players of the fifties and sixties. Parrish's children "foolishly fight over their toys; and they live beyond their means, as the recent rash of player bankruptcies illustrates." But in Joe Durso's *The All-American Dollar,* another pro complains that football is no fun anymore because "players sit around checking their investment portfolios," just like boring old grown-ups. And Oliver chips in with praise for the black players who "knew there was no sense in holding onto their money or sinking it into a bank." What the devil is an adult anyway, and is it a good thing?

Ideally, the exposers' first fight would be with each other. Like all of us, they were raised on at least two completely contradictory moral codes, and can preach from either one interchangeably, and with their ears ringing from clothesline tackles, they can be as confused as anyone. There's another reason for their baggy-pants logic. Happy the man with a book-length grievance—and rare. Each of these books contains one possible magazine article surrounded by more padding than an offensive lineman: every little indignity that ever happened to them, and every two-bit feud, magnified to a Horrible Example to justify a larger printing. Bernie Parrish's article would simply be a demand for a bigger piece of the commercial loot for the players, and he has some nice, dull facts to back him up. But nobody's going to buy a whole book about athletes' pay scales. With bad times here again, it's uphill work feeling sorry for fully employed football players clamoring for their share of the TV cream.

So Parrish tarts up his message with this fuzzy stuff about violence and dehumanization and throws in a chapter about how games *might* be fixed (e.g., the referee could make some bad calls in spite of being monitored by millions of sexually aroused bettors on instant replay). As often happens, the useful part of the books is the dullest, and the sensational part is just a come-on.

In Meggyesy's case, he has some convincingly damning things to say about two particular institutions—Syracuse University and the St. Louis Cardinals. Once again, not enough for a coast-to-coast book. He would like to say more, but so far it's all he knows. Athletes are hampered by narrowness of experience, though, as Benchley might say, not always hampered enough. It seems the Cardinals were a racist outfit, overripe for exposure. But Meggyesy has to do a book exposing all of football as well, and he generalizes feebly. According to a black player, Johnny Sample, in his book *Confessions of a Dirty Ballplayer,* Joe Namath has routed racism from the New York Jets: and no doubt, other cities, other tales, dimly known to Meggyesy.

His real story is about himself, and it's not a bad one. His father's beatings were his first contact with violence, and after that it drew him like Swinburne. He says he hit people to please his father-figure coaches. But Ben Schwartzwalder, his coach at Syracuse, says that "you couldn't go up from behind and tap him on the shoulder. He'd turn around and hit you." So even father figures weren't safe.

Meggyesy had none of the juice or joy that George Plimpton found among the Detroit Lions, or the boozy good fellowship which might make this life tolerable. He just doesn't like the football player type. So he tried solemnly to turn himself into a hippie, for which he didn't have the juice or joy either. The book jacket shows him with a beard and headband and an uncertain frown: and the text is no adventure of an expanded spirit, but a heavy laborious tract written with the help of his new coach—Jack Scott of the Institute for the Study of Sport and Society.

Meggyesy's gloomy grapplings with the counterculture make one wish for a third choice—the clergy, maybe. Chip Oliver, on the other hand, fits cheerfully into both cultures, and anything else that's going. He is an old-line extrovert, who once frightened some tourists by appearing naked in a college corridor, and a new-line love child throwing himself into the latest jargon with a rookie's enthusiasm. Of his new friends, he warbles, "Their philosophy that the problems on this planet are only the effects of acquisitive behavior really turned me on." Wild. Or how about "The Chinese have been eating a rice and vegetable diet for years, and despite the propaganda that they are starving, they don't have the health problems that come from obesity that we do." A rip-off of a book, but a diverting character.

On his high-for-the-game days, old Chip couldn't tell a football from a sunflower anyway. Both he and Meggyesy have dropped acid and it sometimes clouds their message in the clichés of *that* sport. LSD may expand consciousness, but it sure as death shrinks vocabulary, and these two very different characters sometimes sound as if they're talking from the same sack. Also they keep expanding way, way beyond football to call on the whole of straight society to repent—in which case football becomes a silly detail. Oliver would like to turn it into an Elysian love dance, but mescaline can do that for you already, without the game being changed at all.

The matter of pro football is serious enough to be referred to by the philosophers or professional arguers, except that nobody buys their books. (Any clown sporting a jock outsells the most talented noncombatant.) When Ara Parseghian played for a tie against Michigan State, he defended himself by saying, "I think I know more about football than they do." Quite true. The only thing a philosopher could have told him was why people play the game in the first place. Coaches would be the last to know this, and college presidents would be the last to tell them.

The autonomy of the coach with his large jaw and his tiny outlook is the one clear evil that each of our authors agrees on. A coach can mislay or bury a player he doesn't like more effectively than in other sports and can use this threat to manipulate private conduct and thought, play injured men, and work out his own scoutmaster kinks. How much is this un-American tyranny necessary for the best functioning of the all-American game? Unfortunately, our authors are too bogged down in petty grievance to put the question sharply, and so far the pompous football establishment has been able to duck it with, of all things, pious talk about American values. Here's Oliver mulling his damnedest: "The Chiefs played more creatively, and creative people, the ones who do the unexpected, are the biggest winners in football." But here's Oliver vs. Oliver: "Vince Lombardi was a great coach, not because he was a football genius *who was constantly coming up with new things to surprise the opposition,* but because he worked the hell out of his players." (My italics.)

How much of football is played in the head is a moot question, and this probably is not the place to moot it. Our four playing authors (I include Sample) were all veteran defensive players who needed less coaching than most (they were also shifted in youth from offense without consultation, and may harbor resentments; offensive players write dreamy accounts of their coaches). The psychological hold of coach over player belongs to social history. Vince Lombardi probably won't arise again in quite that form. Vince had the world view of a parochial school nun, determined that the Irish and the Italians would not be the slobs that people expected: but those schools are closing. The Chip Olivers wouldn't obey him now anyway. And the Meggyesys must look for a new kind of father.

For a decent perspective on all this, I would recommend two books by authors outside the pit: Neil Amdur's *The Fifth Down* and Larry Merchant's *Every Day You Take Another Bite.* Amdur can be rambling and earnestly sentimental, but he sees the size of the question: football is one more excuse for today's kid and yesterday's adult to have at it—or if the coach tries something new, yesterday's kid and today's adult. Merchant goes him one better. He laughs at the whole thing. Could this be the answer?

Well, the greed can be sent to Congress (Parrish's book is being used in an antitrust investigation, where it belongs), and the violence can be sent to Esalen. But the self-importance, the idolatrous "mystique" that coaches and owners grow fat on must be stamped out in the home, and Merchant's is the brightest and funniest contribution to that task in some time.

1971

32 / *Rhapsodist in Blue*

When the fine picture book *Cole* appeared two years ago, it looked as if a sturdy new fad was upon us. The formula was simple and infinitely repeatable: first round up your flotsam (snapshots, old dance shoes, etc.), then get someone as good as Bea Feitler to design it, a Robert Kimball to edit it, and a Brendan Gill to introduce it, with the gossipy good taste of a career diplomat.

Yet already the fad wilts. Last year's *Tallulah* looked like Hogarth in slow-motion replay: a pretty woman flushing her life away under a peeling mask of whoopee. And this year's *Gershwins* reminds us that what you really need is Cole himself.

Because Porter actually lived a picture-book life, with million-dollar sets, from Old Ivy to the Riviera and Venice, and the finest bit players money could buy. When interest threatens to flag, he takes off around the world with Monte Woolley, the perfect supporting actor—almost as if he knew the book would need it. The slobbering wealth of the twenties comes through in the pictures, and also in the book's production, which obeys the first law of picture books, namely that they should look as daffily extravagant as a Busby Berkeley movie to lighten the flatulence of a Christmas afternoon.

By contrast, *The Gershwins* has a pinchpenny look about it, partly for good publishing reasons but partly because the brothers were too busy working to pile up exotic photos. Between the narrow world of backstage Broadway and of Hollywood stucco, there was barely time for the beach at Belmar, New Jersey—the Gershwins' Riviera—and some awkward group shots with musical luminaries (Cole would have stuck out his tongue to make the scene go; George just looks awkward). The best of *The Gershwins,* as it is the least of *Cole,* is the sprawl of show stills plus some pages of musical notation—the brothers at work. Some of George's paintings are also included, and they struck this tin eye agreeably. All in all, a nice book to get in the mail, but thin gruel for a Gershwin nut.

Even without pictures *Cole* is the more interesting book. Not because Cole himself was more interesting than both Gershwins put together, but because again he was closer to book form, a self-made literary character. The Gershwins got to the social top by talent and stayed there by more talent. Porter began at the top and talent could get him no further. Those last few difficult inches up are negotiated by charm, style, eccentricity—a biographer's delights. To take just one example: Porter's correspondence doesn't only consist, as most show people's does, of congratulatory telegrams or "here we are in Budapest" postcards; in his set, you worked just as hard on a funny night letter as you did on a hit song. Hence more trove for the collector. The Gershwins were built for function, Porter for decoration.

The Gershwins were also built for show business, and their entry to it was as dramatically unsurprising as Porter's would have been to the brokerage business. For real class conflict, one must turn to Porter crashing Tin Pan Alley, turning from duchess to flower girl and becoming useful as well as ornamental. As late as the twenties, this great innovator feared he was too old-fashioned for Broadway: his earliest work had been Gilbert and Sullivanish tea music at Yale, and here he was confronted with street Arabs like the Gershwins, hardened professionals since childhood. Freddy Bartholomew meets the Artful Dodger. Gill says Porter could always be intimidated by a tough-talking Broadway pro and would yank a tune rather than fight. One also wonders whether Cole, a most reticent "perennial bachelor," wasn't afraid that his music would give him away. If so, it must have been a stunning relief to find himself America's most popular writer of love songs.

A good enough story for the most fumble-fingered biographer. And, to top it, Porter also had the steely willpower of a robber baron. He composed one of his wittiest songs lying with his legs crushed under a fallen horse, and he was able to dismiss Scott Fitzgerald as a "crying drunk" for whom he had no time. This willowy fop was, in short, about as fragile as the Edwardian dandies who went over the top in 1914.

It says much about the state of show business biography that no one has done a good one on Porter yet. Gershwin has fared even worse, until recently, though for more understandable reasons. His genius was of the monomaniacal sort that finds total expression in his work, such that when he wasn't being a genius he comes through on paper as a bit of a bore. Fortunately those moments were rare: he clung to pianos like lichen. But his letters and postcards suggest a wheezing jocularity, not to say a terrible prose style, that augur badly; and his liking for golf with "the stockbroker type" almost suggests a young Eisenhower in the making.

Which could mean that once you have heard his music you have learned about all you're going to know of George. Fortunately, it's plenty. For myself, I can think of no composer who speaks his mind more clearly. The generation of Jewish immigrants that hit New York like the Marx brothers, the wildest, vulgarest explosion of talent since the Reformation, found a perfect voice for its wit and drive and melancholy in Gershwin. To a sometime expatriate he talked New York so directly it almost transcended music: yet with no literal street sounds, or whimsical taxi horns, simply a music saturated in its time and place, as true a record as *Gatsby*.

Writings about Gershwin always bog down on the question of whether he was in fact a serious composer manqué or just a pushy songwriter, as if this were the only question to ask about him; but even in this he spoke for his generation, with its cultural pretensions and its gut folk talent. An American genius almost had to express both of these; even James and Eliot expressed both. In music there were lots of deracinated contemporaries who studied classical European composition and who appear now as rather dim provincial figures, with too-perfect manners and too little native juice; Gershwin simply crashed the party like Groucho and stole it. Ask any European whether he'd rather hear an evening of Gershwin or Aaron Copeland and you'll see that George made the right choice artistically.

But it's silly to congratulate George on his artistic choices. His family was of the type that looks around for the arts as soon as it gets its footing, while his East Side neighborhood bustled with Philistine vitality, and

George absorbed it all like young Charles Dickens—but all into his music, not his speech box. "What comes out of that piano frightens me," he said, and well it might: his bourgeois lobes had no say in the matter.

Although constipation and trips to the whorehouse do not a Kafka make, Charles Schwartz's *Gershwin: His Life and Music* is a generally serious attempt to describe the kind of artist Gershwin was: from the rattleybang phrases of the early songs, with brother Ira clinging on for dear life, to the longer line of, say, "Our Love Is Here to Stay," with Ira at ease now and spreading himself. I have my own views about this. Comparisons with Gilbert and Sullivan are especially foolish. The early songs seem designed almost to embarrass his brother—try putting words to "I got rhythm"—and Ira obliged with lines like "The loving she for me" and "He loves and she loves and they love"—until you find yourself muttering testily "the he for she who'll fly to I." Ira always seems to be stumbling, glasses askew, to keep up with his greyhound brother and playing desperate word games without depth or real meaning. Anyway this particular Gilbert proved much better with other Sullivans, such as Vernon Duke ("I Can't Get Started") and Kurt Weill ("Poor Jenny"), and George still sounds better with no words at all—not songs or concert music but just Gershwin.*

The ideal biographer might go even further than Schwartz in reducing Gershwin to pure music, as Alec Wilder did in his ground-breaking *The American Popular Song*. The high price of copyright prevented Wilder from quoting any lyrics at all so he had to analyze his songwriters solely in terms of their notes. The result approaches a kind of musical psychoanalysis. "I fail to see the wit of the F sharp," says Wilder sternly; and when I noodled that particular piece with my one good finger, I failed to see the wit too. Interestingly enough, Wilder doesn't like Gershwin, although he seems to like most of his songs. The dislike is "just personal," as Gatsby would say. The real Gershwin lurks down among the F sharps, and Wilder meets him there like a gentle fastidious upstater on his first visit to Zabar's Delicatessen.

Curiously, Heywood Broun felt the same way about Scott Fitzgerald. These two near-contemporaries, George and Scott, came busting out of the post-World War I confusion full of themselves, in equal parts shy

*Since writing the above, I've read Ira's "Lyrics on Separate Occasions," which shows more good work with George than I'd allowed myself to admit.

and ludicrously conceited, and hell-bent to convey the whole of American experience—a staggering dream that they almost brought off because they didn't know it was impossible. Between them they defined the jazz age for us, though their paths don't seem to have crossed, and their definitions of jazz must have been very different.

We know, because he could talk, that Scott grew up, learned to live with failure and pain and drastically reduced dreams, and died a wise man. But George's secret is locked in his music. Superficially we are stuck with the early legend: the radiant egoist who hogged the piano (all pianists hog the piano) and boasted till dawn, an incandescent presence with nothing to say. Does the music tell us something akin to Fitzgerald's notebooks and his *Crack-Up* essays? My own unmusical guess is that his music was saying something different by the end. When Gershwin died, he was still too busy to be a completely interesting man: but *Porgy* is getting awfully close.

On the other hand, World War II was coming, and he might have been asked to write symphonic pieces about Victory in the Air. And he might have done it. And that would have been awful.

1973

33 / *The Wit of George S. Kaufman and Dorothy Parker*

The lives of the wits make grim reading these days. To judge from John Keats's *You Might as Well Live,* Dorothy Parker had a wretched loveless childhood, got her own back at the world with some fine wisecracks, and came to a miserable end. According to Howard Teichmann's *George S. Kaufman,* little George was coddled and frightened into helplessness, learned to fight back with some splendid wisecracks, and came to a pitiable end.

Both stories may be true for all I know. The odds on any intelligent person having an unhappy childhood are better than fair, and the odds on a sad ending are practically off the board. However, there are a couple of things that bother.

First of all, there is the sheer ease and speed with which these conclusions are reached. Teichmann needs only a few pages to wrap up the Kaufman case. George's guilt over an older brother's death, his lifelong fear of sickness, his inability to play baseball—no wonder he had to be witty. It's all a bit like one of those magic insights in a 1940s' Hollywood psychodrama which show mother drinking, father killing himself, and baby screaming, all in one flashback. That this brand of glib psychologizing passes for biography nowadays is ominous. This sort of thing may be good enough for analyzing Richard Nixon, but surely minor playwrights deserve better.

Keats is not much profounder about baby Parker. His account of her early childhood is largely based on her own recollections given in interviews during her last bitter years. Mrs. Parker was notoriously hard on people who had left the room; and since parents and teachers came comfortably into this category, they got their lumps. But of the kind of adversary proceeding from which biographic truth emerges, Keats offers practically none.

In each case, the author uses only such material as points to a childhood wound. The possibility that Dorothy was a holy terror from the womb who drove her wicked stepmother crazy with her feline cleverness is not explored. Or that anyone who played the great American game of poker as well as George had no need to worry about baseball. (More boys are lousy at baseball than good anyway.) Or that both of them were artists with highly developed personas, and hence unreliable witnesses to their own pasts.

Take Kaufman's helplessness for instance. It seems he couldn't drive, swim, or tie his own shoelaces. But what Teichmann overlooks is that humorous authors have been coming on helpless since at least the days of Addison and Lamb (see Cyril Connolly, *Enemies of Promise*) and were still doing it under Leacock and Benchley. Kaufman was outrageously competitive and you can be sure no one was going to come on more helpless than he, even if it meant being carried from room to room. No doubt he had natural gifts in this direction, but like most successful people he could always be as tough as he needed to be, even to the point of imposing his helplessness on others. Likewise Dorothy's cynicism was at least partly a conscious literary manner—following after Edna St. Vincent Millay "in my own horrible sneakers"—which hardened into a characteristic as life belted her around.

The individualist-psychologizing of the 1940s left out all these questions of fashion and cultural artifice and what other people were doing at the time, and so was particularly at sea with entertainers, who live by those things. Thus we had those films about Al Jolson's tragic flaw, etc., and now we have these books with the same period flavor, as if wit needs a tragic wound to explain it.

All available evidence suggests that *everyone* was trying to be witty in the twenties, just as everyone was trying to be authentic in the sixties. Each era is bullied by one temperament which seems like the only one to have. So, was the whole nation wounded that year? Probably about as much as England was wounded in the Restoration. Anyway, what created Kaufman and Parker was not primarily their warped temperaments, but the vast public demand for wit; and what distinguished them from a thousand aspiring wise guys was simply their success at providing it. If there was a neurotic component, it was in the success, not the wit—particularly in those wit marathons at the Algonquin with everyone whoring after laughs and press mentions, as much part of the period as six-day bike races and flagpole sitting.

Looking at Kaufman's wisecracks now, one is puzzled by the ones that have survived. By what evolutionary law does such a feeble off-Wilde as "a bad play saved by a bad performance" still find itself in print? Or such a mechanical switcheroo as "forgotten but not gone"? There is more wit in a single essay of Benchley's—or a single essay of Kaufman's. But the fact that it was purred or shot back or murmured by a living person gives a joke more value, even in print. (Thus the Algonquin may have spawned our current talk shows.)

The wit *apparat* of the twenties is more interesting than the individual toilers. The Algonquin wits were like comic-strip characters. Many of their lesser gags were almost interchangeable, but their well-publicized "characters" made them seem different—just as Durante and Hope would make the same material seem different. For a Parker line, you add a "she said gently." For Kaufman, one stresses the pause, the deadpan, the devastated victim.

The entrepreneurs, Franklin P. Adams and Alexander Woollcott and assorted press agents, circulated these images and fixed them forever. It was simply up to the originals to stay in type—a stultifying requirement that may have kept them all from growing as they might have. Mrs. Parker, at least, came to hate her comic-strip self. "But dammit it was the twenties and we had to be smarty." She tried to live another life and to stop being a waxwork in a brightly lit window. She spat venomously on the old Algonquin legend. Having to be Dorothy Parker had damn near ruined her.

Kaufman, on the other hand, seems to have been at some pains not to grow or change at all. Hand after hand of bridge, a contracepted mental activity if ever there was one; joke after joke put together like Erector sets—"a lot of bridge has passed over the water," he murmured gently (or was that the other one?); play after play, worked at compulsively, but showing no deepening of mind or leap of imagination.

For anyone who takes the American theater seriously, it is disheartening to find one of its most influential figures with as little inner life as Teichmann's book reveals in Kaufman. It is true that some excellent writers have barely seemed alive when they weren't working. But somehow the very forms they worked in urged them beyond Kaufman's sophisticated Norman Rockwell view of people and life. Kaufman either could not or would not see beyond the limits of the Broadway hit. The only escape for his obviously superior intelligence was in those wisecracks of his, some of which were indeed wonderful, and in playing cards, which was a much more neurotic evasion than his wit ever was. But these activities seem less a defense against some childhood trauma than against the adult thinking and feeling which could have threatened his Broadway career. In modern American style, his job, not his past, defined him.

He may have known best at that. Mrs. Parker's attempts to be more than a wit ended sadly: a few pretty good short stories, following Hemingway in those self-same sneakers, and some smart, formula verses, at the cost of enough derangement of the senses via booze and wanton melancholy to buckle a Rimbaud. The sick room of a minor artist is a glum place. And Keats's attempt to raise her stature only makes it worse, like the twitter of a near relative. Yet she knew the score about herself ("my verses are no damn good") and where she stood in relation to real artists ("the big boys") and that's more than something. The pity of it is that the Algonquin waxwork lives while the real Dorothy Parker has begun to fade. It isn't even a tale of great tragic waste. Maybe with a purer vocation she could have done a little better: but she tried much harder than she let on, and my guess is she squeezed out all she could.

Kaufman at least was perfect of his kind. "He gave me the walk and the talk," says Groucho, and that should be achievement enough for any man. In fact he was the real Groucho, of which Groucho is the imitation or platonic representation. The sequences Kaufman wrote created Groucho, and the latter has been trying to live up to them ever since. "Ah Emily, I can just see us tonight, you and the moon." Pause. "You wear a necktie." Quoted from loving memory. And much more in this vein, finest American dada, heartless, nonrepresentational, humor for humor's sake.

Unfortunately most Broadway comedies had to be adulterated with this and that—sentiment, human interest, etc., so Kaufman took on a raft of collaborators to help out with these, and with the jokes as well, so we'll never know just how true his comic gift was. We do know that he refused altogether to write love scenes, which suggests, not that he was scared of them but that he took his comic vocation seriously and was not going to adulterate himself so long as he could get Edna Ferber or somebody. The best comedy is always heartless, an alternative to rational emotion, and Kaufman dedicated himself to matching this product personally: again, not as a frightened child, but as a ruthless professional.

Teichmann has, about half the time, written the right kind of book about him, i.e., an old-fashioned collection of theater anecdotes. Those people lived in anecdotes, one couldn't imagine a life in between. The anecdotes still entertain, which is all Kaufman ever contracted to do. The life in between, now that we have it, is the usual mess and hardly worth telling. The mysterious psychic springs of humor are not here, and the rest is soap opera.

1973

34 / *Frank Sheed and Maisie Ward: Writers, Publishers, and Parents*

This piece is about my parents, Frank Sheed and Maisie Ward, a couple of writers and publishers who richly deserve one. Since they are both very much alive and capable of kicking, I shall try to keep it light, sticking to their literary selves and leaving personal feelings out of it. Up to a point.

I came to ancestor worship late in life. My mother's family, the Wards, were some kind of big noise in the Roman Catholic Church in England; I didn't want to hear about it. The only one I cared about was a great-great-grandfather who was said to be a cricket champion—a gift that deserted the family for generations after his death. (My uncles were born and raised in a library, as far as I could make out.)

The cricketer begat, in the fullness of time, a big fat son called William, nicknamed "Ideal," and an equally large one called the "Real" Ward: both named after books they wrote. A small plague of writers was on its way. "Ideal" proceeded to become a friend of Cardinal Newman's and the first member of the Oxford Movement to jump to Rome. For which high treason he had his Oxford degrees taken away, inspiring him to sign his letters "William G. Ward, Undergraduate" thereafter. "Ideal" was an altogether formidable Victorian ("Madam, you will find me strong and narrow, *very* strong and *very* narrow"), sometimes called "the buffoon of the Oxford Movement," with a marked tendency to debate people like Huxley and Mill.

"Ideal's" son Wilfrid seems to have been partway dragooned into Letters because his real passion, Opera, was no trade for gentlemen. He made a fair first of it, anyway, turning out a workmanlike biography of Newman, among other things, and editing the *Dublin Review,* where he got caught in the middle of the Modernist Crisis (a brouhaha foreshadowing some of Rome's more recent discontents), which effectively broke his heart, since he had friends on both sides. His wife, Josephine, wrote some pretty good novels, though she has suffered from not being named "Mrs. Humphrey." (Young Scott Fitzgerald recommended one of them called *Tudor Sunset* to Edmund Wilson, but Mr. Wilson doesn't remember reading it.)

My father Frank's family in splendid contrast left no records to speak of and no bearded photographs to worry about. His grandfather had been a sea captain shipping out of Aberdeen to Sydney, origins cloudy: his grandfather's father had been a "ne'er-do-well" (that's all the son would say); and his uncle, one Muckle Wullie, was harpoonsman on a whaler. Frank's own father was a drifting draftsman, as well as one of the rare Marxists in Edwardian Sydney.

Not a literary man in the bunch, you'll notice. My father got what he could of that from prowling the Sydney bookstores and from his mother, a self-educated Irish girl called Mary Maloney who had sailed to Australia by herself at the age of fourteen and who, through the years, must have read every nineteenth-century novel in English. ("If the French were so intelligent, *they'd* speak English," she said.) When she was eighty-five, I introduced her to the Marx Brothers, expecting little, and she laughed herself cockeyed. Also, sure sign of the literary intelligence, she fancied Groucho over Harpo. One could make her laugh up to the day she died just by mentioning Groucho.

The Sheeds, then, were the family for me—Scotch-Irish vagabonds who left no trace, or at least, that's the way I pictured them. My father was the man who wore his hat funny (brim down all the way round) and looked like an amused stranger who'd just landed from somewhere at family functions. "Frank would be in two places at once if there was a night train," said his bemused mother-in-law. And Jean Stafford, who worked for him briefly, remembers him sleeping on top of his desk with his dinner jacket in a shopping bag next to it, prior to speaking at some starchy church event or other.

That style was built into their publishing house, Sheed & Ward, as well as into our personal lives—movement, improvisation, squat where you land. One week you found a butler laying out your clothes and sneering at the underwear, the next you were cursing because the toilet wouldn't flush and you'd just stepped on a roach. It made absolutely no difference to my parents, and it had better not to junior either. If publishers had trunks like actors, I would have been born in one.

It was an ideal temperament for building a small, mainly Catholic (because who can compete with the secular biggies?) publishing house. It meant not only that they could get books out of Dorothy Day as well as Monsignor Fruitcake, it also meant simple survival. They started out in London in 1926 with £2,000 and the dubious help of Hilaire Belloc, who didn't want to edit, whose own books were bespoke elsewhere *(helas!)*, and whose money, like W. C. Fields's, was all tied up in ready cash.

My parents did get books out of the old fraud and from Chesterton and all the big and little names of the English Catholic Revival, not to mention such Continental pistols as Maritain, Léon Bloy, Berdyaev, and even an early Mauriac; but it was a sweat. The two of them edited on packing boxes with one secretary and with my father doing all the business work. (Luckily, he's some kind of prodigy at that. Years later when the adding machine broke down, he did a whole year's accounts in one night.) On top of that, my mother got deathly ill between my sister's birth in 1927 and mine in 1930 and was trying to pursue a writing career on her own. They picked up another editor somehow and a species of businessman and staggered on grimly.

Having mastered these trifling problems and gotten some real chairs in the office, they decided to go through the whole scene again over here. It was 1933, a crumby year, and since America had just gone off the gold standard, all the books came out the wrong price; but they had a fat $20,000 to lose this time and a solid backlist and they were able to pick up some pocket money on the lecture belt. (Both are veteran street-corner speakers.) My father contracted the bad habit of putting this money into the firm and not taking a salary—a habit he has not broken to this day.

So there was always just enough in hand for various swindlers and incompetents to fumble through, and Sheed & Ward hired some dillies.

Yet I honestly cannot remember any heavy anxiety reaching the house, even when a vintage psychopath posing as manager made off with the lot in 1943 and they had to start from scratch. Instead, there was usually a vague sense of elation—my mother had just discovered the *Catholic Worker,* or the Cooperatives in Nova Scotia, or the worker priests in France, and maybe there was a book in it.

She usually wound up writing the book herself. Although she was supposed to be doing a life of G. K. Chesterton (which she eventually did), something was always catching the corner of her eye and she was off like a retriever. She did her own legwork, in the slums of Marseilles or wherever, and came back snorting fire—"Do you realize what's going on there?"

My mother seemed to read three books at a time, and I remember her calling out bits from them that made no sense at all if you weren't as involved as she was. My father would listen like a good publisher without losing his place in *his* three books. He could move his full attention there and back faster than light artillery. Yet Maisie was not bookish as I'd pictured the Wards. (They weren't either, I've since realized.) Books were to wrestle with. They were life itself, as real as their subject matter, as real as the slums or the docks or this preposterous fellow who'd made a perfect bloomer about Cardinal Newman.

I myself came to hate the sight of books—and still wish that they came in a different shape. "Are you going to be a writer too, sonny?" "Hell, no." Luckily my parents didn't seem to care one way or the other, though they put me onto some good stuff if I ever changed my mind. What did appeal to me was the unexpectedness of their corner of the literary life—unexplained little men from the Continent turning up to play croquet, comic priests in black dickeys bellowing songs round the piano (my father played as if his pants were on fire), and always plenty of gossip steaming hot from Vatican or chancery. It was a pretty good life, if you could forget the books for a moment.

The family moved over here in 1940, though my father continued to commute to London, thumbing any rides he could get. He made one crossing on a banana boat, another sleeping in the bomb rack of a B-24. He was always getting stranded in the Azores or Lisbon or some damn place, which kind of thing seemed to exhilarate him, though it worried the rest of us. One morning in London he went whistling to his office, placed his key in the door, and found the whole building had disappeared. A packing boy came up, gazed at the rubble, and threw up.

One stray bomb, presumably looking for St. Paul's Cathedral, had all but wiped out our English branch: 300 books stored in the basement went out of print in a flash. My father's subsequent trips were devoted to raising morale in the skeleton staff—something he does tolerably well—and persuading obliging printers to be even more obliging, which they surprisingly were.

The American office passed a gentler war. They lost a great young editor when Robert Lowell decided to declare himself a Conscientious Objector (the warden asked Frank if Lowell would make a good prison librarian and was reassured) and the vintage psychopath mentioned above did a little bomb damage on his own. But people were down to reading the labels on bottles those years; and although the paper shortage cut into new titles, a house with a good backlist could dump inventory forever.

The first rumblings of the religion boom could already be picked up. *Peace of Mind, Peace of Soul* (readers will have to guess the salacious title I thought of to go with that series) were big postwar books. Sheed & Ward set itself immediately against the sleazier aspects of the boom; there was to be no quack spirituality or three minutes a day with the Man Upstairs. It is often forgotten that there was a hard side to the boom too: the magazine *Integrity*, which preached and practiced ascetic communes; the still uncompromising *Catholic Worker;* the Friendship House Movement in Harlem, which had influenced Thomas Merton earlier; and much, much more.

In fact, Friendship House groups used to hold interracial meetings at our apartment; and I remember the Negro elevator men complaining about the black guests. That was our world, and preeminently my mother's world. Her life of Chesterton finally got finished and became a best seller, and she used that and other earnings to help support two communes and God knows what else. Social activism comes and goes with the tides, and most of those Catholic groups were down to a twitch by the late fifties but hers goes on forever. To bring that side of her up to date: in recent years, she has started a housing-aid society in England which buys old houses and turns them into low-rent flats and which has since grown into a national organization. She has also been taking the interdenominational pulpit to raise money for a village in India, which recently returned the favor by throwing her a three-day fiesta, with huge banners saying "Welcome Mrs. Sheed" and fire dances and much action on the tom-toms. Not bad for her age, whatever that is: eighty-two is her story.

I hasten to say, I take no credit for this extraordinary woman: these qualities skip at least a generation. She has also become more radicalized in later life and has lately been interviewing draft-resisters in prison. To stick to her literary self, which is tougher than I expected: she has written many more books, including a two-volume life of Robert Browning, which was listed among the books of its year by the London *Observer,* and is completing a study of the Brownings' scapegrace son, Pen.

Frank's books include *Communism and Man,* which was praised anonymously by George Orwell in 1936 and the first half of which has been used in Communist party study groups (the second half is, of course, counterrevolutionary muck); and a number of lean and splendidly lucid books of theology which have sold in the hundreds of thousands.

His brand of theology seems to be out of fashion at the moment, a situation that he views serenely; but in the forties and fifties he was considered a flaming radical, if only for daring to poach this clerical game preserve and assert a layman's right to think. (Rome grudgingly made him a Doctor of Theology for his pains, which is like a civilian making five-star general.) It's no business of mine to evaluate his theology, even if I knew how; but I do know that many of the more swinging Catholics of the day have acknowledged a profound debt to him for his writing as well as his publishing.

To get back to that for a last look: the happy amateurism that was Sheed & Ward's trademark in the thirties could have sunk it faster than group theater in the grey-flannel fifties. Symbolically the original brownstone home on lower Fifth Avenue was torn down to make way for a department store, itself boarded over by now. The next office sprang a fire—I think somebody bribed a fire inspector too well. Anyway, fire was almost too good for that dump. Before anything worse could happen, S & W moved to a regular modern office between Grove Press and Praeger and began to behave like a real business with a profit and a direct mailing department and even finally a computer. There is no way this could be as much fun, although it was probably as much fun as Praeger's operation.

Frank had finally found people who could run the place without sending him emergency telegrams: a real businesswoman named Louise

Wihnhausen, an ad-copy whizz called Marigold Hunt, and a fine editor, Philip Scharper. (I salute them all.) Scharper was tuned to Pope John's church the way Scott Fitzgerald was tuned to the twenties. A Golden Age was in the works, and my parents could at last afford to put their feet up (which in Maisie's case means doubling her activities: she always works harder with her feet up).

Came, as the good book warns us, the Crash—not just the normal post-Vatican Council slump which could have been expected, but the Death of Print era (with McLuhanism raging like pestilence) married fatally to the Death of God. Sheed & Ward's clerical readers were getting married, literally, and plowing their books into diapers. (American husbands have always made lousy readers.) Sheed & Ward had been doing ecumenical books for some time and could count on solid Protestant and Jewish attention. But it wasn't enough, suddenly nothing was enough. Religious houses were folding like morning glories or being gobbled in mergers, to the point where, as far as I can make out, Sheed & Ward is now the only independent Catholic house left.

Ah well, retirement never suited my father anyway. He returned to work a year or so ago to see if he could keep the old tub afloat, and by George he's done it, so far. Afloat and then some. He's an incurably cheerful man, figures that if the pendulum comes back just a couple of inches, he's sitting pretty. If it doesn't, if it isn't a pendulum at all but a clock hand moving away, he won't be heartbroken. This, I suppose, is the quality that most astounds me in both of them. They never expected it to last forever. "We did what needed doing at the time," Frank says. "And we had a lot of fun doing it." Anybody got a better boast than that?

1972

PART TWO

And Other Words

1 / *America and the Movies*

"In what sense does the US lead the world in movies? We make more of them than any other country and are I suppose more proficient technically, but have we ever turned out anything that was comparable artistically to the best German or Russian films? . . . The idea of establishing and exploiting the lowest common denominator of audiences has finally killed the movies."

Thus, Edmund Wilson in 1937—little realizing that *auteurs* were already turning out *genre* movies for future *cinéastes.* Ah, what a difference a few French words can make. Within a few years, the French New Wave were poring over the junk Wilson describes and, unhampered by English, finding gems, masterpieces after the fact.

The Anglo-American mind is traditionally poleaxed by French approval, however bizarre. And in no time words which not only Wilson but the directors themselves would have considered pretentious and *wrong* were the coin for discussing Hollywood, with Louella Parsons all but forgotten.

Not a bad thing. Our nonvisual intellectuals had certainly missed a trick or two, if the best of them could dismiss technical proficiency so lightly. But the revisionists could not stop with the pretty pictures and fine individual scenes: they had to find dramatic and narrative virtues that had eluded even the wide-ranging Wilson. And to do this, they had further to fashion a theory of "movieness" so self-enclosed that no previous aesthetic could touch it. Only on these terms could they have their Golden Age.

The *auteurist* wars ended in exhaustion a few years back. But they left a legacy of assumptions about Hollywood that both sides now seem to accept. For instance, to a purist, Michael Wood would seem like a natural enemy: what can a flippant English professor of literature know of movieness? Yet at the outset of his funny book *America in the Movies*, Wood invokes the magic word "style" as an auteurist would, to elevate whatever he wishes. After reciting a catalogue of movie nonsense from the old days, compounded of silly lines and inane plotting, he says it was exactly "right" for the period. Because of Style. He quickly adds that the same sort of thing is dead wrong in *Cleopatra* (1963), when apparently America had come of age.

This contribution to Age of Innocence theory would come as news to the survivors, who thought the nonsense was just as bad then as it is now, although time may have lent it quaintness. The witness from those years is overwhelming, and not just from snobbish intellectuals and sourball novelists. Dwight Macdonald, in his young dandy period, wrote about movies brilliantly in the late twenties, but sat out the whole Golden Age in protest; and if Macdonald is too verbal for you, consider Walter Kerr, a highly visual critic steeped in silent movies, who turned his back on the talkies to find more nourishment in, God help us, the Broadway stage. And so on. It is not just a question of perhaps overvaluing a few old movies but—fatally easy for us—of undervaluing the best taste of a generation.

There was, of course, much oblique merit in thirties to fifties movies, and a new kind of critic arrived to do it justice. James Agee and Otis Ferguson were expert at grading junk according to its kind and finding stray bits of carbon. But their descendants want more. They want to embrace the whole junkyard—for the very good reason that they were raised in it.

Those were the only movies we had, and we had no choice but to love them. If they were aimed, as the director Raoul Walsh says, at the inch and a quarter forehead, we simply had to lower our brows for the occasion. And now, with the glow of our childhood on them, these simple-minded movies seem "just right." It turns out that the director was talking to us sophisticates all along over the heads of the mob—while he was talking to the mob too. As Richard Schickel puts it, he offered "something a child could respond to on one level, an adolescent on another, an adult on a third"—not bad going for an eighty-minute film.

The result is rather like a literary criticism that bogs down in comparing Rider Haggard with Conan Doyle—not altogether bad, if we keep the enterprise in scale. Schickel's boyish book *The Men Who Made the Movies* is a good example of how not to do this. It is based on a series of TV interviews with eight veteran directors, in which a certain amount of flattery may have been necessary to get the old boys talking. But the reverence remains in the text double thick, along with a fawning introduction that would embarrass a reverend mother. It seems that when critics of a certain age come within sniffing distance of the old Hollywood, they lose their bearings and forget what they came for. Once upon a time the old charmers would have signed up Schickel on the spot for PR duties, but now they don't need to.

Yet almost the only interesting thing about these interviews is Schickel's determination to make them so. If we had masterpieces, we must have had masters: so Schickel makes even their limitations a clue to greatness. For instance, he tells us admiringly that the directors tend as a group to be men of action and not of verbal analysis (Wood says that old movies always insisted on this distinction, so that some should walk and others should chew gum), which puts them at a blow beyond their intellectual critics, who sound like dreadful weeds anyway, and covers for a lot of lackluster dialogue. In fact, I began wondering whether we mightn't dispense with dialogue altogether and simply show pictures of the directors fishing or something.

Schickel stresses that men like Walsh and Howard Hawks and William Wellman were real he-men in touch with an earlier America. But what so often struck one about their films was their artificiality even in this, their strength—because their active years embraced not the heyday but the decadence of machismo, when toughness had become pure pose, as in apache dancing. For the first time ever, many Americans did not actually need to be tough, so they made a fetish of it, using the word itself to nausea. And the directors, when they could tear themselves away from hunting trips with Hemingway, gave it to them in ungovernable doses. Hawks's prattle about "who's better" would presumably strike a genuine man of action as corrupt or silly ("Go roll a hoop in the park," as Hammett told Hemingway), but to pale-faced city boys and French cineastes it was nectar.

As with toughness, so with everything they touched. Far from keeping their roots in America, the directors had merely preserved them under glass. Like most people in Hollywood, they lived in their own airtight compartments of friends and rushes and pictures of memories, in a town that was itself airtight. The hard-nosed bullet-biters like Walsh seem to have kept their own road companies of actors and technicians about them to sustain a mining camp uproariousness at all times, as depressing after a while as shiny false teeth. No one in America was doing that anymore if they ever had. This was just old men at play.

Schickel praises Walsh's *Gentleman Jim* because it keeps touch with Irish working-class life. But in all the weird annals of Hollywood Irishness, no movie was ever hokier or further from *any* kind of Irish life than this jolly, funning, brawling, kissing broth of an old sod. I would not have been surprised to hear it had been made behind the Iron Curtain.

The directors were of course serving up myths, which is Wood's theme and we'll get to it in a moment. But one thing Schickel's book makes clear despite itself is that the directors were rather ordinary men with ordinary minds who became geniuses only after they retired, or semi-retired. In their own time, the time that counted, the producer's name was usually the big one, not theirs. And however we inflate them now, the tonal quality is that of clever functionaries, not creative artists.* One would do no better or worse with eight cameramen.

As if to confirm this, the introduction refers to how well the directors worked with "what they were given" and adds approvingly that they had very little trouble with their studios (in the vanity of retirement they make this sound like some sort of sly integrity, but there is barely a movie of the period that couldn't have been strengthened by a little troublemaking). The myths were parceled out by the grotesques in the studios, guessing the public taste from a company village 2,000 miles away and up.

Since we bought the results the assumption is that they guessed right;

*There are exceptions at both ends. One or two of the subjects seem perhaps too old to do themselves justice, while another, Alfred Hitchcock, seems to belong to a different species altogether. As a dealer in deceit, he was able uniquely to express himself even in Hollywood. Incidentally, the others interviewed, besides those mentioned, are George Cukor, Frank Capra, Vincente Minnelli, and King Vidor.

though once we had a choice, their guesses (see Wood on *Cleopatra*) suddenly seemed wrong. Which would seem to verify a Raymond Williams view, that this was fundamentally an entrepreneurial culture and not a folk one.

It is necessary to Michael Wood's thesis that Hollywood had at least some links, however twisted, with the Folk, and that the movies which seemed so hilarious because they spoke to *no one's* real concerns were actually mining shadows in our psyches. And since it is impossible to prove the matter one way or the other with any precision, his book simply ignites a string of arguments which can burn as long as you like —not a bad function for a movie book. What Wood does is place movies and America in juxtaposition, like facing mirrors, or like Groucho and Harpo in *Duck Soup,* and try to guess who is doing what to whom: which at least allows the Williams possibility that Hollywood invented its own America, and the second mirror copied it.

America in the Movies begins as a gloss on Barbara Deming's powerful, lopsided book *Running Away from Myself.* Deming maintained that movies told horrible truths about America while pretending to tell pretty ones. E.g., Bogart's neurasthenic alienation is the real story of *Casablanca,* not his trumped-up conversion to action at the end. And so on. The only problem with this, and it is a nearly fatal one, is that Deming completely ignores the exigencies of storytelling. Granted that a narrator wants to reach such and such a happy ending, then everything along the way must work against that ending. And the strength of his story will almost invariably lie there.

Which is why Milton is always on the side of the devil. Applying Deming's brooding analysis to lighter entertainment, one might suppose that Broadway musical fanciers are obsessed with boys losing girls. In general, since nine plot resolutions out of ten are likely to be contrived and unsatisfactory, one presumes the author's real meaning is somewhere in the middle of the story.

Wood seems to acknowledge the difficulty, though not perhaps enough. He understands that films are so many escapes, but he suggests that, to work, they must first remind us, however glancingly, of what we're escaping from. So his first question would be rather, why this particular happy ending? why these difficulties? And here, as an Englishman who beat him off the boat by a few years, I may be able to help him in one respect at least.

Although at one point he mentions the Motion Picture Code (only to dismiss it rather too swiftly as basically what people wanted. How on earth does he know?), he doesn't ever touch on that other great enforcer, the Catholic Legion of Decency. Perhaps out of delicacy, film historians have not really done justice to the power of this strange organization. Although a few young Catholics used its condemned list as a shopping guide, and learned a lot of French for their pains, most of them went along with their annual pledge to boycott not only these films but the houses that *showed* these films.

This was quite a hammer, and more than enough to flatten a mogul. By chance I once visited a studio in the company of a widely syndicated Catholic reviewer, and all hands groveled, as before Goldwyn. This man, a kindly fanatic, told me afterward that his favorite movie was *The Father of the Bride* and that *The Asphalt Jungle* was a deadly poison.

So before we can talk of the flow of myth through film, we have to consider what was trying to stop that flow and why. For its part, the Church was making a last desperate power play (for which it is now paying dear) to keep its immigrant children in line. These in gross were better educated than their parents, had a bit of money for the first time, and some of them had actually seen Paree. In short they were ripe for secular temptation, with nothing to save them but the reflex of obedience, which was about to be worked to death.

The obvious medicine was domesticity in cloying spoonfuls. And since most of them knew what harsh medicine this can be in real life, it had to be sugarcoated beyond belief for popular consumption. Hence Donna Reed. But this myth was not rising from the public: it was landing on it. And the same goes for "problem" movies like *Pinkie,* which squarely confronted the trials of Negroes who look like white movie stars, and which seemed more like an Army training film than a reflection of anyone's unconscious.

A Wood- or Deming-ite might answer that mythmaking simply went underground at this time to burrow into the middle of the film, the adversary part, and they would probably have a point. The cult of domesticity was so alien to the actual filmmakers that they may have put a little more vinegar into subverting it than even normal storytelling calls for. Perhaps.

Another difficulty that Wood wrestles to a draw is that of finding specifically American myths in movies aimed at, and gobbled up by, a world audience. He is quite right to suppose that "nice guys finish last" (as in *The Gunfighter*) is a typically American thought, but one might argue from dramaturgy alone that the Greeks had it first. Or, if not that, something else which made them typically American—a love and fear of success. (Using Wood's methods one could conceivably prove that almost anybody is typically American.)

He is on firmer ground with the guilt-of-new-wealth theme in films like *Mildred Pierce,* since Americans happened to have new wealth and nobody else did; and because in some sense it came out of Europe's hide—though few Americans probably worried about this. But as with his myths in general, the truer and more painful they are, the fewer movies there are to support them. Naturally enough. If you can find the myth, it hasn't been hidden properly, and if it's been hidden properly you can't find it for sure. Hence the pleasant circular sensation of reading his book.

But sometimes he strains too hard to justify his title: for instance in foisting the legend of the "obscurely motivated" and destructive woman on America. This after all the baffled French husbands we've seen gazing into the Seine is a bit hard to take. Wood's trump card here is Rita Hayworth in *Gilda,* but he complains that her face denies what she's doing, even as she lays waste to her men, and that her mind seems to be elsewhere, as well it might.

Let me suggest another theory, probably no better or worse than his: namely, that this European perennial strikes Americans as plain silly, and that they can't do it with a straight face. I would even add for the sake of argument that, owing to looser social arrangements, Americans get to know what the other sex is up to earlier than many Europeans, for whom the difficulty of mating outside or even inside one's own class provides hordes of mystery women in all varieties. At any rate the type *la belle dame sans merci* is a small part of our canon and has a borrowed look about it. Barbara Stanwyck in *Double Indemnity* is more our kind of woman, and we know exactly what she is up to: the same thing we are.

Here I wish that Wood had opened his inquiry a little to take in (a) foreign movies, and (b) foreign audiences. Which of these myths rang bells in Europe and which clinked? The success of, say, Eddie Constantine in France suggests that the lonesome, alienated hero is even more doted upon there than here, not because of any frontier but because of the lack of one. It could be that the studio sages looking through their telescopes saw that Gary Cooper would be a marvelous export to the cooped-up peoples of Europe—and of the Eastern seaboard, which looks the same at that distance. American myths be damned; the first spaghetti western was made in Hollywood.

All these quibbles (and one could raise a dozen more) are somehow anticipated and neutralized by the author's manner, which is light and unassertive, like a good tailor trying things out on you. Perhaps this theory fits? Ah well. Pity. As sociology this has limited value, since we can only trust the bits we already know, but as entertainment it's fine.

At one point, hopelessly stuck, Wood announces with Fields that he is off to milk his elk. You can't get mad at an author like that: even when he says, apparently seriously, that Charlton Heston with arm aloft outside the Promised Land reminds him of the Statue of Liberty. Even his elk would draw the line at that one. (Presumably a European Moses would have kept his hands in his pockets.)

For the sake of a solid unified subject, the grasshopper mind of Wood has overloaded the myth of American exceptionalism: which I can only say is typically American of him.

To return to the actual Hollywood, where *auteurs* rubbed elbows with baby tycoons: *Life Goes to the Movies* is as good as an archaeological dig, though not always for the reasons intended. The same Richard Schickel gave this book a fulsome review in *The New York Times Book Review* even though he had worked for *Life* himself. I mention this not to pick on Schickel but because it sheds light on the whole publicity apparatus on which Hollywood thrived.

"This book is about a magazine's love affair with an industry," begins the text, meltingly. "From the start, *Life* and the movies were hooked by each other." Which sounds like just the right word. And Schickel, being hooked by both, harks back to an era when even first-rate men took sycophancy for granted.

Life (whoever that is) still talks in the tones of that era and it's a spooky re-creation worthy of the movies. Perhaps it's in order for a magazine to gush over itself posthumously: but all this simpering from the tomb could have a distorting effect on cultural history. Because, for at least part of this period, *Life*'s coverage of Hollywood was almost as depressing as Hollywood itself. In a long section called "The Build-up," we are shown how the magazine conspired to inflate talentless starlets into national figures—"with tongue firmly in cheek," we're now told.

That last touch is macabre. The picture of grown men sitting "with tongue firmly in cheek" as they transmitted this studio garbage makes the flesh creep. But for *Life,* looking back on itself and finding itself good, the whole seedy operation has been transformed into gorgeous "nuttiness," "goofiness," *fun.*

Finally on page 108, *Life* pulls itself sternly together and says, "Despite fun and games with starlets and despite the importance of a star's performance, *Life* recognized that Hollywood's essential ingredient was the film itself." This was very acute of *Life* since they were the ones who had made the fuss about the starlets to begin with. But here as elsewhere, *Life* does itself a disservice by blurring the dates and making itself into a timeless continuum. It could be that the magazine improved as films did after the big studios collapsed, taking with them the whole publicity nexus. The photographers had always been good, because like studio technicians they had never had to speak.

The book immortalizes the earlier tone. "*Life* managed to maintain an affectionate and faintly awestruck attitude toward the famous toilers of the dream factories." This is marvelous period pastiche, and it evokes the whole sickly relationship with movies better than any objective analysis could.

The thirties, forties were an era of mass-produced junk, and all the *auteurs* and editors with tongue in cheek cannot alter that much. It is edifying to note how often talent managed to find its way through the chinks, and no doubt instructive for TV writers to study this. But *Life* and the studios were partners in crime: among them, and all the lesser flacks, they *were* Hollywood, all we had, and the book conveys precisely what this Hollywood was. At the front are pages and pages of stars, then promo, then actual movies—and only later, as the magazine was approaching its own end, a few pages of directors. This Hollywood produced no masterpieces, so there is no need to look for masters.

Yet Hollywood always knew how to make movies, and sometimes this knowledge was enough. What the French *auteurists* were seeing in effect were silent movies, which contained the wisdom of the silent era, plus in a few cases more. After the first problems of mike placement were solved, the camera had begun to move again. And perhaps it took foreigners to notice that there was a technical continuity with the past which sound had only seemed to sever.

For a close look at what the silents knew, Walter Kerr's book *The Silent Clowns* can hardly be praised too highly. Kerr has always been a trying figure for highbrows, partly because of his unnatural importance as daily play reviewer, but partly because he seemed too intelligent for those chronic celebrations of commercial theater with the whiz-bang phrases all ready to quote. His detail work was unparalleled: he could take a scene apart like a watchmaker. But later one felt, so what? It often seemed like too much labor over too little. Did that little scene where Ethel Merman glances away quickly really deserve a paragraph? Like the estimable Andrew Sarris, Kerr seemed to believe that by analyzing something excruciatingly you gave it worth.

Such a critic may be fine at good vs. bad, but untrustworthy on important vs. trivial. And Kerr had something else in common with the Sarrises: a belief in "theaterness," which like "movieness" overrides other values. Thus, for him, ideas as such have no special virtue in a play unless they are also good theater: a perfectly O.K. position for a new movie critic, but by whim of fashion, a disaster for a play reviewer. Thus Kerr was accused of selling out to the well-made play, whose very efficiency delighted him, though this efficiency seems to have polished the life out of Broadway.

One thing that *The Silent Clowns* makes clear is that Kerr has not sold out to anything. He simply got his aesthetic from the same place as the *auteurists*—from the movies. When he sees a scene on the stage, he breaks down its movements physically, as if it were silent. Speech, one feels, may be an immensely useful adjunct to movement, can even in some sense *be* movement, but movement came first in his own awareness and speech remains its servant, its Jeeves. This presumably was why he gave up on talkies: because they reversed the order at first and movement almost died.

So it's clear that silent comedies are his perfect subject since importance does not arise (these films are 100 percent unimportant, bless them) and technique is transcendent. It is the one subject that can worm a masterpiece out of him. And if *The Silent Clowns* isn't quite that, it is only because it isn't organized to be one. It reads more like a series of his best Sunday pieces stitched together, so that it lacks momentum, i.e., you can read it backward without missing much. Overall, the book is so dense with proposition and example that it's like reviewing Euclid. The subject is comedy, but before we get to that, the possibilities of a flat screen and a camera have been explored, as if for the first time by a gifted child: or as they were by the first moviemakers.

Kerr concludes that, after the treasure chest had been ransacked, dramatic movies still needed speech to complete them, but comedy didn't: for everything words could add to a joke, they took away more. Chaplin with his tormented ingenuity kept his silence into the talking era; Keaton and Lloyd were killed by sound, as surely as any dramatic actor with a bad voice; Fields survived, but he honored his silent lessons. Speech is still Jeeves to Fields's action, even if Jeeves steals the show.

Kerr at his best can write about comedy with all the deadpan solemnity of Buster Keaton. He talks once of being "trapped into laughter" and that's how it is with connoisseurs: the relish builds from within and erupts reluctantly. As Kerr gravely describes a sequence he causes the reader to do roughly the same: to hold the laugh until it explodes in multiple bursts. No one writes about comedy better than Kerr; Alex Comfort on the orgasm doesn't come close.

His book also tells talking directors the absolute least they must know about silent techniques and about the groping evolution of screen comedy. If Peter Bogdanovich had read it with understanding, he could not have made one frame of his woebegone *What's Up, Doc?* In short, it is criticism of a very high order indeed lavished on the purest of our popular art forms. Ironically, the words tend to crowd out the pictures, and the postage-stamp stills in the margins are too small to convey anything except information. But the fine larger ones confirm the point that actors then existed to our minds solely in action, and not as exhibits stuffed and mounted.

Which brings us back for a moment to *Life Goes to the Movies.* This is primarily a picture book, and probably only a pervert would read the whole text. The selection and layout are quite conventional, and perhaps so much the better. Because Hollywood and its magazine extensions, brimming over with the best talent of an era, never did quite as well as they could. And this book records precisely the size of corset Edmund Wilson's two ogres, Hollywood and the Lucempire, allowed their minions to work in. One looks back on Walter Kerr's world of the silent clowns with a longing.

1976

2 / *Toward the Black Pussy Cafe*

Of all the subjects that don't need de-mythologizing, one would have thought W. C. Fields was preeminent. With comedians in general it seems important that their life and their work be taken as one. "I hear he writes his own lines" is a phrase that echoes from childhood. The lot of the gag-writer is a bitter one: unless he consents to be a performer himself, like Mel Brooks or Carl Reiner, we don't want to know about him.

Hence, most books about comedians tend to be unsatisfactory. Either they service the myth and give the clown a brain he doesn't deserve ("The trouble with Groucho is he thinks he's Groucho," says one of his old writers) or they tell the truth, as John Lahr did of his father, Bert, in *Notes on a Cowardly Lion,* leaving us with a somewhat shrunken functionary, barely worth a book, though Lahr got a good one. Comedians are actors, and in dealing with such there is rarely anything between fan magazine falsehood and terrible disillusionment.

Books about W. C. Fields, on the other hand, tend to be satisfactory even when they're bad. For instance, his mistress's book about him, *W. C. Fields and Me* by Carlotta Monti, is hilarious for wholly unintentional reasons. Any book by a chorine that starts out "I can't deny that he was an anomaly" is going to be hilarious. Fields's own voice rumbles like this through every phrase. Because Fields really was a comic genius. There was no question where the lines came from or the style, and some of this had to spill into the private life, leaving a fund of great anecdotes that even a good-hearted starlet couldn't ruin, so long as she followed the master's directions.

Still, we demand more of Fields than even comic genius. We have to believe he meant it. We want certification that such a one existed: a mean, child-hating con man who was so funny about it that he made these things all right. Staged comedy exists partly to resign us to evil, but for this to work we want more than playacting. As Groucho says of professionals, we want a real old lady crashing downhill into a wall in her wheelchair—only to walk away unharmed.

Robert Lewis Taylor produced a few years back one of the best books ever written about a comedian, *W. C. Fields: His Follies and His Fortunes.* In it Taylor tells just enough truth to qualify as a biographer, including the unfunny horrors of Fields's alcoholism. But his dominant strategy is to accept Fields's own version of Fields, which was a work of art built on a dungheap, like so many artists' lives. He gives us a Fields meaner than any ten men, and yet somehow funny and harmless, where he was probably bitter and brutal. People get hurt and yet they *don't* get hurt. Wife and child are deserted, Fields screams with the DTs. Everyone exits laughing.

Since his early years were the least verifiable, it is here that Fields's remodeling of himself, as transcribed by Taylor, was most thorough. Over the years, Fields spun a version to his cronies, Gene Fowler and the like, that made him sound like a Dickens child: a vagabond, shoplifter, jailbird. This gives his life the convenience of a movie biography in which everything can be explained by filmable incidents: thus, he got his meanness from being swindled by a crooked manager; he got his voice from this and his nose from that. It only needs sketches by Boz to illustrate the turning points. Fields's devotion to Dickens affected not only his art, as we shall see, but his life, and his fans were quite content that this Dickensian version should be the Fields of record. We conspired in accepting it as the real old lady in the wheelchair.

But now his family has come along, in the person of his grandson, Ronald, to tidy him up in a book ironically titled *W. C. Fields by Himself:* if only he *were* by himself. But Ronald bounds alongside, keeping a close eye on him at all times, reminding one of the family in

The Bank Dick who try to make Egbert Sousé respectable. It seems he did not hit his old man with a shovel and run away from home; he did not do time in the slam (Taylor has admitted that there is no record of him in the Philadelphia jails, but puts it down lamely to his many aliases); he did not even hate children. Photos are introduced showing him rather gingerly dandling his grandson, which can only dishearten his fans.

In short, like many a doting widow, the family has cruelly stripped Fields of his legends, obviously failing to understand what made him great in the first place. If this were all there were to him, we would not be reading books about him at all, let alone this one. I had almost said Ronald Fields has done the impossible and made him dull; but here, since Fields scholarship grinds on and rational inquiry is thrust upon us, a grudging point must be admitted. It is not as difficult as one had supposed to make Fields dull. Without the subject's face and voice to guide us, we find ourselves staring directly into his subject matter: and the effect is one of a nagging, terrifying boredom.

In fact, I can think of no famous comedian outside of Jack Benny who skirted dullness more perilously than Fields. People who don't worship him tend to be bored even by his best stuff and to see no point at all. For he is always threatening to sink back into his material—that world of drunken fathers and harridan mothers and squalling brats that is not funny at all, but desperately bleak. Older children may like Fields for what they take to be his congenial anarchy, but smaller ones are apt to be alarmed by this brutal, boozy adult, smelling of Victorian row houses and failure. The only anarchy allowed in that world was the freedom of a father to strike his children and this W. C.'s father, James Dukenfield, availed himself of early and often.

In trying to clean his grandfather up, young Fields has linked W. C. once and for all to that gray world—and not as a rebel, but as a sullenly dutiful son who repaid his bullying father with a trip to Paris as soon as he could afford to. W. C.'s early letters are not particularly funny but are tinged throughout with the sourness of genteel poverty. The flavor is perfectly captured by Ronald when he describes W. C.'s father as "a commission merchant dealing primarily in fruits and vegetables," i.e., a fruitstand vendor. That this bogus respectability should linger on through three generations suggests how cloying it must have been and how hard for Fields to hold it at laughing distance. Like Thurber's relatives in Columbus, whom one suspects of being cold and meanly eccentric in real life, Fields's family needed a prodigious swipe of the wand to become funny.

Since one must assume for now that Ronald Fields's documentation is unarguable, the colorful street urchin has to go, and we must look elsewhere for the genius. One startling possibility emerges. Although Ronald shows no mean gift for sniffing out W. C.'s unfunniest material, there is enough of it collected here in sketches and letters to suggest that comedy did not come easily or even naturally to the great man. It is an article of faith among Fields fans that he is always funny: and one remembers the racking chortle of Ed McMahon and the thin strained laughter of the studio audience as a not particularly funny piece of Fields was run on the *Tonight Show.* But some of the material Ronald has assembled, e.g., an early sketch in which a scabrous family battles the London underground, or those leaden, one-joke exchanges with Edgar Bergen (vastly overrated), might tax even the susceptible McMahon. To make them work, one has to keep imagining the Fields persona; without it, they would be weaker than the output of any journeyman gag-writer.

The persona itself was the work of genius, and Ronald's book suggests that this was more consciously arrived at than we like to think. Fields's native gifts were industry, physical coordination, and mental retentiveness, plus a downright anal stinginess. The two kinds of retention were possibly connected, and together they account for much of his greatness and misery. Their immediate effect was to make him a master of music hall and vaudeville, where shticks and bits of business had to be hoarded like miser's gold. I am told it was not unknown for comedians to pull knives on each other when they suspected their acts were being stolen. One's act was all one had, and it had to last a lifetime. Fields was superbly equipped for this cutthroat world: or if not, he became so. Very few kindly men can have emerged from vaudeville.

Without detracting from W.C.'s uniqueness, I believe it would be rewarding to study the other comedians of the era for technical similarities. For instance, Fields's habit of throwing up his hands and hunching his shoulders when anyone threatens to touch him might be explained as a reflex flinching from his father's blows. But if memory serves, Leon Errol had a similar style; and before either of them, God knows what forgotten comedian working the London halls in the 1900s when Fields was starting out who may have inspired them both. In payment, Fields's hands fluttering at the throat may have taught young Oliver Hardy a thing or two. And so on. Just as the genius of comics is customarily overrated, so their craft and attention to detail is proportionately ignored. In an allied field, it is often forgotten that Sydney Greenstreet was a D'Oyly Carte veteran and that he played the Fat Man precisely as any Poo Bah would have, while Peter Lorre was a member of Bertolt Brecht's ensemble. Thus *The Maltese Falcon* was a mating of acting traditions, and not just of individual actors.

Fields once called Chaplin "a goddam ballet dancer," but it is no coincidence that they both came out of this London tradition, where techniques in physical comedy had reached a high polish.* All commentators agree that Fields had ferocious dedication, spending up to two years learning one juggling trick. And his first approach to comedy was probably similar: a dogged humorless mastering of each movement, until his body work was so good that he could make side-splitting *silent* movies. To this day, there is no actor I would rather see just enter a room and sit down, with the possible exception of Fred Astaire.

The vocal side of his act was carried at first by the physical and has a consequent freedom and experimentation about it, akin to Will Rogers's offhand patter during his rope twirling. The people had paid to see a juggler, so the commentary was gravy; and Fields used it partly to cover his mistakes and hold the crowd's attention, but partly, one suspects, semiconsciously, as a man mutters to himself when engaged on an intricate task—I suspect Fields would have talked the same with no one around. The result is a dreamlike free-associative quality closer to poetry than to the world of gags.

With both Rogers and Fields it is worth bearing these origins in mind. Rogers's offhand delivery always implies a man doing something else—playing with a rope or looking up from a newspaper. (In those pre-monologue days, a comedian was expected to be usefully occupied.) In Fields's case, the keynote is a narrow concentration on his own concerns at the total expense of everything else. Many of his asides are not heard by the other actors at all and would not be understood if they were. And they have no connection with the needs of the plot. "Either they'll have to move that pole or vaseline the joint," he murmurs as he slides into the Black Pussy Cafe; and we are reminded of the solipsist beginnings of his act.

*Since Bob Hope left London as an infant, it is scarcely plausible to connect him with this tradition. Nevertheless this master of the double-take and the hasty retreat would have been physically if not vocally at home in the British music halls.

Buttressing this effect of majestic irrelevance is another quality derived from his stinginess: he would not let any of his old material go, but insisted on inserting it willy-nilly into movies where it had no business. Taylor reports a running dialogue between Fields and Mack Sennett, which would start with Sennett declaiming on the organic nature of comedy, the need for everything to have a reason, and would end with Fields saying, "I think I'll work my golf act into this two-reeler about the dentist." The result is an *oeuvre* of dazzling bits and pieces, but only one great movie *(The Bank Dick).*

If this artistic stinginess was based on artistic insecurity, the instinct was probably sound. Fields had hoarded very well, but when he moved away from those tested routines his comic taste remained uncertain to the end, and he made some uncommonly disappointing films. His most reliable work, to my taste, consists either of his early vaudeville routines —the golf game, the pool game, the fatal glass of beer ("It's not a fit night out for man or beast")—or their offshoots, i.e., sketches of generic similarity, in which the movements are stylized and the tongue is free to ramble. Conversely, his weakest moments come when he tries to let his visual imagination out a notch, as in the airplane sequences in *International House* and *Never Give a Sucker an Even Break,* where his urge to let fly, artistically, clashes with his native narrowness and his juggler's affinity for commonplace objects.

When Fields fails, the effect is peculiar: it is not as if a joke hasn't worked, but as if it has not even been made. That is, one wonders why he thought that particular idea was funny to begin with. It is as if his art were trying at times to be something other than comedy. (Those gruesome little scenes between husband and wife—funny?) Comedy was his mode, the thing he had learned so bloodily, but one wonders whether the handsome young chap in the early photos, who looks as if he's posing for the Andover yearbook, wouldn't have liked just a little bit more.

What we do know is that he worked uncommonly hard to educate himself, taking an autodidact's delight in long and unusual words, which later did him a comic favor but may have started out more seriously. Linguistic pretension is a staple of American humor as it is of cockney, but the taste is not confined to comedians. (A reading by Fields of the later Henry James would about cover the range of cultural aspiration, in an era when even fastidious Americans had to go and overdo it.) Anyway, one senses more than once that Fields is sniffing around literature itself with a poor boy's wistfulness. Fields: "That's a triple superlative. Do you think you can handle it?" Mae West: "Yeah, and I can kick it around." Alas, literature in any form other than parody would almost certainly have been beyond him. His early letters are incredibly stilted and illphrased, and it is something of a miracle that he wound up such a master of phrasing. But he could only be a master in comedy; and perhaps he used fancy words humorously because he could not get them quite right seriously. His noncomic writing remained as stiff as a schoolboy's to the end: not the least of reasons for hating his family.

Fortunately for everyone he discovered Dickens, and thus found a quasi-literary mode for his gifts, which would have to do. His Mr. Micawber was a masterpiece: and if critics object that he was just being himself—well, that is the whole point. He read Dickens constantly and wanted to play Dick Swiveller next. This he could also have done as himself. For all Dickens's variety, his orotund word-mad windbags have a strong family resemblance.

Oddly enough, Carlotta Monti, the fun-loving mistress ("Our respective senses of humor dove-tailed," she says solemnly, as Anne Hathaway might mention her sense of rhythm), does the most justice to the Dickens connection, possibly with a little help from Cy Rice, her collaborator. She notes the similarities between the funny names they both used—though fails to note that this is one further connection with the larger cockney tradition. Dickens was a great frequenter of London theater, where the humor of quaint names coupled with braggadocio goes back at least to the sixteenth century. Ronald Fields, in one of his brighter moments, observes that "Fields stole as much from Dickens as Dickens took from people like Fields; he plagiarized Shakespeare's Falstaff just as Shakespeare copied an Elizabethan like Larson E. Whipsnade."

Placing this in a Far Western setting, as in *My Little Chickadee,* Fields reproduces the host of English swindlers and con men who ripped off the territories. Yet this is only one aspect of Fields and should not be overstated.

I would not dream of claiming this flower of Philadelphia for England, although his grandfather did have a cockney accent. Fields cannot be reduced to techniques and traditions, even if these have been scandalously overlooked by the trauma-mongers. No technique, for instance, could account for his nose—though it might account for his voice (has any commentator really told us what he sounded like in real life or when young?). But there is something about the inner Fields that is elusive and bothersome, and holds our attention in a way that mere talent could not. Put it like this. I have always felt that the idea of Fields is funnier than Fields himself; that even the face and voice he has taught us to remember are not quite the real ones. (I am always surprised when I attend a Fields movie by how wrong his imitators are, and by some troubling quality in his face that no cartoonist has captured.) There is something about Fields himself that leaves one staring vacantly after the laughter is over.

"Goddamn the whole friggin' world and everyone in it but you, Carlotta," are the last words Miss Monti records. The same comic techniques can be used for vastly different purposes: when Oliver Hardy fluttered his hands, it expressed embarrassment or foolish pleasure; with Fields, it was naked distaste, a horror of being touched, equal to Twain's and Kaufman's, plus a reaching for his wallet—touched in that sense too. He hated people, all right, although in fits and starts. His bursts of generosity and meanness alternated so violently as to be almost physically painful to watch. No one has properly calibrated this to the rhythms of his drunkenness—e.g., when he calls FDR "Gumlegs, our President," we know it's sanitarium time—but even on his good days, and with friendly biographers like Taylor and Monti on hand, there is a gray bile in the air that must have tormented the good-natured side of him. I tend to shy away from Freudian terminology (Freud on humor being even more undebatably disastrous than Freud on women), but if Ben Jonson was, as Edmund Wilson says, the greatest of anal playwrights, Fields would have been the perfect actor for Jonson, just as he was perfect for the extravagances of Dickens.

To some small extent, his misanthropy, like Groucho's, was a product of stinginess and not just its cause; if you like someone, you may have to give them something. (Also, as with Groucho, his misanthropy was professionally necessary, the essence of his comic point of view, so there was every reason to cultivate it and none to restrain it.) In an incredible lifetime of letters to his estranged wife, sunnily explained by Ronald as showing "the strain of trying to maintain a relationship largely by letter," W. C. whines and curses about the money he has to send her and cries poverty, even when he is doing handsomely with the Ziegfeld Follies. The self-pity and sheer hatred of giving come close at times to hysteria. Ronald says, "Only a few people knew of the love he still harbored for [his wife]," so out of deference to the living we'll leave it at that: except to say that publication of these letters will not add to the number.

So loving someone briefly (his wife, Hattie, became a vaudeville widow almost immediately) had cost him plenty: and the itch was raw until he died, leaving Hattie virtually disinherited. Yet it is worth noth-ing that he did keep the connection with his wife going and that he did not divorce her to marry Miss Monti—and that he left Miss Monti, his loyal mistress of fourteen years, even less money (twenty-five dollars a week to be precise, bequeathing the rest to an orphanage for "white boys and girls, where no religion of any sort is to be preached"). Stinginess was his ultimate weapon against his near ones, a fluttering of the hands against their embrace; yet it was mixed with a punctilious sense of obligation, of hanging on to them even if it cost him. Domesticity had a horrible fascination for Fields, as one might guess from his subject matter, so long as it was kept horrible enough, "with the wedding knot tied around the wife's neck." That was the only kind of home he knew, and he could never quite leave it. He lied about running away as a boy, and he lied about running away as a grown-up. The de-mythologizers win that one. Fields was secretly respectable, during the gaps in his drunken dreamlife.

"On the whole, I'd rather be in Philadelphia" was his chosen epitaph, and one's mind travels back to the Dukenfields' household to see what he meant by Philadelphia, and the first sound one picks up is James Dukenfield's big hand rattling off little Claude's ear. If that was his earliest view of humanity, it can't have appealed to him much. And if he loved his father, he might have decided the returns on loving weren't worth it. A lifetime of parodying and downright imitating his father and his whole wretched family would seem more to the point.

And yet. There is a jaunty confidence and determination in those early photos that argue against any sick-room theory of Fields and his comedy. And he left too many heartbroken friends behind to have been the deformed clown of romantic legend. His humor is not just some neurotic compensation, but a cunning assault on Art, in the limited conditions of his life, and in its way a triumph of character. By his prime in the 1930s he had so welded his act to his life that he could "think he was W. C. Fields" and get away with it—though Ronald's book reminds us that he couldn't always. One must, like Taylor and Monti, follow the master's own selections. Never mind. A man who can slash his Jack roses with his cane, snarling, "Bloom, damn you—bloom for my friends," cannot be tamed by any number of relatives, even the horrific ones of W.C.'s nightmares. The family in *The Bank Dick* stand stiffly on the porch in their Sunday best: Egbert Sousé, Fields's dream of himself, his masterpiece, escapes down the driveway to the Black Pussy Cafe and freedom.

1974

3 / *The Twin Urges of James Baldwin*

When James Baldwin goes wrong (as he has taken to doing lately), it usually seems less a failure of talent than of policy. Of all our writers he is one of the most calculating. Living his life on several borderlines, he has learned to watch his step: driven at the same time by an urge to please and a mission to scold.

In his early days, the twin urges came together to make very good policy indeed. White liberals craved a spanking and they got a good one. But then too many amateurs joined in the fun, all the Raps and Stokelys and Seales, until even liberal guilt gave out. And now the times seems to call for something a little different. *The Devil Finds Work* shows Baldwin groping for it—not just because he's a hustler, at least as writers go, but because he has a genuine quasi-religious vocation. In the last pages he richly describes a church ceremony he went through as a boy, akin to attaining the last mansions of mysticism: and you have to do *something* after that. Your work, even your atheism, will always taste of religion.

And this is the first problem we come across in the new book. Because the subject is movies, and most movies simply do not accommodate such religious passion. So his tone sounds false. He may or may not feel that strongly about movies (it's hard to believe), but sincerity isn't the issue. A preacher doesn't have to feel what he says every Sunday: rhetoric is an art, and Baldwin practices it very professionally. But the sermon's subject must be at least in the same ball park as the style, or you get bathos, the sermon that fails to rise.

Since Baldwin is too intelligent not to notice this, we get an uneasy compromise between old habits and new possibilities. The folks pays him to preach (to use his own self-mocking language), so he turns it on mechanically, almost absentmindedly, lapsing at times into incoherence, as if he's fallen asleep at the microphone. But since getting mad at the movies is only one step removed from getting mad at the funnies, he escapes periodically in two directions, one bad and one good.

The bad one is to change the subject outrageously in order to raise the emotional ante: thus there are several references to how white people like to burn babies that totally stumped me. A prophet should disturb all levels of opinion and must therefore be something of a precisionist. But this stuff passes harmlessly overhead. Blacks have been known to kill babies too, in Biafra and elsewhere, but nobody said they like it. People apt to be reading Baldwin at all have long since graduated from this level of rant. He may write for the masses, but he is read by the intelligentsia.

But his second escape at times almost makes up for the first: which is simply to talk about movies according to their kind, with amusement, irony, and his own quirky insights. More writers should do this: we were raised as much in the movie house as the library, and it's pretentious to go on blaming it all on Joyce. In Baldwin's case a movie case history is doubly valuable because his angle is so solitary, shaped by no gang and deflected by no interpretation, and shared only with a white woman teacher, herself a solitary. Nobody ever saw these movies quite the way he did, or ever will.

Unfortunately the childhood section is tantalizingly short, and the adult's voice horns in too often, but some fine things come through: in particular the way the young Baldwin had to convert certain white actors into blacks, even as white basketball fans reverse the process today, in order to identify. Thus, Henry Fonda's walk made him black, and Joan Crawford's resemblance to a woman in the local grocery store made her black, while Bette Davis's' popping eyes made her not only black but practically Jimmy himself.

This is vintage Baldwin: and if he lacks confidence in his softer notes he shouldn't (his sentimental notes are another matter). He does not automatically *have* to lecture us on every topic he writes about. In this more urbane mode, his racial intrusions often make good sense. For instance, in checking *A Tale of Two Cities* against what he has learned in the streets he perhaps inadvertently suggests to this reader, at least, how Dickens might have veered away from what *he* had learned in the streets. In fact, Baldwin's whole treatment of this story suggests a potential literary critic, if he'd calm down for a minute.

This section ends with a valuable addition to Baldwin's early autobiography: a corpus to which one had thought no further additions were possible. He discovers the theater and loses his religion almost at the same moment. The reality of stage actors playing Macbeth is enough to blow away even that encounter with the Holy Ghost. And as if to symbolize this, he literally tiptoes out of church one Sunday and heads downtown for a show: taking, as he says in another context, his church with him.

If stage acting could transplant God, it utterly demolished screen acting for him. "Canada Lee [in *Native Son*] was Bigger Thomas, but he was also Canada Lee: his physical presence, like the physical presence of Paul Robeson, gave me the right to live. He was not at the mercy of my imagination as he would have been, on the screen: he was on the stage, in flesh and blood, and I was, therefore, at the mercy of *his* imagination." If you're raised an incarnational Christian (and it's hard to image another kind), flesh and blood can easily become food and drink to you. Henceforth in even the silliest play, the actors' presence would thrust reality through at Baldwin; conversely, only the greatest of actors could insert physicality into a movie, and that fleetingly.

His own course was set. Embodied reality, thick, hot, and tangible, is Baldwin's grail, even jerking him loose from his own rhetoric. So he became a man of the stage, dealing with real people and not their images; and he wrote some of his best work for it—including my own favorite, *Amen Corner,* in which he uses the stage to exorcise the Church once and for all. Only to come out more religious than ever—only at random now, passionately foraging for Good and Evil in race, in sex, even in Norman Mailer.

Perhaps, then, not the ideal man to write about movies. The magic element which is their particular genius is precisely what maddens his fundamentalist soul the most. Like Pascal at the real theater, he sees nothing but lies up there. Although he seems to know something about the craft of movies, it doesn't interest or charm him in the least. His book has no pictures, which is unusual in a film book, but quite appropriate for this one. Because even the stills would be lies.

Specifically lies about race. And here we have a right to expect the latest news from Baldwin and not a rehash. I assume he is still a black spokesman in good standing. Although his book is disarmingly datelined from France, which is nearer the *pied-noir* country, there must be a victims' network of information which keeps him up to date. But his personal witness, his strength, has begun to sound tentative. He talks of being terrorized in some Southern town, but he can't remember what year or, apparently, the distinction between one town and another. "It is hard to be accurate concerning the pace of my country's progress." Very hard from St. Paul de Vence. We can get fresher testimony than that every day of the week.

Anyhow for Baldwin there is still just something called the South, unchanging and indivisible, and the liberals down there might as well pack up shop. It's a bleak picture and if Baldwin sees any lift in the clouds he either isn't telling or he rejects it as a dangerous illusion, an invitation to drop one's guard. For instance, in the dopey film *In the Heat of the Night*, there is a scene where the white sheriff humbles himself to carry Sidney Poitier's bags, and Baldwin sees for a moment something "choked and moving" in this, only to round on it sternly as a dangerous daydream. "White Americans have been encouraged to keep on dreaming, and black Americans have been alerted to the necessity of waking up."

So paranoia, as before, is his message to blacks, and a white reviewer is in no position to question it. Since no improvement is to be trusted, the implicit solution is revolution, and Baldwin talks airily of seizing property as if this were still the slaphappy sixties when all seemed possible. For the moment, revolutionary rant seems as remote as the evangelism that used to pacify blacks: but again, Baldwin isn't quite calling for it, only toying with it. His new position is still very much in the works.

Meanwhile, offscreen, geographical distance may have obscured some of the social nuances Baldwin usually pounces on so swiftly and surely. He talks, for instance, of whites being terrified of blacks, and blacks being enraged by whites, as if this blanketed the case. But one of the odd things that happened in the sixties was that the blacks became largely de-mystified, for better or worse. By accepting such drugstore rebels as Rap Brown and Stokely Carmichael at their own valuation, we let ourselves in for one of the greatest letdowns in memory. The black enigma was transformed overnight into the black chatterbox. Although, as Claude Brown once said privately, these men could not have rounded up ten followers in Harlem, they told us they were leaders, so we took them for leaders. And we were relieved to find they were not the brooding giants that Baldwin had conjured, but just average publicity hounds.

Because of this comical misunderstanding, many whites ceased being impressed by blacks altogether, except such as carried knives, and a new psychic alignment occurred that Baldwin should come home and tell us about. The problem now is not so much fear as deepening indifference. Baldwin still writes as though our souls were so hag-ridden by race that even our innocent entertainments reflect it. And he gives us the old castration folderol as if it were piping hot. But the news I hear is different. Many whites now go for years without thinking about blacks at all. The invisible man has returned. And as *de facto* segregation continues to settle like mold, his future seems assured.

On the black side of the fence, one simply has to take him on trust. Young blacks today *seem* more confident than Baldwin's prototypes but it might only take a few full-time bigots plus some ad hoc recruits—as in South Boston—to chip the paint off this. What one can question, by the current division of racist labor, is his account of the white psyche. Because here again he simply says nothing that a contemporary reader can use. His white men sound at times exactly like Susan Brownmiller's rapists, whom that author also transformed into Everyman, and in fact like all the hyperaggressive bullies you've ever met: and these surely come in all colors.

Of such movies as *Death Wish* or *Straw Dogs* or the worst of Clint Eastwood (if such there be) or black exploitation films—in short all the movies that validate bullying on one side or another and make it chic —he says nothing except, tantalizingly, of the latter that they "make black experience irrelevant and obsolete" (his own, or everyone's?). If by chance he has not seen the others, in particular *Death Wish,* the mugger-killing wet dream, he has wandered unarmed into the one subject Americans really know about.

Baldwin's weakness as a prophet is to suppose that the rest of us experience life as intensely as he does; and his strength is roughly the same. If his overall sociology is suspect right now, his ability to enlarge a small emotion so that we can all see it is not. And this perhaps rescues him even as a writer about movies.

Throughout, his eyes swarm greedily over the screen, scavenging for small truths. And although brotherhood epics like *In the Heat of the Night* and *Guess Who's Coming to Dinner* were flailed insensible by white critics, leaving precious little to pick on, in each case he finds some scene or other even richer in phoniness, or closer to truth, than we suspected. For instance, in the latter film, he has a passage on a successful black son's relation to his father that probably no one else would have thought of. While for the former, he provides such a droll plot summary that the absurdity jumps a dimension.

He is also good on *The Defiant Ones* and *Lawrence of Arabia* though here one senses that he is not saying all he knows. He talks at one point of the seismographic shudder Americans experience at the word "homosexual," but he handles it pretty much like a hot potato himself: talking around and around it without quite landing on it. Again this is policy (the word homosexual does go off like a fire alarm, reminding us to put up our dukes) but in this case, I think, too much policy. When Baldwin holds back something it distorts his whole manner. The attempt to seduce is too slick. And this, just as much as his compulsion to preach when there's nothing to preach about, diverts him from his real lover, truth. He is not seeing those movies as an average black man, but as a unique exile, and the pose is beginning to wear thin.

So, the tension remains. He has been away a long time and I'm sure he has a story to tell about that, perhaps his best one yet. It is hard to believe that in Paris and Istanbul his mind was really on American movies: but they might have been something in the attic that he wanted to get rid of. And the attempt is worthwhile if only for the sake of some sprightly lines, to wit, "J. Edgar Hoover, history's most highly paid (and most utterly useless) *voyeur,*" and random bangs and flashes. He even talks several times of *human* weakness (as opposed to white weakness) —including his own: which suggests that the hanging judge may be ready to come down from his perch and mix it with us.

But for now he remains up there wagging his finger sternly at the converted and the bored. And with so many clergymen, he too often deduces Reality solely by intelligence in this book, and while he has more than enough of that quality, it tends to fly off in bootless directions unless anchored by touch. He is right to love the stage. His art needs real bodies. But anyone who sees reality as clearly as Baldwin does must be tempted at times to run like the wind; and perhaps, for just a little while, he's done that. After all, that's what movies are for—even for those preachers who denounce them the loudest.

1977

4 / *I Am a Cabaret*

If they keep doing versions of Christopher Isherwood's *Berlin Stories,* someday they're going to get it right. The saga of Herr Issyvoo and Sally Bowles has turned up by now in every form but roller-skating ballet, for all the world as though it were one of the sturdy myths of the West, instead of a wispy nuanced memory that has to be told right or not at all.

Granted the dawning possibility that the original has no dramatic possibilities whatever, the movie musical *Cabaret* may be about the best that can be done with it—certainly better than the play *I Am a Camera,* the movie *I Am a Camera,* and the stage musical *Cabaret*—though still many moons from the book. Each of these versions reflects the period it was produced in much more than it reflects the period Isherwood wrote about (as if the story itself were a camera), and perhaps 1972 can see itself truer in Berlin of 1930 than previous years could; or, if not, we can at least make a Berlin in our own image that has its own entertainment possibilities.

Anyway, these purveyors of mutton soup, who make their living adapting things from the forms in which they belong into forms where they taste awful, are the quintessential hacks, so it follows that the

Bowles cycle is a gruesomely instructive guide to our worst show biz conventions. John van Druten's play reads like a ghostly parody of a forties or fifties Broadway hit. While managing with lunatic ingenuity to pack in as many lines from the original as possible, van Druten zapped every last one with an emotional cliché of his own period. For instance, when Sally, the aspiring nymphomaniac, has her abortion, she says, "It's like finding that all the old rules are true after all." The original Sally would have gagged on her Prairie Oyster over that one.

Later, van Druten's Herr Issyvoo, the camera, waxes bittersweet on the same event. "It'll seem like another of those nasty dreams. And we won't believe or remember a thing about it. Either of us." *(He starts to put the cigarette in his mouth. Then he stops and looks at the door.)* "Or will we?" *Curtain.* It's all there in the script, even the unlit cigarette, left over from *Call Me at 9* and *My Heart's in the Heather.*

The play emphasized Sally at the expense of Berlin. Broadway reveres a big female part and will feed anything to the flames to build a roaring one. It also likes an eccentric it can identify with completely. Thus, the year being 1951, you get amoral Sally analyzing herself like a Rose Franzblau column. "Mother never stopped nagging at me. That's why I had to lie to her. I always lie to people, or run away from them, if they won't accept me as I am." The original Sally only mentioned her mother in order to lie about her and her social connections; otherwise, like Cole Porter's *Gigolo,* she had no mother but jazz.

The actress being Julie Harris, Sally became a nice girl on sabbatical instead of a hopeless stray. When the play was plowed into a film in 1955, it still featured Julie Harris and her apple pie anarchy. It dissolved, as I recall, into one of those fifties cliff-hangers about how naughty can a film get, will she say "slept with" or what? Very hard to show big bad men preparing for World War II in such a setting. Since Hollywood wasn't even ready for Franzblau, the male part was beefed up to par (if you can call casting Laurence Harvey "beefing"). But this only took us further from Isherwood's world, with its underlying theme of perversion and voyeurism. The original Issyvoo, the camera, may talk like an English schoolprig but he takes the most amazing pictures. He is magnetically drawn to corruption, where he nests and clicks away happily.

So far, the pale, unassertive quality of Isherwood's book had made it an ideal "property" to be mauled into all the standard commercial shapes. Time, now, to set it to music. By the mid-sixties, when *Cabaret* was spawned, the drama of private sensibility was bearish and the Broadway musical had taken to grappling with extra-large themes and vast social groups which could do those great panoramic stomps and choral numbers—a day in the life of a grapepicker, or whatever. So Sally and her camera were shunted side stage to make way for German decadence and the Jewish problem. The plight of the harassed Jew, used honestly, if smotheringly, in *Fiddler on the Roof* earlier the same year, was slapped on rather crudely here, to demand a tear that, aesthetically speaking, belonged to some other story. One character was revealed melodramatically as a Jew, one as a Nazi. Horrors! But this wasn't Isherwood's point. In the book, even big-hearted, nonaligned Sally Bowles says: "I've been making love to a dirty old Jew producer." *That* was the point.

Which brings us to the current movie, in which all the constituent parts—German decadence, Jew and Nazi, Issy and Sally—seem to me both more honest in themselves and better balanced with the others than in previous versions. Some of the pathologic dishonesty of Broadway and Hollywood has, of course, been sucked off by the networks; but besides that we are now so far from the original that it is possible to introduce a fresh imagination, instead of chewing down and down on Isherwood's. If one must have adaptations, complete disregard for the originals is the safest rule.

There is one superficial problem to deal with first. Sally's big selling point is decadence, and how does one make a movie about decadence these days? Now that we're allowed to do it, it's too late. Thus, when Sally and her camera make love to the same man, it seems no worse than group therapy. And when Joel Grey, the sinister nightclub MC, swings into a transvestite number, we of the Myra Breckenridge generation can only murmur, "This led to *war?*"

Bob Fosse, the director, and/or Jay Allen, the screenwriter, seem to understand this, so they do not try to double the decadence and reach for some last, overlooked area of shock, but concentrate instead on the gallant clumsiness of the cabaret routines, the lumbering attempts at style and at Parisian gaiety. Instead of swelling his stage to a Nazi *Bund*-rally grossness, Fosse shrinks it to small vulnerable frames, themselves easily blown away in the storm troopers' dust. These also fit the off-Weill tunes of John Kander, which are meant to sound like a trombone played in a phone booth, or at least like an understaffed band trying to sound portentous, and which lost all their point in a full Broadway pit. The film suggests that these little shows did not boil up into sadistic hysteria, but were a rather touching alternative to it: as Sally Bowles's Windermere Club was in the book.

By picture and voice overlays which are as heavy-handed as anything in Fritz Lang, Fosse makes the whole story part of the cabaret program, sharing its brief sanctuary. When the Nazis break in there, the story will be over. Meanwhile, the decadence of Sally and her friends is no worse than a nightclub turn.

The artificiality enables Fosse and Allen to slough another problem —the danger of making the Germans, whose children presumably go to movies, real enough to hate. But this could have been sloughed even better by sticking to Isherwood's text, for once. Fosse and Allen allow Issy and Sally to be led astray by a charming German nobleman, but in the book it is a rich American drunk. In fact, all the most corrupt characters in the *Berlin Stories* are foreigners—an English psychopath, a Polish boy-swindler, Isherwood himself—and not Germans at all. Issyvoo wasn't writing about German decadence (after an English public school, what else is new?) but about a shattered society where parasites of all persuasions nibble until antibodies in brown shirts begin to form.

The film handles the Jewish question itself with care. The early days of the Solution pack so much horror on their own that they will dominate any movie they're in, even if they are played way down. Here the secret marriage of the two Jewish characters and the glimpses of street beatings are played more or less to scale with the rest. Yet each one is worth a thousand volts of Sally and her green fingernails. The film follows the book in making the principal victim (Marisa Berenson) aloof, rich, and otherwise unlike ourselves, and the street goons are presented as a bad cabaret turn, unreal as anything else. And still they knock Sally and Issy out of the box and upset Isherwood's eerie emotional symmetry.

As for these two (Issyvoo has mysteriously become "Brian Roberts," a fine lending-library name, but also a small sign of the film's independence), they are obliged by filmic law to go through a form of romance with each other, but far from bestowing a Hollywood blessing, this is turned to further sinister effect: Issy is simply promoted from no sex to two. No sex was better, with its unstated note of homosexuality, but big commercial movies have not reached the stage of unstating anything.

Issyvoo's role has been a problem in every version—what kind of conversation do you expect from a camera?—but Michael York at least conveys the manner: a Cambridge Brownie mounted on a tripos, who combines social poise with almost constant embarrassment, and who is always "on" for a good orgy yet never forgets to brush his teeth. Where the literary Isherwood switches from dumb to pompous to sophisticated to suit a scene's focus, York sticks close to dumb. On the other hand, he looks and sounds so much like James Mason that one assumes he knows something he's not saying.

As to Liza Minnelli as Sally—there is no way of liking Miss Minnelli as someone else, you must try to like her for herself. Sally's schoolgirl precocity, her well-bred attempt to master the demimondaine manner, there is no trace of these, and nothing to replace them with either. The movie Sally also has a Franzblau past, but Liza might be lying about it. When you say your lines with that metallic brightness they could all be lies. Miss Minnelli even flunks (agreeably) the most basic of Sally's attributes: Sally had (and it's important) absolutely no performing talent whatever. Miss Minnelli has a little. She is a reasonably talented stage musical performer and like many better ones (Bolger, Merman) looks just plain lost on screen. Until, that is, she goes into a Judy-plays-the-Palace routine at the end, which has no connection with anything.

Of the rest, I liked Helmut Griem as Mr. Facing-both-ways, the double seducer, because he plays it without guile. He is forced to hold still for endless meaningful close-ups—confrontations in serious musicals tend to be portentously long and awkward, as if the characters were singing at each other, and real awkwardness is conveyed by a veritable dance of the elephants—but Griem retains, as a good seducer should, a sense of real unaffected friendliness.

Footnote: When I reviewed the play *Cabaret,* I rebuked Joel Grey, as the MC, for being too playful about his decadence. This is a reviewer's cliché (the satire is never biting enough for us—unless it's in bad taste) and I was wrong. Some of that German decadence probably was playful and nothing like as sinister as we thought in the days when *we* were so nice. Since it also gave us the German expressionist filmmakers and Kurt Weill and so much else, the moral question becomes whether it was done well or badly. Grey's performance seems a little harsher this time, and he's better in medium shot than close-up, but his instinct for the part is right, and he remains the best thing in the show.

1972

5 / *The Interview as Art*

This is partly an act of reparation. A few years back, I wrote a somewhat lofty piece about the second collection of *Paris Review* interviews, suggesting that the information therein was neither better nor worse than Hollywood gossip. I was mortally sick by then of hearing about Hemingway's number-two pencils, and I felt they had about as much to do with literature as, say, whether Aldous Huxley slept in pajama tops or bottoms.

It was a dishonest piece (I was too young to be honest) in that I artfully concealed how much I had enjoyed the volume—which meant it had some kind of value, if not the kind I was looking for. It was also an ingenuous piece because I did not yet realize that gossip is the very stuff of literature, the *materia prima* of which both books and their authors are made. From Homer to Bellow, gossip is simply what authors *do,* in books and out; and no fine distinctions are made between craft gossip and the wisdom of the keyhole. In fact, Aldous Huxley's sleeping arrangements would have interested Flaubert a good deal more than Hemingway's pencils. Literature is the one subject in the world one cannot be priggish about.

Can the interview as a form pass beyond the realm of necessary small talk into art itself? Perhaps. Whenever a good writer uses words, literature is a possibility, and the interviews in *Writers at Work: The Paris Review Interviews,* Volume IV, the subjects have a distinct interest in producing literature. Because the interviews represent the authors' contributions to their own gossip: these are their own fair copies of themselves, and this is the way they would like to be talked about. Hence, their idlest comments take on the urgency of missing pieces. If a movie star says that he sleeps with the windows open, we are probably getting a coarse reading of his present image. But if an author says so, he is adding a workmanlike stone to his monument. He is telling you for one thing that he is the kind of author who doesn't mind talking about the mundane personal—whether archly, as one might expect of Nabokov, mock eruditely à la Burgess ("the Elizabethans didn't even *have* windows, you know"), or with the exhaustive candor of a Jack Kerouac. In any event, he knows as movie actors do not that such details can immortalize a character for better or worse, and he is taking no chances. It is his business to know it. Novelists in particular spend a lifetime sabotaging their characters with one loathesome habit or ennobling them with a perfect gesture. So they are careful when they dress themselves for the public. As their own most important characters, they deserve the most attention.

This is not to suggest *The Paris Review*'s urbane corps of interviewers pepper their victims with inane questions—far from it. But as one moves from the artful table setting that introduces each interview through one's first glimpses of the great man into the actual questions, one senses a continuity of self-creation that would reveal itself equally in small or large matters. This author will be a grouch, that one generous; and they will not slip, unless intentionally. For these people are masters of disguise, of controlled performance, and this is the record they want to leave.

Which doesn't mean there are no real people in the book. The real person includes the magician *and* his tricks. Novelists begin life as liars. It is their apprenticeship (and I'm not sure that poets aren't even better at it); but by their maturity they don't need to lie anymore. The truth itself is a trick. The mask of a Vladimir Nabokov is welded seamlessly to his face: the persona in the interview is as real and unreal as Humbert Humbert himself.

I stress Nabokov because the greatest novelist gives the greatest performance. He is, to the tip of his tongue, the Nabokov man: a dispossessed nobleman whose blood runs irony and who will never stoop to being likable. (He is likable.) W. H. Auden, playing for the poets, is not far behind. His interviewing self is, or was, an extra person, like the Holy Ghost, generated by self-contemplation. Auden could apparently answer questions forever in a serene stream, without lapsing from character. He has given so many interviews that his answering service could give a perfect Auden response to anything.

Auden's self-monument was complete, and he wasn't about to tamper with it. Consider in contrast his old friend Christopher Isherwood, still trying on faces like a boy in a prop department. In fact his boyishness is his mask. He talks about his discovery of Eastern spirituality as if it had happened yesterday and not back in the thirties when he and the rest of the class, Aldous Huxley and Gerald Heard, discovered the East on the American Gold Coast. Yet who seems younger? The owlish, born-old Auden or Isherwood, the professional boy?

Novelists, since they need so many, perhaps settle less well into a single face than poets. Because the other quite spectacularly boyish interviewee is John Updike—still young, of course, and, as an American, full of vital blank spaces that are filled in for Europeans (prairie versus garden), yet earnest and eager for any age. Updike answers the questions as though it were for a very important exam and with a guileless sincerity that seems, like something in Henry James's *The American,* both provincially earnest and somehow more sophisticated than a European smartie like Nabokov. Like *The New Yorker* magazine at its best, he is beyond sophistication and even makes the latter seem rather a callow thing in itself, a trap for *arrivistes.* Of all the subjects, Updike gives the most honest day's work and worries the least about how he's doing.

For sheer vulgar performance that in no way cheapens the actor, Anthony Burgess remains something of a model for writers. He can go on the most rattle-brained talk show and make it sound exactly like a *Paris Review* interview, if you subtract the gibbering host. One feels he would be bored to hold the same opinion two nights in a row. These are his rules: it is a game, and Burgess is a game player. Just as Auden satisfies with his eternal Audenisms, Burgess could be interviewed nonstop for five years and continue to surprise.

Robert Graves takes this style to the end of the line; Graves is such a professional surpriser that only a conventional opinion from him could still shock us. It has been a unique privilege of our time to watch the building of Graves, from shell-shocked schoolboy in World War I to

Mediterranean warlock, encanting at the moon. As an expatriate in Majorca, Graves remains a bit of an Edwardian tease, as willful and unflaggingly facetious as a Sitwell; yet in another sense, he has grown more fully and richly than is given to most. His literary opinions are so quirky that they seem designed solely to start lengthy feuds in the London *Times;* yet in terms of his own art they are not quirky at all. As evaluations of other poets, one may find them arbitrary to the point of uselessness; but as definitions of himself and his task, they are as illuminating as his beloved moon. Perhaps this is true whenever writers criticize other writers; from Tolstoy to Gore Vidal, they are simply telling us what they themselves plan to do next or defending what they've done last.

So understood, their crochets take on serious value. Writers make admirable critics (Vidal, since I've dragged him in from left field, is superb), but their subject is nearly always themselves, and how they reflect off others. "I wouldn't have done it like that" is their unspoken refrain; and what remains after they have chiseled away everyone else and every other possibility is a statue of themselves.

It is possible that the malice of writers has been overrated (by myself among others). Reading their ruminations on their craft, one sees why this writer could not possibly like that one, would indeed consider him a menace. Literature is a battleground of conflicting faiths, and nobler passions than envy are involved. Even those writers like Nabokov who are crabby by habit usually have a powerful aesthetic to back it up. (Nabokov's self-statute is chiseled so fine you can run your finger along the smirk.)

Concerning these craft ruminations: a beginner might alternately find them useful or fatal, depending on his own genius. Anne Sexton, for instance, was taught by Robert Lowell to make each line of verse perfect before going on to the next. Likewise, Anthony Burgess polishes as he goes and never looks back. I myself consider this practice deplorable, leading to fine sentence-by-sentence writing at the expense of form; but for writers like Sexton and Burgess, who have an innate sense of form, it seems to work. (When it doesn't, watch out.)

Hence, the value of a collection of discordant voices, each hawking its own dogmas. At the end, one wants to set up one's own stand. Where any one author might indeed be a menace, taken together they testify benignly to the richness of the enterprise. The Sexton interview, for instance, reminds one, so that you can almost feel it on your skin, of how the Spirit was blowing through Cambridge that year, for those who had the wit to use it. The confessional poetry she and Sylvia Plath learned from Lowell later turned in on itself like monoxide in a garage; yet at the time it had the scent of liberation. But the rambunctious George Seferis receives very different breezes in Greece. And Jorge Luis Borges, like a timeless satyr in a high-walled Roman garden, feels none at all.

It is not my aim to catalogue each interview and tap it on the head with my gavel but to indicate the range of meditation that each inspires. One could, as with a good novel, find a thousand other stories in the shadows, from the wistful reticences of Isak Dinesen to the desperate garrulity of John Steinbeck—so right when he's being funny and off-hand, so wobbly and windy when he strains to be major (Nathaniel Benchley's introduction suggests a comedian trapped in a reputation). The interviews tell stories that even the watchful subjects may not have wanted told; but also, and really more valuably, they tell each subject's favorite story about him or herself.

The interviewers presumably prefer to remain faceless, and we'll leave them so. But it is worth noting how much this particular skill has refined itself since *The Paris Review* started (although these interviews are not necessarily the latest chronologically). It is not easy to play the straight man, with a touch of the DA, to a famous writer; your own cunning must very nearly match his. And then at the end, you must be prepared to disappear altogether, leaving his answers standing alone on stage. Otherwise there is no art, only chat.

Having never attended one of these *corridas* myself, I cannot say whether the authors really talk as fluently and aptly as they appear to on the page. I'm sure some of them do, the inarticulate author being a romantic myth, like the deaf composer. But I fancy that for others, this is not so much how they talk as how they would like to talk: a further self-creation and self-concealment. Having been given the chance to revise their words and to erase the banalities of spontaneity, they are free to invent not only themselves but their way of presenting themselves: Stammers are ironed out, contradictions reconciled, mumbles turned into roars. A shy man like Dos Passos becomes airily confident; Conrad Aiken becomes young and John Berryman peaceful. This kind of magic is their stock in trade, and the rewritten interview gives them a rare chance to apply it to themselves—not in the rambling form of autobiography, which usually brings us yards of information that nobody asked for, but in the specific twentieth-century form of interrogation.

In a democracy, *we* ask the questions; *we* determine what is interesting. Within this cage of questions, the artist prowls, looks for exits, expresses himself somehow. The result (as with poets fettered by meter) is often better, or better for *us,* than their own mysterious wanderings would have been. That is what zoos are for. That is what art is for.

Most writer interviews are not art at all, but a sort of cultural packaging. The cages are too small, the questioner's powers too sweeping; what we want to know obliterates what the speaker wants to say. But in this case, where the subjects seem virtually to question themselves and to collaborate in their own limits, the zoo is at worst a low-security one. And perhaps this amount of constraint enables them to show their plumage to better advantage. At any rate, several of the interviews wander in and out of art (if I can use that impossible word one last time) and may even rank among their subjects' finer recent work, which is much more than I would have admitted in my *a priori* slumbers of a few years ago. Even the least ambitious of them constitute the finest in literary shop talk and exegesis. (No one should henceforth read Eudora Welty without consulting her carefully measured program notes.) And all sixteen of them are self-portraits of the artist of a kind scholars are lucky to piece together, much less satisfactorily, from diaries and letters. Speaking for my frivolous self, I would trade half of *Childe Harold* for such an interview with Byron and all of *Adam Bede* for the same with George Eliot. And if that is not precisely literature, it will do.

1976

6/GRAHAM GREENE: *A Sort of Life*

Most novelists start lying early and often, to protect and amuse themselves in childhood and later to clothe, house, and otherwise appease their surly dependents. It must be one of the most immoral arrangements in nature: all the lies told to parents and teachers serve to polish the novelist's art, while the little George Washingtons are probably getting nothing out of school at all. And then, there is the vicious joy of finding a regular grown-up profession that caters to one's vice: it's like being paid to pick your nose or steal candy the rest of your life.

Of course, the Hays Office in the sky makes sure that thinking up fresh lies becomes an excruciating torture eventually, and one is tempted at last to commit a truth, in the form of a memoir. Graham Greene has reached this stage.

But luckily, the old wizard is so sunk in deceit that it sounds as if he is making it up anyway. The truth has everywhere been pruned and teased until it's as good as a lie, to pass the time on a wet afternoon in a dingy nursery.

Greene's secret has always been to concoct an atmosphere in which only a Greene character can breathe; in fact, his characters are made of atmosphere, as a star is made of gas. Little boy Greene is composed of sinister English village, the streets you couldn't go down, the man who cut his throat before a gawking crowd. Mr. Greene senior, a school principal, is defined by a green baize door which cut him in two. A bored father on one side, a godlike authority on the other. Mrs. Greene is a great coolness, silence, the occasional tolerant letter. Graham doesn't say a harsh word about his parents, and doesn't have to.

As the atmosphere congeals to form an adolescent, it seems only natural that the boy should try to kill himself several times, out of fear and boredom: and that these two vultures will perch on his shoulders forever. The green baize door drove him to an early breakdown. The boys in his father's school distrusted him because he came from the wrong side of it; yet his father was no ally either. The writer's sense of himself as a double agent, and all the lost agents and drained souls this sense was to spawn, began there. His famous saying, that a writer's first duty is disloyalty, is another lesson learned at his father's cold knee.

A novelist has seen it all by the age of twelve. All that remains is to gather the corroborating details. At Oxford, Greene did some actual espionage, of a slightly farcical nature, which gave him the night trains and midnight callers. His first job took him to Nottingham, his basic gray industrial city, and to the shabby Greene lodgings. Even sexual frustration was managed, and no one has ever conveyed the futility of first love more convincingly. Other, more general things must have happened to him, but those are another story. The thread running through a man's books must be accounted for. The rest is self-indulgence.

Thus, only *A Sort of Life:* an artifact, a fiction, and one of his finer ones at that. It even bears his characteristic defect—the stated theme that doesn't quite seem to fit. He says that the book is about failure, but if he hadn't said it, I wouldn't have noticed it. Failure, like loss of faith, fascinates him, and he drags it in, like an ugly child that nobody really wants to see.

If he is trying to strike up a bond with other failures, he won't: they hate superstars horning in on their territory. If he is talking of some private failure, he has left it out of the book. By any normal definition, this is a story of sly triumph, of art feeding itself shrewdly off circumstance. The Greenes as described sound like the kind of lumpen ruling-class family least likely to produce a novelist. Yet Graham has made the most of every eccentric uncle and every unexplained aunt to prime his sensibility and fill his gallery. And he has lived a life, utterly unlike that laid out for him, fastidiously suited to his talent.

Something else comes through, almost from the left hand, and that is an extraordinary courtesy. The reference to the bit characters of his life are almost unfailingly generous. Memoirs are for settling scores, but he passes up the pleasure again and again in a way that would have been called manly in his father's world.

Also from the left hand, humor and a surprising, insinuating charm.

1971

7/ P. G. WODEHOUSE: *Leave It to Psmith*

Somewhere between the Romantic Revolution and the Great Victorian Exhibition of 1851 in England, suet pudding entered the English soul, after which it became almost impossible for that country to produce a pure artist. Despite generous help from Ireland, America, and even Poland, any Englishman who had been to a public school felt and looked like a perfect chump, a tourist, in the world of Flaubert and Rimbaud.

It was almost as if these schools, founded in the 1830s, had it for their main object that Shelley and Byron would never happen again. When such a one showed up, he was immediately laughed at, plunged into cold water, and taught to laugh at himself for twelve grueling years; after which he was either hopelessly maimed or would retreat with the crowd into humor, crossword puzzles, detective stories, and the burdens of facetiousness.

Hence the English aesthete from the *Yellow Book* nineties through Bloomsbury is a sorry figure: either a thick-skinned humorless survivor (or Sitwell) or a wounded bird, limping around the wounded-bird preserve with the others. While overhead soared the inverse aesthetes or anti-artists: Kipling, W. S. Gilbert, Conan Doyle, and preeminently P.

G. Wodehouse, a hack and public-school troubadour, who would have considered "art for art's sake" an unbearably soppy and pretentious sentiment, while he practiced it with an intensity that would have startled Flaubert.

It is only fair that such a barbarous school system, which had drowned so much talent in cold baths and laughter, should finally have coughed up its own kind of genius, and Wodehouse is absolutely the best it could have done. But a genius turned out by people dedicated to stamping out genius is necessarily a strange one, and Wodehouse, squirming around Parnassus with his hands in his pockets, must be at least the strangest since Jane Austen.

Yet, if one can turn off Wodehouse's goofy, haunting tones for a moment and run his life through silently, one finds something not unlike a romantic artist's life, right down to the ruthless monomania which turned its back on two world wars and ninety years of history. His childhood was objectively miserable. He barely knew his parents, but was farmed to a sequence of aunts whose quality may be judged by the aunts in his books, or by Lady Constance in *Leave It to Psmith.* On the rare occasions that he saw his mother, she seemed like an aunt too, so that the very word rang with horror; and it is no surprise that he spent his life (again, forget that the subject is humor) savaging such creatures in print. All in fun, of course, but to the end of his life the gentle Wodehouse could not be induced to say a kind word for his real mother.

In the last days Wodehouse observed mildly that his childhood seemed to be just like Kipling's, except that he'd rather enjoyed his. But this was some triumph of will and selection. For just as George Orwell made a hell of his schooldays by fanning the right memories, Wodehouse made a heaven of his; and it is a clue to how close these processes are that Orwell and Kipling, the laureates of unhappiness, were among Plum Wodehouse's most ardent admirers. They knew the score.

Wodehouse's artistic mechanism was set in motion by the need to exclude unpleasantness. He was a quiet, lonely boy and became a quiet, lonely man who escaped into joy at his desk. By all accounts, he was a friendly and obliging fellow; but no less an admirer than Evelyn Waugh described him privately as the dullest man he ever met. And socially he was famous for fleeing the kind of jolly scenes he wrote about to walk his dog. Generations of visitors were astounded that this taciturn blob could have produced such streams of liveliness. In true Victorian fashion, Wodehouse had grown a second soul back in his workshop, while the first one remained as shy and unformed as a bank clerk's.

Whether or not the sheer exclusion of pain can produce great art, it can, when pursued as cold-bloodedly as Wodehouse pursued it, fashion a very pure and rigorous one. His only entry into public history was in World War II when he was interned by the Nazis and gave some barmy broadcasts saying it wasn't all that bad, and his friends put this down to his incurable innocence: but if so, it was the merciless innocence of the artist who has subordinated all reality to his own work. Again, Flaubert could have done no more.

Nor was this some elderly aberration, like mislaying one's glasses, but a perfectly typical performance that might have happened at any period in his life. He told his biographer, David A. Jasen, that he had tried to enlist in the Royal Navy before World War I but was turned down for defective eyesight. Yet later when England was less fussy, and was looking for any warm bodies it could stuff into Ypres and the Somme, Plum was safe and sound in America, turning out such items as *Picadilly Jim* and *Oh Lady, Lady.* One shouldn't overdraw the matter: Wodehouse was a devoted husband and stepfather and dog owner, and he left no such trail of ruin as Shelley (his headmaster would have frowned). But his work towers eccentrically above his life in the style of a James or Proust. He had no children of his own, and no real homeland outside of his imagination. And one suspects that in his heart he felt, like Faulkner, that a good Bertie Wooster story was worth any number of old ladies.

Was the actual work worthy of such steely dedication? Not, it seemed, if he could help it. Nobody ever struggled harder to suppress his genius in the interests of amiable tripe. *Leave It to Psmith* is an interesting turning point, among several. Wodehouse had, at this time, been writing for more than twenty years, and had never really let himself go. (Forster's "undeveloped heart" goes for clowns too.) His comic gift would come prancing out for a page or two, but each time Plum would give it the hook. Psmith had first appeared in 1906 and seemed like the beginning of a comic avalanche; but Wodehouse put him back in the toy box and proceeded with romantic comedies of a pleasant but far from explosive nature.

Indeed, he was not certain that people would pay for pure farce—and Wodehouse wrote first and last for money. If he finally became a sort of artist, it was only because it paid to. And again this reflects the somberness of his real life. Paralleling Orwell once more, he had won a scholarship to Oxford, only to be deprived of it by family penury, with the further twist that his elder brother went up there instead. In those days Plum wrote Latin and Greek verse as easily as English, and one wonders what kind of writer would have emerged from four years of academic security. Instead, Plum found himself writing for his life. His father had put him to work in the Shanghai Bank, an institution as grim as anything in the annals of self-pity (although naturally he made it sound frantic and jolly) and in a short time he would have been shipped East, where no publisher has trod.

So Plum's early writing was a desperate pitch for a market, and any developments in craft were governed solely by public demand. If readers wanted school stories, school stories it was. Romance, comedy—the trajectory can be traced through his private ledger, where he scrupulously recorded seventy years of sales figures. He couldn't afford to mess around like those arty chaps.

And so it might have remained if he hadn't discovered America not long before World War I. He was immediately drawn to the place, not only by its bulging fees and fresh subjects but, I suspect, by its businesslike efficiency. Wodehouse especially loved the stage, and the American musical was about to develop into the formidably oiled machine which has since flattened us. And Wodehouse played a big part in this development. Up to then, musicals had been closer to variety shows, with the chief comedian carrying the load between disjointed musical numbers. But the team of Wodehouse, Guy Bolton, and Jerome Kern began to integrate the songs and the story and, ironically, to de-emphasize the comedian, starting us on the long greasy road to Rodgers and Hammerstein.

Wodehouse's work in the theater had a profound effect on his novels, which he proceeded to write in the manner of a company preparing a play out of town. No one has ever written more *efficient* novels than Wodehouse, and a lot of this can be traced to their theatrical structure. He himself called them musical comedies without the music, and they are almost literally that, since he was writing musical comedies *simultaneously* with them. The Wodehouse Golden Age, which *Leave It to Psmith* helps to usher in, was, in fact, preceded by such feverish stage work that a less driven man might have given up print altogether in its favor.

The other thing America gave Wodehouse was even more valuable:

that is, an audience which found Englishness funny as such. This steered Wodehouse back into his past, where he rummaged for comic servants, funny phrases, odd schoolmates, and those invaluable aunts. To judge from their photos, his mother already made a perfect Lady Constance and his father a sublime Lord Emsworth. From an American distance they took on a sharpness and strangeness they might have otherwise lacked: so much so that the English laughed at their own Englishness too, as if they had never seen it before.

The World War I years were the incubation period for his art. Around then, Jeeves took his first faltering steps, Beach the butler began to shimmer, and Beans and Crumpets stirred in the womb. Rough sketches of Blandings Castle and the Drones Club could give way to the real thing. By the twenties Wodehouse the artist was ready, was almost obliged, one might say, to roll.

Leave It to Psmith is an interesting transition book, because it still carries the trappings of romantic comedy with it into the uncertain future. The scene where the girls sit around discussing their chums' misfortunes has the frothy tenderness of an earlier Wodehouse. Likewise, Psmith's canoe wooing almost cries out for a Jerome Kern song to clinch it. And Aunt Constance is not allowed yet to be a perfect comic monster, but must remain a good woman underneath.

Even Psmith himself is not quite a finished character, but a compendium of mannerisms that will dissolve and issue into several comic characters, including the later Jeeves and the notorious Uncle Fred. This is a last chance to see Wodehouse among his blueprints and prototypes. The elements are ramshackle, as they still were in musical comedies, but they are all there, ready to be shaped over the next twenty years into a comedy so narrow and fastidious, so lacking in strain and the clown's need for approval, and so ruthlessly unadulterated by other emotions that they deserve to be called classic art. And blessedly, Plum made a bundle from them.

Even the famous phrasing, which is a bastard mix of slang and classical quotation and any English phrase Americans might be expected to find funny, is a closed language. One knows instinctively what words and constructions he would not have used: not only for reasons of sound (at which he was pitch-perfect) but attitude. It is interesting to note how tyrannically Wodehouse uses language to steer us through objectively wretched situations like a guide with a fixed smile, or a nurse determined we shall enjoy ourselves.

Blandings Castle, for instance, is really the same old class-ridden upstairs-downstairs jailhouse that sensitive writers have been railing at for generations. Wodehouse gives only the merest glimpse of this (Eve Halliday, hired as a librarian, does not feel free to talk to one of the guests; Eddie Cootes, the gangster, is whisked off to a nether world called the Servants Quarters and can speak to nobody) before we are moved on by the iron grip of our determinedly sunny host. *There will be no unpleasantness.*

Thus the horrors of a class society, where dotty, monomaniac peers and their idiot sons littered the landscape and leeched off the rest of England, are magically made to vanish, to be replaced by the more manageable horrors of schoolboy convention. For instance, the only character outside the servants' hall who actually works for a living, namely, the secretary Baxter, is promoted into a monster, because he's too *serious.* Efficiency, which is good in Jeeves, is bad in Baxter. The author's commentary, which is as musically insistent as Jane Austen's, assures that we will feel this. Likewise, when the benighted Lady Constance does something decent by inviting a foreign poet to stay over, we know right away that this is potty and pretentious of her and that the poet will be a fraud. On the other hand, when Lord Emsworth, a ghastly bore, tells Psmith, a posturing wastrel, that the latter is all right because he doesn't look like a poet, we wholeheartedly agree that this is a good thing. Emsworth in fact can't follow a word Psmith says, but he knows a gentleman when he sees one. And since Psmith turns out in the end to be the son of the Smith of Corfby Hall (his *uncle* sold fish, but uncles like aunts must carry the sins of the parents), Emsworth's judgment is confirmed.

In short, our own liberal standards, if so they be, have been totally and painlessly reversed, and I can't imagine the most fanatical Marxist objecting (in fact, I know one and he doesn't). Aesthetes are another story, and I have heard more than one of them object to Wodehouse's brutal philistinism. It is not just that poets are mocked, but that they are mocked by the likes of Psmith, who is himself a parody of an aesthete. Public-school boys might not be allowed to be arty in those days, but they were allowed to make fun of being arty, and Psmith is a walking caricature of a *Yellow Book* dandy. Once or twice, in moments of impatience, Psmith shows the innate cruelty and exclusiveness of this type, which must have made life hell for artistic little outsiders. In fact, the Psmiths, for all their campy high style, were often the policemen of those public-school prison camps.

But Wodehouse will have none of it. Even his Psmiths will be nice. He swears they were, that he remembers no bullying, no boredom. And for a couple of hours we share his amnesia, a boon to Marxists and fascists alike. A real exorcism has occurred.

What makes it doubly all right is that although we are briefly adopting a schoolboy's values as to who's ripping and who's ghastly, there is no hint that these values meant anything special to our author, let alone that he would fight for them. They were just a capital viewpoint for telling some stories. His only business was art, and according to his friend Denis Mackail, he talked in real life about nothing but writing, to a degree that would have exhausted even the Goncourts. Even in his letters to his stepdaughter, he wrote about his writing in a manner which, in a less casual-sounding person, would have been considered slightly insane.

So the system had produced a pure aesthete despite itself, although an unlikely one. Balzac once said to a friend whose father had just died, "And now to serious things. Who's going to marry Eugénie Grandet?" And this same note echoes discreetly through all of Wodehouse's collected correspondence. Beyond that, there are hints of a real painter's eye in his dithyrambs to Blandings Castle, and his description of Psmith's arrival at Market Blandings rivals the best of Evelyn Waugh for pastoral prose; but more typical of his sensibility, perhaps, is his blast of outrage at the tacky suburban villa that Psmith's friends the Jacksons have to live in because of their poverty. Recurrent through his work is a comic but genuine horror at bad taste in clothes, houses, human faces which was apparently matched in real life by little squalls of disgust and impatience recorded by Mackail, which were this stoic's only concessions to artistic temperament.

A couple of final points. Wodehouse's mastery of language has been so much discussed, and sources traced, that not much needs adding, except that an Anglo-American right then had the run of the world's two richest slang systems in their primes, which, laid on top of a classical education, gave him unrepeatable equipment. One fresh surprise for me was the parody of American slang used by the gangster and his moll. "I'll never forget you, Eddie! There's only one tintype on *my* mantelpiece" could have come straight from *No, No, Nanette.* Wodehouse was back in England when he wrote this book, and must have seen how Americanness could be made almost as funny as Englishness. And if the result is not quite successful in the Damon Runyon sense, the very attempt is pleasing.

Finally, the plot. Admirers are bemused by how seriously he took these plots, but surely Wodehouse was right about this. The movies of Mel Brooks and Woody Allen are recent reminders of how even the best jokes sprawl when the string breaks. Wodehouse's lines stand up sturdily on their own. "His crookedness was such that he could hide at will behind a spiral staircase" could turn up anywhere—and did. Like other Wodehouse standbys, it can be found with variations in several books. But he knew he was not superhuman: his second-line stuff needed help and got it. Character and situation always kept pace, sometimes too hectically, but ever on hand to prop up a joke. This in the end is what makes his books comic masterpieces and not just comic occasions.

In *Leave It to Psmith* the plot flirts with the detective novel, which was just then coming into its great flowering under Dame Agatha Christie. And this brings us back to the real-life Wodehouse for the last time. Although he read widely and intelligently, his taste for trash remained ravenous, and only his imperious sense of humor can have kept him from attempting straight detective stories himself. The offhand ingenuity of *Psmith* shows how he might have done at it.

But his real gift had surfaced by then and been recognized and paid for, and with his rock-ribbed sense of limits, he stuck to it. Right to his death at ninety-three, which took place in his muse's homeland, namely, England as seen from America, he continued gamely to bat out these gems—a wonderment to hacks and a glory to anyone. He left his money, in this suffering world, to the Bide-a-Wee home for pets, the final refuge from unpleasantness; but who cares if Wodehouse by then had become a bit of an auntie himself? To my mind, *Leave It to Psmith* is worth any number of old ladies.

1975

8 / V. S. PRITCHETT: *Midnight Oil*

V. S. Pritchett insists on remaining a minor figure in the teeth of the evidence. "I have talent but no genius," he says on one page, and on another, sounding like the bluff salesmen he writes about so well, "I am no thinker or philosopher." And most poisonously modest of all: "I often wish I had had the guts to get into debt." The gamble in life that announces the high-roller in art.

Since his second volume of memoirs reveals enough guts for all the regular bets—enough to strip himself of class, family, religion, and country before he was twenty-one, not to mention nearly starving to death—he must be talking about some other kind of guts, some aristocratic quality that character can't buy: a death-wish "guts" much on the mind of the generation that just missed World War I. Or he may merely be seeing how he looks as a typical V. S. Pritchett character. "There is the supreme pleasure of putting oneself in by leaving oneself out," he says of his fiction; and what is good for a story may be good for a memoir. The Pritchett in this book could be a dummy, and the man behind the curtain may be the man to watch. As usual, beware the fictionist writing his own life. Even candor becomes a strategy.

Pritchett's is first of all the candor of the honest Rolls-Royce salesman, going out of his way to point out small defects you might miss yourself. His extraordinary first memoir, *A Cab at the Door,* was an impossible act to follow, and it is typical of him that he not only knows it, but tells us exactly why. Childhood lays itself out, like a novel, he suggests, complete with central observer, fixed characters, and linear plot. Later, life disperses itself into anecdotes. After twenty-one, it no longer strictly matters whether the author went first to Ireland and then to Spain, or Spain first. And after thirty, he could stitch the pages in backward for all we care. Even his references to his outrageous parents will seem arbitrary now that he has left that particular novel.

As if that wasn't enough trouble, "the professional writer . . . finds he has written his life away and has become almost nothing." The author cuts his adult experience into usable lengths and throws the rest away, leaving only the bottomless well of childhood. So *Midnight Oil,* like Graham Greene's *A Sort of Life,* tapers off as the author's career gets into gear—except that since Pritchett has never "succeeded" in the usual sense but has reached the top by a million Japanese-size steps, his book straggles to a halt somewhere in the middle of the track.

These are the handicaps, and they are precisely as debilitating as Pritchett says, no more and no less. Nobody criticizes Pritchett like Pritchett. There are new and excellent tricks to look for but the old ones will not be quite so effective. The early episodes of life in Paris are expertly told, but the polish is almost too high on them. They are halfway into fiction already—as if the author had considered them as stories, done some work on them and decided to put them back into life. And stories cannot breathe when you throw them back in the stream.

But who understands this better than the salesman himself? The book "is a selection . . . my 'truth,' " as he calls it. And the anecdotes, with their perfectly timed punch lines and their suspiciously quaint characters, are not so much reality as sketches of reality by a rapidly improving art student. The narrative thrust, to replace the natural ones of childhood, comes from the growth of a writing sensibility, from hearty middle-brow to something more delicate. And if you can keep your eye on that thread, through the rich mix of theory and example—well, you'll have one thread to look at. Pritchett is not the type to make a whole carpet just to hide one thread.

His early career was as unlike the American dream of the Big Talent preparing for the Big One as possible. He backed into France, thumbing his nose cautiously at his Christian Science family; his first contacts were not with the official greeters, Ezra Pound and Ford Madox Ford, but only with more Christian Scientists. And his basic Paris scene was no can-can by gaslight but a Christian Science meeting room, emblem of exotic crankiness and strangled imagination. He was spared literary company for a mercifully long time. "When I read in memoirs about the Paris of the Steins, Sylvia Beach, Joyce, Hemingway and Scott Fitzgerald, I am cast down. I was there. I may have passed them in the street; I had simply never heard of them."

A break for us. At this point, I'd as soon read about the Duke of Windsor as another evening at Gertie's. Instead of that, he was unconsciously discovering his own literary turf, among the boarding-house widows and dubious small businessmen and the losers kept alive by the One Big Secret. The sense in which he remains minor is defined by his subject matter: the doorway to his world is too low for a major figure to enter. It takes, of course, all the guts in the world to refuse the magic mushroom that makes a man bigger than his material.

Yet *passim* there is the sense of frustration that, having escaped the middle-class world of childhood, he should find that this was indeed still his material. "If I had moved among cleverer and more instructed people," he says as stiffly as Mr. Kipps himself, "I would not have been so late in developing an original imagination." This is surely the sigh of the autodidact who thinks he's missed more than he has. It cannot be emphasized too strongly that an evening with Gertrude Stein is just an evening with Gertrude Stein.

From France, his course wobbled to Ireland, with Victor still blessedly unsure of where the hell he was heading. "My only interest was in describing scenery, and I considered myself very bold if I introduced a human being into it." Unconsciously, he was following a rigorous aesthetic that Flaubert would have approved, starting with still-lifes before going on to the human figure, and finally to "the very different task of making people talk not to me, but to each other." So that with a Pritchett story you always get the right furniture and the piece of facial landscape you need, plus the effect of a person talking to himself, plus the effect of that person on others—all at the highest level of technical, midnight-oiled accomplishment.

In Ireland, he had the chance to enter our Top Talent Literary Big Leagues, meeting Yeats, James Stephens, and whoever else was lying around. But by now temperament had completely blocked off all the little entrances for opportunism, and he got nothing out of the big boys at all. In fact, for all his superb recording equipment, he can barely remember a word they said. His art simply wouldn't function with them. Instead, he ran into a salesman "with one of the flattest minds I had met up to then" and from him got (years later) a great short story called "Salesman." His talent had settled itself. His next port of call, Spain, would be yet a third country calculated to rub away at his English, small-shopkeeping muse, but it was too late, fictionally speaking. In the most romantic corner of the globe, he would always find the salesman with the flat mind and record him perfectly and forget the local Yeats.

Maybe it was always too late. "I strongly wanted to belong to this world of small trades," he writes even of his Paris days. "The only talk that got into my writing was . . . simple, commonplace remarks." But too late for what? It was Joyce himself who claimed to have the soul of a grocer's assistant. To call such material minor is to impose a class system on literature; and perhaps the most intriguing thing about Pritchett, self-consciously middle-class and self-taught as he proclaims himself, is that part of him seems to do just that. There is a touch of the Edwardian self-made man about his modesty, dazzled but retaining his small, stubborn pride, as he finds himself among the top people. Again: "Scott and Balzac acquired huge debts." Aristocrats are always in debt; maybe that's the difference. As writers' *personae* go Pritchett's is a singularly attractive one; but writers are too often accepted at their own evaluation, and he sometimes suffers next to the more confident climbers.

His fictional self squatted down where the divining rod indicated and refused to budge. But curiously, his nonfiction mind continued to move with ever greater gusto and to set up as an excellent author in its own right, quite different from the fictionist. In Spain he discovered political ideas, in wartime England he became (because everyone else had left and someone had to mind the store) a masterful literary critic, and of course he had always been a fine travel writer. But he doesn't seem too interested in all that now, unless there's a good story in it, or a person that would make a good story. His political involvement, in particular, pales to vanishing in retrospect.

What he is interested in is himself as a work of fiction and as a maker of fictions. *Midnight Oil* is, he says, the story of an old man (he ages himself slightly for the purpose) trying to figure out a young one. He approaches this young puppy firmly but patiently, like a good confessor dealing with an inscrutable delinquent, taking absolutely no nonsense from himself. The younger man slips in and out of focus, revealing himself most when least self-conscious and disappearing altogether when he looks at himself too hard. The old man adds up the contradictions—brave but shy, proud but modest—and shakes his head in wonderment. Was that really me? Oh dear. The book, says Pritchett, is finally about embarrassment—his own at having been young then, at not being young now.

That is the best *story* he could find in his life, never mind if it's the truest: an artist's duty is always to tell the best story. The angle of old man gazing at young one gives his book the depth of mirrors facing each other. And as a tale of embarrassment, he adds a further subtlety, by seldom mentioning the subject—it just breathes quietly through all the episodes, making them stories, artworks, and not just Funny Things that happened to me. And that, if you turn back to the beginning, is precisely what the salesman promised; a modest little Rolls-Royce of a book.

1972

9/ JAMES THURBER: *Men, Women and Dogs*

Thurber in his heyday was one of those international names, like Garbo, Bip, or Mussolini, that immediately summoned up a point of view: partly, no doubt, because he sounded like one of his own characters (as did Benchley, Perelman, and Damon Runyon—comic writers seem to begin with their own names and build on that), but more certainly because of his drawings. These were mostly drawn in the 1930s—a Golden Age for American humor, mainly because everything else was going so badly. The wisecrack was the basic American sentence because there were so many things that could not be said any other way.

Dorothy Parker's original introduction to *Men, Women and Dogs* is itself a period piece, as enviable and unreachable as a face in a train window. In real life, Thurber was then reeling from one eye operation to another, losing en route most of his sight and his mental perspective, while for Parker's problems, personal and political, you would have needed a broad-minded abacus. Yet you won't hear a whimper of this in her essay. For the occasion, she has put on the old greasepaint of the 1920s belletrist to toast the new magic man in town, Mr. James

Thurber, a man without a past, a background, or even a physical existence.

These conventions of concealment and artifice were as good for humor as they were bad for sex (n.b., the orgy of film comedies brought on by censorship in the 1930s). As in Victorian England, the clowns were still freer than most people; Lewis Carroll and Edward Lear could bring the psyche news it would tolerate only from a jester, and Thurber did the same for us in the puritan twilight of the Depression. The one restriction on such humorists is that they have to tell it in code—the more frabjous the better. Carroll's "slithy toves that gire and gimble in the wabe" are like a message from a prison camp. So *that's* what's going on in there.

Thurber's words alone seldom hit quite that kind of black magic, but combined with his pictures they do it repeatedly. Like Disney and later Walt Kelly and Charles Schultz, he produced universal archetypes fit for a T-shirt. But fine as Pogo and Snoopy are, they do not wake you with palms sweating the way Thurber's people do. Beginning as a *New Yorker* staff man from Ohio, who learned sophistication from E. B. White, like boys smoking corn silk in back of the barn, and staying pretty much within the stylized limits of that magazine, he stumbled upon a vision of man, woman, and dog that even an Eskimo (perhaps especially an Eskimo) would recognize and run from.

Thurber was a marvelous comic writer, but alone among such he was able to sketch the phantasmagoric goo from which his funny ideas came. If Henry James or Dostoevsky had done their own illustrations, the results could hardly have been stranger or more illuminating. *Men, Women and Dogs* is like a writer's head with the back open; the fact that it's *funny* back there is as spooky as anything in Jung. Thurber did not make up his jokes in his mouth, like so many clowns, but somewhere between the optic nerve and the unconscious, an area where the slightest tilt can lead to torment and madness.

As it did, we now know, in his last years. But this book belongs to the sunny period before he literally lost his sight and had to move into his own skull for good, with no fresh images to lighten the nightmares. At this point his defective eyesight was still an asset conjuring up useful if scary visions of rear admirals on bicycles and dogs guarding window ledges, which he describes in one of his essays.

Characteristically, Thurber made light of his drawings. A man likes to be responsible for his own creations and these were, in a literal sense, "found art." The remarkable E. B. White, having taught him how to write prose, and having turned him in the process from a bumpkin into a byword in sophistication, proceeded in the late 1920s to scoop up his doodles and turn him into an artist as well, whose nonmastery of line came out magically close to Matisse in at least some critics' opinions.

Someday White's role as a hayseed Professor Higgins will be fully acknowledged for the artistic miracle it was (Thurber's early letters show not one trace of his masterful urbanity and his last blustering years demonstrate how paper thin it had been all along), but the subject right now is Thurber and the particular gifts he brought to the operation: fitting White's neat prose to his own wild dreams of men and women until his master was comfortably distanced. The captions of his cartoons are not always so far from the stuff that White used to write for *The New Yorker* under news breaks (e.g., from memory—*News-break:* "And then little Diggins, only 15 pounds, scored the winning touch-down." White: "Little old Diggins, by Gad!") but the total effect was quite different when acted out by Thurber's unbaked cookies (as Parker called them) in befuddled alignment.

Although Thurber's prose had its own unique glories, it could not endure the loss of his sight, as White's surely could have, but fell off tragically and bewilderedly. There was a brief, gallant period in the early 1940s when he mustered his last clear visual memories and produced at frantic speed his finest work. Then a period of wild word-play in which he strove vainly to make the words do it all but couldn't quite swing it. And finally those last stories in which people pour drinks upon drinks, and the author can no longer *see* things for them to do.

So his comic genius hung by a thread to his flickering vision, which had already been cruelly reduced by a childhood accident involving a bow and arrow. His life was in fact a sickeningly literal enactment of The Wound and the Bow theory (namely, that to draw the magic bow of art, one must have a disabling wound). Thurber's wound gave him a funny-looking world to draw and write about, and then his wound took it away again.

Thus the beguilingly blurred figures undercut by the incisive voice of the half-blind man, perhaps not quite sure where he is even in his own drawings. Some of these pictures are downright accidental. The notorious first Mrs. Harris was supposed to be crouched on a staircase not a bookcase: but it seems the artist's perspective failed him into a masterpiece. No wonder Thurber downplayed his art. Yet an openness to the accidental is a mark of genius. And precisely because it is accidental, Thurber blunders into effects beyond the reach of controlled draftsmanship. (For the last months of Walt Kelly's noble life, someone else did his drawing for him. But who could imitate Thurber's mistakes?)

Yet if his eyes were a crucial part of his comic machine, they were not the only part; his ears were in there too. The blurry women who menace the Thurber male, and the shaggy dogs that comfort him, are respectively strident and quiet as snow. In real life, Thurber was surrounded by his share of menacing women, starting with his mother, who set the trend, and one imagines their voices crackling out of the fog as harshly as the blind man's crackles back at them. But it is too simple to say that Thurber hated women. A close look at the creatures he drew suggests a fondness and a bizarre companionship. If some of his women are a bit on the tough side, they need to be to help the Thurber male across the street. (This would be a screaming grievance later when, in real life, he had to be led to the bathroom, but shouldn't be read back too far. In this book men and women carry each other inexplicably home about equally often, and the monsters are more than made up for by gentle spirits "from haunts of coot and hearn" and good-hearted blondes and nude pianists.) Although the Thurber woman is most triumphantly herself as the back part of a house lunging toward an apprehensive male, she is not always herself.

At his crudest ("Goddamn pussycats"), Thurber reflects the hearty misogyny of the frontier, echoing Mark Twain and his own boss, Harold Ross, who periodically blamed the state of the nation on women schoolteachers. As such he is merely a footnote to social history: sensitive boys from the macho country, blaming their mothers for making them sissies and lunging around speakeasies getting even with Wellesley girls and other effete Easterners.

But his feeling for women is usually more complicated than that. Their abiding gift is the power to baffle; Thurber's women may be illogical, but they are seldom stupid—and there is always a sense that they are probably right, that they "know" something. This imputation of mystical qualities may still be maddening to feminists, but at least Thurber's women are never inferior, and his response to them is closer to fear than contempt.

Furthermore, in emphasizing his alleged hatred of women, commentators have overlooked his equal and similar hatred of men. Riffling through the cartoons again, one notes that the males are just as liable to wild flights of illogic and of fiendish malice as the females. The only constant is warfare, culminating in the crashing cadenza in the back, "The War between men and women." Yet even this is complicated by strange collusions and crossings of sex lines. The dreadful Thurber couple hunting in pairs puts in several appearances: e.g., the unholy twosome who have broken into someone's apartment to perform their mad dance. ("I don't know them either, dear, but there may be some very simple explanation.")

Checking with Thurber's prose pieces, one finds the same people with the gloves (Thurber's) off: the couples who stay all night, zestfully wrecking homes and marriages, the swinish practical jokers and dotty women poker players, and—significantly often—a goodly measure of men picking on men. Life for Thurber was as competitive as it was for any hustling Midwesterner or for those compulsive games players in the Algonquin set, but it was softened by his goofy eyesight; as he said of the drawing captioned "Touché," "there is obviously no blood to speak of in the people I draw."

In his stories they bleed and bleed, and without the gloss of the drawings he would be remembered as a sardonic provincial in the Ring Lardner manner—a valuable American tradition in its own right, but Thurber didn't bite clear through like Lardner. Yet the stories plus the drawings give us the extra angle that reveals a genius. The stories are like the engine behind the drawings. Thurber came east with his mouth as wide as Scott Fitzgerald's, and for a while he reveled in what he took to be the glamor of it all. But then under pressure of booze and intelligence the mouth collapsed in a snarl and he became unfathomably bitter. When his eyes closed for good, he lost his most cheerful feature and joined the Lardner-Fitzgerald stream of disappointed Americans—than whom there is no one in the world more disappointed.

But thank God, he compiled *Men, Women and Dogs* first, while youthful high spirits could still put funny hats on his nightmares and the intoxication of humorous invention was glamor enough. The dark themes are there in embryo—in especial, the husband and wife who, having exhausted the competition, round on each other for the finals, the death struggle. But he could still be diverted by jokes that had nothing to say about anything, and Thurber is at his best when he isn't saying anything about anything. "I said the hounds of Spring are on Winter's traces, but let it pass, let it pass." I used to repeat this line so often as a boy that it lost all humor, and finally all meaning, and still I loved it. That's art and that's Thurber.

Later on he became famous, and it's harder to be an artist then. By a cruel coincidence, fame and blindness arrived almost together so that fame had to do everything for him and he made too much of it. He had once written a story about a kid who flies around the world but is too obnoxious to be a suitable hero, and sadly he proceeded to live out this story himself. Like his aviator, "Pal" Smurch, he didn't know how a great man was supposed to behave, it was so far from natural bent. Worst of all, critics convinced him he had been "saying something" all along, as indeed he had, but now he began saying it consciously, and it was nothing much in that form.

So this book comes just in time to rescue an authentic comic genius from the flat taste of his last works, and from Burton Bernstein's coroner's report of a biography, which no doubt had to be written, but which badly needs a chaser. At a period when jazz had been flattened into swing and the Hays Office sat on Hollywood's head, such as it was, humor was possibly the only American popular art that the rest of the literate world took seriously. And what they saw first and liked best was this strange fuzzy window on the American soul, the drawings of James Thurber.

1975

10 / ERNEST HEMINGWAY

The collapse of Hemingway's reputation was in the wind well before he died. His serious admirers had retreated by then to defending the early short stories and parts of *The Sun Also Rises* and snippets of *A Farewell to Arms,* and retreat usually leads to rout in these matters: the short stories could not hold out by themselves forever.

Hemingway must have sensed it. His nose for how he was doing was as delicate as a basset hound's. And of course he tipped his hand grossly by blustering at his critics and at the opposition, while simultaneously feigning gargantuan indifference. His son Gregory's kind pharmaceutical explanations of his later paranoia may be true, but not necessary: Ernest knew the score. The vultures were waiting for him to die.

At least he managed to leave it in his will, or wish, that we still discuss him that way. The trail of carcasses left behind by him and his set has been duly noted; but at least he left his own among them, Goyaesque undoubtedly, and smelling of the museums, as Gertrude Stein put it, but the only place his talent could go. It deserves a better memorial than his wife and son have given us so far.

At least there's this: in his own sardonic way, which was not as dumb as it looked—but then, not as bright as a second look promised—he beat them to it. In *Across the River and Into the Trees* he made a complete ass of himself. Everything since has been a clumsy gloss on that. Mary Hemingway's *How It Was* can only be described, in the *lingua finca* and from the title on down, as bullshit once removed. The tinny tones of Papa are duplicated by a writer who lacks grip. "Noisy, badly ventilated U.S. Army food"; "self-packed suitcases" (where, oh where, does one find those?)—the simple Hemingway sentence, which is at best the height of artifice, becomes a brute necessity for such a writer as this.

There is one blood-curdling and encapsulating sequence in the book in which Mary spells it out to Ernest that no amount of humiliation will make her quit. And she proves it. His Italian mistress could sit in the front of the car while she took the back; she would play Tonto forever to his Lone Ranger on hunting trips; name it. She liked being Mrs. Hemingway, with all its perquisites, and presumably still does. But whether someone who seems to try periodically to get rid of you is the ideal subject for a memoir is a vexed question; although Mary looks on the bright side at regular intervals, the overwhelming impression of Hemingway is of sodden, peevish ruin, worthy of one of Papa's own hatchet jobs.

Words fail when it comes to the perquisites themselves—the *finca,* the baby talk, the jolly ship *Pilar.* What Mary Hemingway understandably elides is that she married an artistically desperate man. Her account of their first meeting in 1944 suggests that he came as a darkling surprise to her and swept her off her reluctant feet à la mode de King Kong; yet as a star reporter for *Time,* she had the book on him if anyone did. He was already the world's most obtrusive author, a querulous boozer, and a Catholic convert ready to divorce his third wife at the speed of Gable —in short, a handful, and she undoubtedly paid a murderous price for him. But who can tell what value someone else might place on a curio like Hemingway?

Unreality is, of course, the essence of Hemingway memoirs, his own and others; but the quality of the myths had deteriorated so badly by then that the truth hardly seems worth finding. For instance, it may be true that Mary knew that *Across the River* was bad all along, and that she persuaded Ernest to give *The Old Man and the Sea* an upbeat ending. But even if she was the wise old owl that Hemingway painted her, it doesn't matter: the Old Man's fate could have been settled by the toss of a coin. The author of *A Farewell to Arms* had refused advice from Scott Fitzgerald. But by 1951, the question of whether the Old Man was a triumph of the human spirit or of piscine persistence could safely be left to Miss Mary.

In contrast, the book by Hemingway's son Gregory is a useful addition, because it does give flashes, as in a child's dreams, of an earlier more dazzling Hemingway. But for the most part he is left wrestling with the same hulk as Mary: proving alternately that Papa was capable of kindness, like several million others, and of cruelty, at which he was a little special. Hemingway may have been more alive to his sons than to his women, out of a sheer sense of duty, and he gave them a marginally better book in *Islands in the Stream;* but how thin it all finally seems, sealed off with his fish and his Gary Cooper, with the world of speech abandoned for good.

It will take more than any late memoir to salvage Hemingway and make him seem worth the fuss. Roger Sale has proposed a simple way out: that America in the twenties wanted great writers, so it invented them. There may be something to this: we invented pretty much everything else. But if Hemingway's early patrons, such as Ezra Pound, Ford Madox Ford, and Gertrude Stein, wanted great American writers, the search could not have been simple-minded. The real question is whether what excited them so much was a writer or merely a method.

Hemingway's method, smacking as it did of the teletype and the cryptic newspaper cable, may well have taken less streamlined literati off stride. In fact, his first stories, collected in *In Our Time,* are like news reports gone strangely wrong: by means of omission and artificial selection masquerading as objectivity, Hemingway produced a disquieting, apparently extraneous effect, for which the young Edmund Wilson used words like "poison," "sinister," "moral falsity and tragedy"—though none of these words might be justified by the story as such. All this was accomplished in a style which Ford compared to spying white pebbles on the bed of a clear stream. So many bad writers have since muddied up this style that it's hard to remember how fresh it once seemed. But is that all it was—just fresh?

Hemingway did not help much by falling on his face almost immediately. Our Middle Western geniuses (Lardner, Fitzgerald, Thurber) tended to be instantly paralyzed by fame, presumably because they had no culture to retreat to, no tradition to tell them what to do next. In each case, the solution was to resort to method; whatever had made them famous must reside in that. Even as early as *A Farewell to Arms,*

Hemingway began to look like a confabulation of tricks, which would be laid on double with each subsequent failure.

Yet dismissing Hemingway's decline as a simple loss of nerve does not quite satisfy. His attempts to regain his touch in the thirties were gutty and occasionally sly: *The Snows of Kilimanjaro* in particular is an ingenious blend of his old style with more sophisticated material. So if he failed in the end it may be that the task he set himself was simply too much for anyone. In which case, it might be more useful to speculate where even the strongest of men could have gone with that particular talent. And this is where Scott Donaldson's book *(By Force of Will; The Life and Art of Ernest Hemingway)* comes in extremely handy. Although it adds little to Hemingway criticism proper (it's hard to know what could be added to that mighty body of palaver), it is the first fresh news we've had in years about the play between the actual man and his work.

There is, as one might expect, an almost salacious feast for revisionists. Gregory has confirmed that Hemingway couldn't box worth his hat but Donaldson adds that he could barely stumble through football, and that he threw baseballs "like a hen," although he later claimed to have been a mighty pitcher. In fact, until he grew big and noticeable in his senior year, he preferred reading to any outdoor sport.

The point is that Hemingway did not take to lying in later life: the young Hemingway was almost as phony as the old. This is good news about a writer. At least it explodes the notion that he wrote entirely from experience, and that when that gave out, he was through. It seems he had precious little experience to begin with.

He came from the abnormally stuffy suburb of Oak Park, Illinois, and his legendary summers in Michigan were no more than the camping trips a city kid might take today. He did know an Indian girl, with the sobering name of Prudy Boulton; but his picture of himself as a young sexual vagabond was punctured pretty thoroughly one night in Paris when a whore approached him and he blushed helplessly.

If this last gives the impression that Donaldson is enjoying himself just a bit too much at Ernie's expense, he probably is. Although Hemingway does seem to ask for it, there is no good reason why he can't have his Indian girl. Nevertheless, the general picture is correct and even sympathetic: a man who did all those things would be all the boor that Hemingway seemed; but someone who made them up—and then believed them—might just possibly be a great writer.

Similarly, Donaldson is a bit stingy with Hemingway's war experience.

True, there was comically little of it for the Voice of World War I disillusionment; but one feels that Donaldson would get him out of the Italian campaign altogether if he could. Yet again the mistake is in the right direction, and is neatly corroborated by Michael Reynolds's fine small study, *Hemingway's First War: The Making of A Farewell to Arms.* It seems that though the famous retreat from Caparetto in *A Farewell to Arms* is accepted as gospel even by Italians, Hemingway knew practically nothing about the real thing. Which raises the question of why someone with such an imagination could not have gone on writing forever. But the problem was never one of material, but of inserting the appropriate moral poison, the malaise that, as Wilson says, undermines "the sunlight and the green summer landscapes of *The Sun Also Rises.*" And for this, less material (as in "Big Two-Hearted River" or "Soldier's Home") would have been more. The clutter of expertise in, for example, *The Old Man and the Sea,* smothers one's imagination in a pile of fishing equipment. It is as if the author hoped to find his magic in the very names of objects.

Reynolds and Donaldson also document the tell-tale fact that, in real life, the model for the nurse in *A Farewell to Arms* jilts the captain because he's too young. The bathos is unspeakable: Frederic Henry at nineteen being told to shove off by a twenty-six-year-old nurse. Fortunately, fiction can always straighten these things out, and in the novel, Catherine dies bearing his child: but there is something unpleasant about this distortion. Certainly there's no call for the exact truth, but this is such a mean victory. A premature canonization is a capital way to settle scores with a woman.

Which brings us to the core of his lying and his fiction, which were the same thing to begin with: the compulsion not just to settle scores but to change them after the game was over. Everyone knows the famous examples: how it turns out that *he* helped Fitzgerald and not the other way about; how *he* did his best for poor Gertrude, etc., etc. Donaldson also elaborates on how much Harold Loeb had assisted Ernest before the big fellow flattened him out good in *The Sun Also Rises;* and he throws in a gem of mischievous research (new to me anyway): to wit, that the joke "the very rich are not like you and me . . . no, they have more money" was first used at Ernest's own expense. He, of course, palmed it off on "poor Scott." In other words, the sportsman was a cheat.

It went against the grain. But the code of honor Hemingway celebrated so vehemently was violated almost every time he entered the ring. Even in literal ones, he was notorious for hitting people who weren't looking and otherwise acting up (luckily he was so slow it didn't matter), and in personal rings, he was murder. But what could he do? Much as he must have reproached himself—he didn't become a Catholic for nothing—it was the wellspring of his talent. When he begins a story with that "poor Scott" crack, we know he will be in top form; and when *A Moveable Feast* rises like Lazarus from the Cuban mausoleum, we can guess that malice will be its Holy Spirit, the life force behind it (unless, as I suspect, it was written earlier: even so, the principle holds).

In all this, he reminds one bizarrely of his great admirer Evelyn Waugh. Waugh was also at his best when he was at his most contemptible. And although he hated himself for it, it's too much to ask an artist to give up his ace, so he joined the Catholic Church instead, the Church of perpetual forgiveness, and hoped for the best; and so did Hemingway. Donaldson sticks a toe into all this, as Anglo-Americans are prone to do with writers' religions, and pulls it out fast; but at least he does that. In fact, Hemingway's latinate taste for Catholic liturgy and bullfights might tell us quite a lot about his art—both forms being sacrificial, self-contained, ominously decorous: universal but not really "about anything"* but themselves.

But where did the meanness, the cheating come from? Money is probably the best symbol we have in these matters, and Donaldson's research is at its liveliest at this level, among the pots and pans. Hemingway's father was infuriatingly stingy, allowing the children a penny a week multiplied by their ages, thin pickings even in the 1910s. And when Ernest got to Paris, he turned out to be quite the scrounger himself—preying off the likes of Harold Loeb, and never picking up a tab anywhere. Donaldson records the number of cash exchanges in *The Sun Also Rises* (thirty) and this tells as much as backstairs criticism can of what Hemingway saw when he walked into a café. Later he became prodigally generous, but in such a man, generosity is always a calculated statement. It goes into a ledger and will be paid back one way or another.

But theories of Hemingway's nastiness need not be multiplied indefi-

*Catholic readers may respond that the mass is about Calvary, about the Last Supper. Just so: all art is about something in that sense. But I believe the attempt to make the mass purely representational, instead of a discrete event, has done more to de-mystify it than all the common-sense reforms put together.

nitely. People who have never tried it have no idea how pleasant being nasty can be. And being good at it is the only motive required. Hemingway may have added to this the hysterical competitiveness of a Midwesterner with a Thurber mother (it helps to think of him as a Thurber character sometimes) who had routed his Thurber father and would eventually get him too in some form or other—as wife, critic, maricon or make-believe friend. And who knows, he might even wind up babbling baby talk to her someday.

But there has been altogether too much of this bootless psychologizing about Hemingway (his bad luck to have lived through the Freudian epidemic) and it adds up in sum to an insult to the autonomy of literature. Writing problems usually have writing causes, most outstandingly so in Hemingway's case. His manic frenzies weren't what brought him low, if anything they kept him going; what they couldn't do was tell him what to write next.

Donaldson begins his book, quite correctly, with the problem of Hemingway and thinking, but he is too easily satisfied with the answer, already suggested, that Hemingway was brighter than he looked. Unfortunately, intelligence was never the problem.

Hemingway's purpose (and he repeated it as often as a street-corner orator) was to produce an art as pure as painting. When he called Cézanne his inspiration, he wasn't simply high-hatting other writers as usual. He was truly after an art in which the creator could be as intelligent as he liked, but in which intelligence must be transmuted entirely into form, so that no lumps of thinking are left showing.

An admirable ambition, although hardly the way to compete with Mr. Tolstoy, and to my mind he was brilliantly successful at it; the very small daubs of light and color (always, as Reynolds Price has pointed out, much smaller than one remembers) establish a psychological landscape in which the thought is merged perfectly: clearly there, but indistinguishable and unextractable.

The problem was always to find a consciousness that actually sees things this way and embody it in a plausible person. Hemingway's bifocal theory of fiction demanded such a presence for the close-ups at least, with a language to match, whether pidgin Spanish or cigar-store Indian. He proved most successful when he used the standard American boy Nick Adams or that masterful device, the shell-shocked soldier, forbidden virtually by doctor's orders to think. (Philip Young claims that Hemingway *was* that soldier, and that his art began with that. If so, it might explain his extraordinary predilection for head injuries thereafter.) Later, he would try the boy again in *The Old Man and the Sea,* and the old soldier in *Across the River and Into the Trees,* but even drunk and reeling from his latest bang on the head, the author himself had changed too much to get the primitive impersonations right. In these late books the boy is a cipher, the soldier is a dummy stuffed like a turkey with Hemingway's opinions, trying not to think and to lay down the law at the same time.

In between, Hemingway had tried to accommodate his own inevitable growth and change in such halfway houses as Jake Barnes, Frederic Henry, and Robert Jordan, and the declining graph of their quality speaks for itself. Donaldson reminds us that each of these heroes is in some sense a literate person, but this is a technicality: giving them college degrees no more makes them intellectuals than a mail-order degree from Bob Jones University would. They are still trying not to think, which more and more meant trying to keep Hemingway out: and he was getting brutally insistent.

Heaven knows, he tried not to think himself. His sojourn on Cuba reminds one of Peter Pan's magic island, with Papa straining excruciatingly, almost Teutonically and by the numbers, to stay young, to stay simple, forever. And he rehearsed his goofy private language as conscientiously as Waugh rehearsed his Super-Cad. Alternately Hemingway courted large doses of primary experience, too fast and shocking to be assimilated by intelligence. If he couldn't re-enact the primitive consciousness, he could at least re-create the direct experience, which just might jar the consciousness alive again.

Thus, all the hunting, fishing, and war-sniffing were not altogether fatuous, but gallant attempts to keep his prodigious sense of vocation in business. As a parent of the existential novel, he believed, with the early Camus, that sheer quantity of experience had value, perhaps the only value left to us. And he laid it on, like a good American, with a trowel.

Ironically, the best Hemingway novel was finally written by Camus anyway, namely *L'Etranger,* just as the best old Hollywood movies were made by the French New Wave. But Camus also had the wisdom to realize that this was a young man's game, that for a middle-aged man to go gulping down sensation without thinking can be dangerously like a Shriner on a spree; so he allowed something like thinking to enter his subsequent fiction.

Hemingway, alas, clung to his method, partly out of pride, and partly perhaps because it was all he had. It would be nice to be sure of this latter: but as early as *The Sun Also Rises* there are signs of potential freedom, of an exit into adulthood, that he never availed himself of. This was his last book before fame settled in to stay and clamped his style into place, where it grew warped and gnarled like a tree in a cave: but that it was a splendid style, and that his pursuit of it was honorable, if muddle-headed, to the end, I have no doubt.

1977

11 / F. SCOTT FITZGERALD

Scott Fitzgerald is a sound you like to hear at certain times of the day, say at four in the afternoon and again late at night, and at other times it makes you slightly sick, and no one was sicker about it than poor Scott himself. It isn't music to march by or make speeches by, and we didn't hear it much in the sixties when all that seemed important. But Gatsby's neat sad waltz seems to be back and even if it makes you sick, sick was never quite so good before.

That paragraph, if I did it right, daughter, is meant to suggest that Hemingway's style actually runs into Scott Fitzgerald's at certain points, so that one writer leads to the other, depending on your mood and temperament. The great Scott cult of the forties and fifties came partly out of the temporary exhaustion of the Hemingway cult. Writers (and we were all writers then, baby) had caught enough fish and watched enough cigarettes burn down and made love like enough zombies to be ready to move indoors. Our Ernest imitations were still as clean and fine as ever, but they smacked of wartime, when there wasn't enough vocabulary to go around.

Right now we wanted something a little more expensive looking. And Fitzgerald's style was the Hope Diamond and the Plaza honeymoon suite rolled into one, a prose for the man who has everything. We didn't precisely imitate him, mainly because we couldn't, but he was *the* influential writer of the fifties for many of us anyway, dead or alive. And what writers felt about the prose, other people felt about the life-style. That first Fitzgerald boom coincided with a national group-grope for style after the war and depression, a grope that, alas, didn't come to much: there was a new run to be made on Paris (you soon had to beat the Americans off with a stick—which always suits the French fine) and the Riviera was opening up for beautiful-people business again. And what better guide on how to do those things heartbreakingly, Americanly wrong than Scott? Back home, there were also some fitful attempts to revive the twenties—one of those ritual resurrections that have since become a national tic—and it felt good, between Charlestons, to gaze at the fatally flawed golden girl and realize that you would never be quite so happy again.

So Scott had high and low appeal, and no fad can ask better than that. He was a uke on the banks of the Nassau and the tourist being thrown out of Harry's Bar in his opera hat and a catcher full of rye. He was also a marvelous writer. We don't have that many cult writers to choose from at the best of times and Scott was able to service several myths at once. He was the last of the romantics and the first of the promoters. He went down in flames like a Byron and wrote it up in *Esquire* like a Mailer. He also had lung trouble like Shelley, constipation like Flaubert (or was it the Goncourts?), booze trouble like Baudelaire, and wife trouble like everybody. He was a one-man library for the busy student. And in fact he even died too young and too old, with the face of an old man and the hands of a girl.

For the cherry on top, there was the irony that he needed us to discover him in order to complete the story. He had seen himself as a boat beaten back by the currents of history, not knowing that the American current goes round in a circle and that he would be passing the reviewing stand again shortly. Hence the fad was part of the fable, the last act, the O. Henry twist. Scott died with a million-dollar check that he couldn't cash at the flophouse. Poor sonofabitch.

So much for us. We resurrected Fitzgerald like a spring god after the long winter of war. Besides, his books were few and easy to read. The fifties suited him almost better than his own period had, with their hurry-up English courses and their scavenge for a usable past. Scott was usable to a fault. He was apolitical and so were we. He preferred the private life and the paper-thin heartbreak and so did we. He was forever analyzing himself. Check.

That was the heyday of the "I was a" books: I was a teenage vampire, atheist, sherry addict. Freud and Joe McCarthy and Rabbi Fulton Peale had all struck at once and the traffic in unhappy childhoods and political naivete and all-round what-a-fool-I-was was fierce. The bookshelves groaned with ex-Communists harking to the hound of heaven and alcoholics drying out in convents and a great wailing procession of penitents decked out like a Spanish Good Friday, flailing themselves to ribbons. And there was poor Scott who'd done it all in *The Crack-Up* and no one had listened.

So much for us, yes. By 1960, we had limped off the stage, dragging our Charlestons behind us. So why has Scott, of all our hobbies, bobbed up again now? To be sure, his self-pity puts him in the mainstream again. But it was the wrong kind of self-pity. It wasn't political, but as Gatsby said, "just personal." He had no one to blame but himself and his crazy wife, Zelda, and right now many people are blaming him for her too. In his latest reincarnation he is something of a sexist pig, a combination male oppressor and whimpering boychild: still, at any rate, servicing legends in all directions.

"A novelist is many people, if he's any good," said Scott. And Scott was good. What we have now is definitely not the same Scott we had last time. As with any recessive cult, he is already the copy of a copy. In reviving the fifties (surely the most pointless fad in history) we perforce revive the twenties that the fifties were reviving—a possible reason for dropping this whole thing, before we have the eighties wearing seventies clothes that were really fifties imitations of twenties designs.

But beyond that, the new Scott is missing a quality we no longer have an ear for—a kind of witty exuberance that has all but dropped out of memory. The new Scott is a rather lifeless fellow after all those resurrections. Nancy Mitford's fine book on Zelda takes the fun out of even the good part, the campy but ardent response to popular tunes, the midnight cartwheels on Joseph Conrad's lawn (the world's greatest writer, therefore its greatest man), the country weekend which Edmund Wilson describes when Scott had the butler groan and rattle chains to prove the house was haunted—all these now seem like ominous symptoms of a manic-depressive crash: which maybe they were. But the diagnosis still sounds a bit like your

Aunt Prunella saying "Don't get too excited, dear. You know how too much laughing turns to crying."

"Scott was funny—funny and charming. That's all I remember," says someone who knew him slightly. And Zelda once interrupted a schizophrenic tirade to break up over one of his answers. The fun could turn sour and destructive at times, but it may also have helped to keep him going. His defenders have made much of his stoicism in face of trouble (which was certainly impressive but sometimes stagy), but they underrate those flashes of pure humor which nourished him and completed him as a writer.

The new Scott is all case history as fits our strange mood, and God knows he's an ample one. Whichever way Women's Lib finally turns out, pity the wife who competes with a writer. He will gladly destroy them both before he lets her stand in his light. Sexist? Sure, but he'd do the same to his brother. And then for more case history, we have Scott the drunk, gray-faced and hands twitching, gallantly turning out his movie scripts for brutish movie producers—yet still, stubbornly, his own executioner, because he believed in movies and tried so hard to please. And finally to round out the penitential cycle we have his collected letters to his agent and editor, two relationships which commonly show any writer at his screaming shameless worst. The manic Scott is all but gone and the depressive is left to moan and rattle his chains.

For a writer, the moral may simply be that this is what you get for being a pioneer in the celebrity culture. Scott went public early, and his legend remains as a public utility for later generations to use as they will. But for his out-of-season fans, the real Scott is to be found in his notebooks and working papers, where he elaborated so patiently at turning the mess of his life to gold. "To observe one must be unwary," he wrote, so he took experience straight without a notebook. But he later hoarded it like a miser and pored over it like a monk illuminating a manuscript and produced enduring work. When a writer explores emotions to danger point like Scott, it is worse than philistine to talk about weakness of character. The whole moral test is in the books. *The Great Gatsby* and *Tender Is the Night* are all the character reference a writer could want.

Meanwhile, his reputation continues to seesaw rather foolishly with Hemingway's. Since Papa has been down for a while, we can expect him to rise shortly with Scott dipping to measure. Even our tastes are competitive, and if you like scotch you're expected to hate bourbon. This can lead to dismally excessive judgments in both directions. For instance, the recent denigration of Hemingway has been hysterical and vindictive, as though a tyrant had been deposed. (Moral for that: everyone feels superior to a suicide.) Likewise, the sneers of the Hemingwayites at "poor Scott" are like a festering echo of the dead man's voice, claiming that the town isn't big enough for both of them. Well, writers don't have to like each other (especially when, as in this case, they sometimes came to the party in the same hat), but their admirers should show more sense. Hemingway and Scott had, of course, very different sensibilities, but they were never better than when they were most alike. Interestingly, Scott admired Ernest for this and Ernest despised Scott: but that's gossip, not literature. Anyone interested in the tone of American writing in the twenties, that sense of a party going wrong, of sudden tears and dash for the bathroom, must accept both these men, in a harmony they could never create for themselves. Together, they make one hell of a writer.

1973

12 / *Letters of E. B. White*

New Yorker writers have always denied that there is such a thing as a *New Yorker* style, and by now they are probably right. (All rumors about that magazine are automatically denied, but some are false nevertheless.) But in the heyday of Gibbs, Thurber, and White, readers knew better. There was such a style, and its name was E. B. White.

Not that all the writers used the style (in fact, most of the best avoided it). But White's notes and comments established, as they say in Rock, The Sound. "Harold Ross and Katharine Angell, his literary editor [and later White's wife], were not slow to perceive that here were the perfect eye and ear, the authentic voice and accent for their struggling magazine," wrote Thurber in 1938 before his blindness had stiffened everything into private myth; and no one knew sounds better than Thurber. In fact, he was a bit of a mimic on the side and presumably without trying, he himself took White's style and ran with it. But from comparing their juvenilia, there's no question that White got there first, by about twenty years.

Enough. White doggedly downplays this kind of talk because downplaying is his very essence. A nimbus of modesty surrounds him, as it does the magazine itself, because boasting is so second-rate. But if you read these letters with half an ear, the jig is up. White's notes to the milkman achieve effects that the others sat up all night for. If the present editor has allowed the style to semi-retire, it is not just because of his own raised consciousness, but because too many people were sitting up all night to too little purpose. They don't make writers like White anymore, and rather than plug on with inferior imitations, Mr. Shawn has wisely let in new subject matter with the new voices to match.

Still, it was, and is, an intriguing style, and any American writer, from pastoral to Spillane, who hasn't learned from it has missed a trick or two. Essentially it combines the English sensible (as crystallized in Fowler's *English Usage*) with the rustic colloquial. Look for phrases like "horn in on," "going some," and "mighty" followed by adjective: look, in short, for an imitation of a New England farmer, and a darn good one (or jim-dandy). This inspired concoction removed at a blow much of the lace and stuffing from American belles lettres and even commanded the respect of the British, who have yielded their language rather more grudgingly than their empire. On the evidence, White began writing this way around the age of eleven.

Not exactly of course. One of the grim pleasures of reading collected letters comes in watching a style being built year by year until it resembles a model prison, with the writer on the inside. Only in this case, White had a magazine in there with him. Because, since you could only say certain things in White's style, light dry quick things, the magazine tended only to say those things too.

Which was fine so long as humor was the main order of business: but humor is a young man's game, after that it is just a chore, and by World War II we find White declaring himself heartily sick of Eustace Tilley, the dandy with the monocle who personified *The New Yorker.* Yet it proved hard to convert Eustace to serious purposes. This fretful fellow was accustomed to feeling "jumpy," "edgy," and plain "scared" over things like the disappearance of ferryboats and double-decker buses; now suddenly he was asked to feel jumpy about the erosion of freedom and such, and it didn't sound right.

So one turns to White's letters first off to find how much of this was manner and how much White; and the first thing you discover is that he is indeed jumpy, edgy, and nervous about just about everything. Where Thurber had used edginess as a purely comic device (the edge of a tantrum as often as not) with White it was a simple statement of fact. He is, it seems, so finely strung that keeping his sanity has been a struggle at times and writing brightly for *The New Yorker* a potential torture. No wonder his stuff seemed almost preternaturally sane and well-balanced. It had to.

All this puts into new perspective White's retreat to Maine in the thirties, which had seemed the ultimate in fastidiousness. In fact he was closer to running for his life. Near breakdowns in his thirties and forties left his head feeling funny, as if something bad was running around in the attic (a painful image: he had been scared of the attic in his childhood home in White Plains). In such a state he took, like Hemingway's shell-shocked Nick Adams, to fishing and doing simple country tasks well.

Much of this he describes here to his friends in such painstaking detail that it could be a boy writing home from camp. The act of description seems itself a country task, a necessary branch of farming. Just as you could barely tell by the end whether Hemingway was writing or fishing, White hammering a nail and fashioning a sentence looks more and more like the same fellow.

The effect was obviously good for his prose and his nerves, and a treat for his friends (he is clearly a charming man). Yet, as nature writing goes, White's still gives off a slight sense of a city boy writing about the country: not precisely a Eustace Tilley, but someone just a little too delighted with everything, whether the birth of a lamb or the ways of the titmouse. This is an urban mind in exile, trying to find the same quaint excitements among animals that it used to find on the sidewalks.

Fortunately White hit on the perfect form for this: the children's book in which the animals double as people, forming their own city. In *Charlotte's Web* especially, White's world is perfectly rendered. There is evil in it, no blinking that: the bad stay bad (Templeton the rat), and Charlotte the spider dies. But the evil is housebroken. These are farm animals and by contract an extension of civilization: that is the price they pay for living. White is more than happy to point out their discords and loneliness because this confirms that these defects are manageable by people too. Later, as part of the sobering up of Eustace Tilley, he extended this Victorian daydream into real life, with a gallant theory of world federation published in *The New Yorker.* But that's what happens when you try to write children's books and editorials at the same time, and it should not be held against *Charlotte,* his masterpiece, or *Stuart Little* either.

In fact, the worst thing about his federalist period was that he felt it necessary to get into that stuff at all. Unless he is holding something back here, there is no evidence that he read any books on politics—in fact, he makes an impressive point of his intellectual sloth—or had worked his way through the historical and cultural barbed wire; yet in the best gentleman amateur tradition he waded in anyway.

Why? Perhaps because this country is merciless to good small talents. A writer who doesn't take chances and swing for the fences (whether or not he has a prayer of reaching them) is less than a man. White must surely have been aware of this. In the mid-thirties he took a year off to write something "major" and found that he just couldn't. Maybe it rattled his nerves too much; maybe the creature in the attic would have got loose; most likely, it simply went against the grain of his style. So instead he made the common mistake of enlarging the subject matter while playing the same basic notes: like a minuet in honor of Napoleon.

The tactical mistake may cost him a bit among younger readers, who don't remember how windy *everybody* got around World War II, from Roosevelt to Archibald MacLeish. White himself was asked to help write a pamphlet on the four freedoms, and at least he saw the joke of that and of committee writing in general. But he did do some bloviating for the Human Spirit, before returning to what he does best: the hammering out of fine sentences about small matters. In later years he returns fitfully to the big picture only to find that liberty entails responsibility and that pornography leads to censorship, but these Boy Scoutisms are just exercises in citizenship like remembering to vote.

One reads the *Letters* for the words, which should be good enough for anyone. The studied informality of his *New Yorker* style turns out not to be studied at all but bred in the bone. And it loosens just the right bit more for his friends. Hemingway's writing "reminded me of the farting of an old horse." (Too bad he couldn't have said things like that out loud.) A famous trick of his, of doubling back on a word or phrase and playing with it like a cat shows up early. To wit: "The only Earp I ever knew was neither Wyatt nor Henry—he was Fred Earp, a copyreader on the *Seattle Times.* All this is getting us nowhere, all this Earp business. It earps me. I suspect it earps you, too." This is the secret of *The New Yorker*'s famous one-line news-breaks and, formula or no, no one else has been able to do it. In fact, being inimitable within a formula is the very definition of White's genius.

Letters by a living man are a bit like a stately home with the owner around—one isn't sure how much one can touch. Keeping psychohistory to a minimum, we are confronted with a passion for independence that seems alternately fearful and almost truculent. In the twenties he breaks off from a girl with a curiously icy letter, and in the thirties he appears to send his wife packing for a year, with a similar *demand* for loneliness. That was to be the year of his masterpiece, which called for a crescendo of isolation in an already quiet life.

In that same ambitious decade (his thirties and ours), he even tried to distance himself from *The New Yorker,* once again for breathing room. Being identified with a great magazine was no substitute for being a great writer, and he made a brief break for *Harper's* and freedom. In the same prickly vein, he has always refused to be exploited, to make money on the cheap or to have his children's books butchered by the media. His recent show of integrity in the Xerox case (Xerox had commissioned an outside article in *Esquire,* as it might place an ad) was not just the old *New Yorker* hand striking one more perfect pose but the expression of a whole life.

That is the plus side of his gift for saying no; but on the other hand is a sorry stream of negation, a refusal to do virtually anything at all, from lecturing to joining the American Academy of Arts and Sciences. He had his good reasons: the few times he ventured out he erupted in a wild array of disorders issuing from head and stomach. But the malaise seemed to spread to the magazine itself, whose psychohistory *is* fair game. One had a picture of *New Yorker* writers (whom one seldom saw) vying with each other in feats of hypochondria and shyness: also of flinching and shrinking, jumping at small sounds, and holing up in the country. American writers will compete at just about anything.

Not White's fault, of course: he never tried to influence anybody. But his retreat from life sounded so tasteful and amusing that it cried out for imitation. When the Whites phased up to Maine in the thirties and forties, they became gray eminences with a vengeance. It was rumored that they disapproved of Thurber's book on Harold Ross, a harmless enough ragbag of too-often-told anecdotes; but then one fancied that they didn't approve of much that was written about *The New Yorker.* When Tom Wolfe did a feckless spoof of the magazine for *New York,* a slew of contributors, including White, dashed off indignant letters which, while more than justified, unwittingly bore out Wolfe's image of *The New Yorker* as an old person with bad nerves. The young magazine would have handled it better.

But White's era at *The New Yorker* was a great one, unique in magazine history. Surely never before has a house style influenced the prose of a generation for the better—even if White isn't strictly speaking a house. And his personal era continues of course as chirpy as ever, as he rides out sickness and the loss of friends with good humor, kindness, and courage. A valuable man, but beware of imitations. His letters are equivalent to a weekend in the country and should be read as such. The shorter, sharper ones he wrote in the city give hints of another kind of writer, but we may never know for sure. Meanwhile, the one we got is fine with me.

1976

NOTE: *After this appeared, Katharine White wrote me a generally friendly letter in which she said that there were several inaccuracies in my review, but gave no specifics. Regretably, Mrs. White has since died, and I can only register her complaint here.*

13 / RING LARDNER, JR.: *The Lardners: Remembering My Family*

"I was struck by the enormous deference that the Algonquinites felt for Ring Lardner . . . he was somehow aloof and inscrutable, by nature rather saturnine, but a master whom all admired, though he was never present in person. It may be that all any such circle demands is such a presiding deity, who is assumed to regard them with a certain scorn." So at least says Edmund Wilson, our late flowering Pepys.

Curiously, the man whose very absence so impressed the killer sophisticates and one-line hit-men of the Algonquin was a Midwestern sportswriter who wrote, among other things, funny items about his children for the papers, captions for a comic strip, and the kind of dialect comedy some of them must have come to New York to get away from. Never mind. Lardner had class, whatever he did; and everyone, on up to highbrows like Wilson and Mencken, was convinced he could do better things anytime he wanted to. The myth was that he was too proud to try.

It looks, from a reading of his son's fine book, as if the highbrows should have left Lardner alone. Although his stories fall maddeningly short of formal perfection, squandering stupendous gifts of language and observation on formula structures, there is no reason to suppose he had either the wish or the capacity to improve them. And meanwhile all this urging to higher things can only have discouraged him with what he was already doing and made it seem cheap.

Whatever the reason—and he was certainly too proud to say—Ring seemed to lose interest in writing at almost the moment the intellectuals discovered him. "He had stopped finding any fun in his work for ten years before he died," said his friend Scott Fitzgerald, who adds that Lardner's real wish by then was to write a hit Broadway musical. Ring spent his last days denouncing the dirty words in popular songs, which might have cut him off from the sophisticates for good. But no: silent, absent, or plain silly, Lardner was aces with them. These parvenus of the Jazz Age seemed to see something in him of an earlier time that they missed sadly.

Much of Lardner's class still comes through in his writing, even while he is miming illiteracy and venality most furiously, because even his bad taste was perfect; but in the flesh it must have been truly awesome, as Fitzgerald reports. Almost too shy to speak, he yet radiated "Standards" as imperiously as a Philadelphia dowager.

And for a strange reason: in a sense, he was one. The Lardners were an old Philadelphia family that had gone to Michigan as one might retire to the colonies and Ring the rough-mouth was tutored at home. If his grandfather hadn't blown the family money, it is unlikely that Ringgold Wilmer Lardner would ever have met the ballplayers and low-lifes that made him famous, or acquired his unique point of view—which is that of a dispossessed aristocrat looking at the scruffy world he has entered, with amusement, fear, and contempt. When Wilson talked of Lardner's "aloof superior intelligence" he perhaps didn't recognize that it had the same social base as his own.

This explains a good deal about Lardner: how, for instance, he could dazzle people in the arts while remaining doggedly philistine. Philadelphia families can produce gentlemen in the International Class, but not, on the whole, artists. And Ring's upbringing was as uncultured as the British Royal Family's. So by some strange transmutation he became an anti-artist instead, mocking his own pretensions as if he were two people. His politics, when he deigned to have any, were grouchy conservative. And when he denounced pornography from his lingering deathbed, he was only being true to his ancestors.

But in the meanwhile, besides producing a body of work that is possibly the best writing about America since *Life on the Mississippi* in a voice that contains a continent, he had done something that possibly no other writer anywhere has done—he produced four first-rate children. Now that takes talent: either one genius, or two very gifted people, plus of course a heap of genetic luck.

One of the quiet pleasures (and it's a quiet book) of *The Lardners* is to discover their mother, Ellis Abbot. It's unfair matching her words with Ring's, she wasn't a pro, but they are supple enough to suggest a woman who could sustain a four-year courtship—breakneck for the time—through the mails. Ring wrote much of his side (sometimes two letters a day) in comic verse—which might be better training than going to writing school—and she shot back well enough to captivate this rambling drunken sportswriter with the impeccable taste.

Lardner himself had a pen in place of a tongue, and this trait was handed down to all four sons. A girl neighbor later said that she was fourteen before she knew that small boys could talk. Yet on paper they all became magically lucid. Their father's "class" was released in them by the act of writing. John became the best stylist sportswriting has seen since England's Bernard Darwin (nose to nose with Red Smith); David became *The New Yorker*'s maid of all work, doing movies, nightclubs, and sports more or less simultaneously until his death at twenty-five; Ring Jr. wrote the Oscar-winning screenplay *Woman of the Year* and then, after an unsightly interval, M*A*S*H, plus his jail-induced masterwork *The Ecstasy of Owen Muir,* a novel; James died in the Lincoln Brigade in Spain too young to show his stuff, but his letters already displayed another Lardner particularity—that he wrote just like his brothers, and unlike anyone else. These four talented men seem to have communicated with each other like deaf-mutes, but they supped at the same source: their father's standards.

It is no accident that the Lardner boys seemed like identical twins. Heredity had worked some prodigies: identical weak eyes, weight problems, and taste for the same girls (reciprocated), but silence, prudishness, and good writing are more likely passed on by code. The chief transmitter seems to have been elder brother John, who modeled himself consciously on his father, down to predicting that he would die at the same age (and almost doing it) and who was both the most silent and the best writer.

Among the occasions of transference were family plays and skits enthusiastically abetted by Ellis, in which tongues were loosed and John wrote song lyrics somewhere between his father and W. S. Gilbert, and those eternal letters where the taciturn ones gabbed like salesmen in a saloon. Later, Ring Jr. talks of getting to know his brothers slightly better, as if these were touchy diplomatic relationships. There is no suggestion he ever got to know his father at all except, like God, by his emanations—and on paper.

And even there, the family meeting place, there was much manifest fondness and gruff kidding but nothing explicit. Even whiskey could not cure Ring's reticence: in fact, it made it worse (he must be the only man who ever got drunk to listen better). And some of this reticence carries into his son's book. The reader must learn the sign language.

If so, he will meet an extraordinary family, the kind one rather imagines growing up in England before 1914 and being wiped out in the trenches. It went without saying that all the Lardners were courageous. Jim was killed reconnoitering a Fascist emplacement single-handed; David died in World War II, taking an overconfident shortcut in a jeep; John, the myopic war correspondent, actually walked toward bomb glare to see better.

And Ring Jr., perhaps the bravest of all, defied the House Un-American Activities Committee with the immortal words "I could answer the way you want, Mr. Chairman, but I'd hate myself in the morning." Typically he takes no credit whatever for the nine months of jail and fifteen years of obloquy that followed: the unfriendly witnesses thought they would win, he explains simply. But this does not account for the ones who broke and ran, under the sheer terror of any inquisition. His stiff upper lip gets in the way of the truth here, and Lillian Hellman's narcissistic *Scoundrel Time* conveys the period mood better.

He does convey his brothers very movingly, though there is some effect in this of the same film running over and over. After one gets over the wonder of this, one begins to wish slightly for another *kind* of Lardner. All of them quit college halfway, plunged straight into journalism ("Isn't somebody in this family going to do something else besides writing," groaned Ring Sr.) and into what look like identical love lives. Two, Jim and Ring himself, became outright Communists, while John and David stayed on the left side of neutral. In all this, Ring seems to feel they were being true to their father's spirit ("six feet three of kindness," Fitzgerald had called him) while reversing his beliefs. So it goes with radical patricians. But even if one finds their politics aloofist-abstract, like the Mitfords in England, the Lardners always put their bodies where their mouths were—or more often weren't.

It is as an ensemble that they really sparkle. The steady exchange of wit, and concern for each other, and idealism for everyone is (there's no other word) ennobling to read: one good mark for the twentieth century. Ring Jr. cannot explain his family, it would shatter their code, but he describes them splendidly in a prose like his own light-comedy writing, not so much quotable as steady and pleasing: to wit, "Some of us [witnesses] were less serene than others, but not even the gloomiest of us (that sounds like a figure of speech, but his name was Alvah Bessie) foresaw the paranoia of the next seven years." Or "there were enough of us [black listees] who survived to create a whole new subversive threat to . . . American movies. The erosion so far is invisible to the naked eye, which is the way we prefer it."

Better things have and will be written about Ring Sr. For instance, as if hobbled by filial piety, Ring Jr. solemnly insists that the old man's drinking was a disease pure and simple, which would be fine if Ring had been the only alcoholic American writer. But Ring's uncertain sense of vocation made his drinking as deadly as Benchley's and Fitzgerald's, as opposed to merely a nuisance like Faulkner's. (On the other hand, it may have helped his free-associating humor, as it did Joyce's.) Ring's literary misanthropy was not visible in the nursery and is therefore too lightly dismissed. The author of *Champion* had a killer streak of his own.

But on the rest of this extraordinary family this is simply the Book, all you're going to get and quite good enough. In fact, while the glow lasts, I'd suggest there are worse ways of whiling away the Bicentennial than reading about these quintessential Americans in their own special language, the Lardner family style.

At least it's a change from *The Adams Chronicles*.

1976

14 / MARY GORDON: *Final Payments*

George Orwell called the novel a Protestant art form, and insofar as protestant means simply breaking away and declaring oneself, this is obviously so. The novel is a supremely handy kind of declaration to nail on a nursery door, a parents' tombstone, a crucifix, on anything that has let one down.

But the Protestant novel is by definition a tale told by a refugee. Protestants, once they have settled in, are not really more interesting to write about than other people, although their lives may shape themselves into neater stories (that being the point of individualism—to be a self-contained story like *Pilgrim's Progress,* with a single Judgment). They have only the one unarguable advantage, which is the freedom to tell the story in the first place.

Conversely, such communal orthodoxies as Communism, Judaism, and Rome may actually provide richer subjects than Bunyan's nuclear pilgrim, but they cannot be used, except on the way out. A parish or *apparat* will simply not be itself in front of spies and informers, so talented believers must bite their tongues as the material glides by. It's enough to make one defect, just to write a book. Because the wealth of oddity in any group can be secured only by what Graham Greene calls "the novelist's duty to disloyalty": i.e., a duty to betray friends and family and all the confidences ever placed in one, in return, if all goes well, for fame and money.

Hence the ex-believer's natural advantage: and hence his usefulness. Just as the world needs spies to keep the balance of leaks at par, so even a Church needs its James Joyces to tell it its own secrets and complete the story. Of course there are certain things you always have to watch out for with defectors: all their secrets will be shameful, to justify their telling them at all, and all will be sensational, to catch your attention. A history of the world told entirely by defectors would be an Inferno; and so is a literature. The liberalized Church (if one can give a concrete name to an impulse) at least seems to realize this, and the message a young Catholic writer gets nowadays is that perhaps you don't have to be an ex-believer to talk, and if you are an ex-believer you don't have to go away mad.

Mary Gordon's *Final Payments* is much more than the latest thing in Catholic novels, and I hope preambles such as this do not accompany it everywhere it goes, but it does show brilliantly the effects of the new dispensation on American Catholic fiction. It gives a picture of certain Catholic lives (its aim is convent-school modest) more ambiguous than anything either a loyalist or a heretic would have had a mind to produce a few years ago. In the European manner, the Church is seen not as a good place or a bad place, with batteries of the best lawyers to prove both at once, but as a multilayered poem or vision which dominates your life equally whether you believe it or not: which doesn't even seem to need your belief once it has made its point. Santayana once called himself "a Catholic atheist," as if there were a rubric even for that, if all else fails.

Gordon's heroine, Isabel Moore, is an ex-Catholic who still carries the vision on her person like radiation. She has sacrificed her life from nineteen to thirty to a fanatical right-wing father, nursing him through strokes and dotage, like a nun presiding over the last days of the pre-Vatican Church. But, like such a nun, she doesn't regret a minute of it. By secular consensus, the old man sounds as murderous as Jaweh (God is not a liberal): a McCarthyite reactionary, who accepts his own and other people's sufferings with inhuman serenity—placed next to the City of God, they are less than nothing. And unblinkingly, he has broken his own daughter's life, driving away her first boyfriend with Jove-like curses and accepting her sacrifice as if he were God himself. The worst of him is that, senile or not, he knows exactly what he is doing.

Yet astonishingly he emerges as the most impressive and attractive character in the book—especially astonishing since he is never onstage but has to dominate from the clouds, and from memory. Gordon has conveyed his mere emanations, his perfectionism, his intelligence, his sheer size of spirit so well that the reader too half sees that after him the outside world would seem trashy and pointless. The religious vocation has been made incarnate.

Which means that Isabel cannot begin to explain it to her friends. Her father the Church dies at last, and she finds them waiting for an explanation. Where has she been all these years? A father fixation? Female masochism? She finds the questions themselves trashy and unanswerable. Her answer must be acted out. The novel is an exploration of whether the years with God were wasted.

The nun parallel needn't be pushed too far. But it pushes very well, even on a prosy level. For instance, after her father's death, Isabel becomes dazzled by the clothes women are wearing, as if she had been literally locked in with the old man. Although she had been seeing a worldly friend all that time, they had apparently never once talked fashion. Likewise, she is suddenly perplexed by the minutiae of housekeeping, although she has been doing it herself for eleven years, albeit sloppily. If all this does not make her a nun-in-disguise, it might as well. If Gordon's point is that *all* Catholic girls are nuns in disguise she certainly goes to extremes to prove it.

More seriously, if we take the nun away and make Isabel's father too much less than God, we land at the level of her friends' questions, and find ourselves reading yet another book about female masochism. The surrender of the soul to God knows no sex, but looking after a cranky old man usually does. And this is decisively not a book about that. Or not *just* a book about that.

The author's problem here is to get the book out of the heroine's head, where everything works perfectly, and into situations where her actual existence can be verified. Since Isabel is telling the story herself, her outside self has to be deduced from the looks on her friends' faces, and their stabbing conversation, which is perhaps the hardest task in fiction.

For this reason, many first-person narrators never develop an outside at all. Isabel develops plenty, almost as if Gordon had started from the outside and worked her way in. Isabel comes across as an overgrown schoolgirl, in equal parts snippy and ardent. Her friends find her vaguely "strong," masochism or no, and wise in an unfocused sort of way. She seems extravagantly both to need help and to overflow with it. The question, as with the wisdom of LSD or opium, is whether the experience of a religious love can be applied to anything else, or must constantly return to itself. "My father is dead," she repeats grimly to herself. She *cannot* return to that. Her love, fastidiously fashioned for one purpose, one sacrament, is at large now, ravening for an object. And so the book begins.

The world of sex fails predictably—but rather more, owing to an author's lapse, than it has to. Gordon's own master is Jane Austen, and she shares some of Austen's difficulties at depicting young men. Most writers can at least render you a passable cad, but Gordon (put this down to her art perhaps) seems edifyingly never to have met one. Her villain is too awful to be true: although he is some sort of social work administrator, and a good one, he hasn't a decent bone in his body. When in a fit of muddled ardor she allows him to seduce her, he responds with all the grace of a tire salesman "You were really dying for it, weren't you . . . I was afraid I was going to have to pop your cherry," etc. And later when she decides that it is high time to repel his brutish advances, he goes off vowing vengeance like Dick Dastard in "Tied to the Railroad Track: a drama." There is no need for this even in plot terms; he could have had his vengeance without ever calling it that.

Her Mr. Right fails more by omission. Outside of a "classic back" and a walk that demands nothing (I had trouble picturing this), he is hard to get a handle on. His fits of petulance are less masterful than they are presumably intended to be, and indeed verge uncomfortably toward the cad's childishness. The only explanation, outside of late-blooming sex, for the man's fitful hold on Isabel is that he reminds her of her father —but this is a tactic of despair. *Someone* had better remind her of her father around here, or she'll boil over and fling herself into his grave.

Fortunately the men take up very little space and are perhaps about what you'd expect on the first day out of the convent when everybody you meet seems a little more significant than he ever will again. In fact, Gordon seems less sure with her own generation in general. Isabel's two women friends, though adequate, are respectively too pale like her hero and too narrowly drawn like her villain. But she makes up for this triumphantly with the people Isabel really would know well: old people, who replicate her father, in that they're dying and helpless, and teeming with strategy.

She takes a job with the swinish social worker, which entails visiting these people and checking on their nursing care. Now at last she can use her eleven years of wisdom. The Christian proposition is that you must love the unlovable, or it doesn't count. Anyone can love the lovable, it is like sending money to the rich; but Christ has located himself like a Hans Andersen prince in the sick, the poor, and the ugly, the people who actually need it, and who have a million ways of warding it off.

Mary Gordon's gallery of addled old people is funny, exact, various: her intense, humorous prose, which gets her over some thin ice with the other characters, here finds its subject and seems magically to become more mature and sure of itself, as if the author became older around old people. Having sacrificed her youth once, Isabel seems anxious to get on with her own old age, and her concept of sacrifice oddly includes getting fat, slatternly, and helpless. Yet for all her introspection, she sees this as duty, not as a contagious disease like leprosy.

That senility is catching might be called an accidental theme, strong but not quite the point. Nor is the book precisely about Isabel's scruples, encyclopedic though these be. It is more about such matters as the *arrogance* of loving the unlovable, and the resourcefulness of the latter in breaking their saviors: hence the hard-faced nurse and the wily invalid, the survivors of the nursing home wars; hence their victims.

Worse yet, Isabel discovers that loving the unlovable is largely a charade one plays for one's own benefit: because for all her quivering sensibility she doesn't seem to be helping them in the least. The happy ones would be happy anywhere, she decides, while the mean ones would still be trapped in their meanness. "People were happy, people were unhappy, for reasons no one could see, no one could do much about." And what one could do was so random and intellectually unplannable. She shows an old man her breasts on request and bureaucratically facilitates the death of an old woman—not the things she was raised to do, but the things that need doing. Charity is small and tactical and has nothing whatever to do with any conceivable government program she is supposed to be working on. It is, as she always thought, one person sacrificing everything to give just a tiny bit to another, with the only reward being the cold comfort of being thought "good."

With her father's cranky absolutism (he is a jealous god), she finally rejects even this reward as a stain on Charity and moves in with an old woman who hates her and who gobbles love without tasting it like a tapeworm, the *reductio ad absurdam* of her father. Margaret Casey used in fact to be her father's housekeeper and had wanted in a dim, crafty way to marry the old man, and Isabel had gotten her fired years ago. So our heroine can be punished for this now too. Miss Casey even does Isabel the kindness of bad-mouthing her so that nobody can observe her by now spot-free sacrifice. Her humiliation is as thorough as anything in *The Story of O*.

Yet sacrifice for its own sake is idolatry, and she cannot enjoy even that, like a good pagan, for long. Her father, her justification, is dead: she cannot see his face anymore. Which means that this is not religious abnegation and transcendence, but vulgar masochism, something the old man would have despised. A nun without a God is a fool. Isabel comes to see this by way of an interior monologue—and as anyone knows who had tried it, it is terribly difficult to show a convincing change of heart in this form. In Gordon's case, it might be a little more convincing with a little less talk. Because the novel has been so sturdily set up that it doesn't need captions. Isabel's doddering pastor, Father Mulcahy, indicates that such super-Christianity is wrong, and a boozy shake of the head from him is quite enough.

In the end, Isabel seems to accept the regular world of loving the lovables, who will certainly give her as much chance to sacrifice and suffer as all the old people put together. But she still carries her strange, pseudo-nun's equipment with her. For instance, she cannot understand property, or why people should be collectors; she has no patience with nature, a quirk common to those who have once seen nature as a mere shadow of God. Even with her girlfriends, she is happiest talking of schooldays when they were all Catholics together. When that narcotic is used up, she will be as hard on them as she is on herself, a pain and a comfort like religion itself. In any plausible sequel one pictures her at permanently perplexed odds with the secular world, still going about her father's business.

It is entirely appropriate that *Final Payments* should be written in a comic mode. "She was performing her Catholic high school girl trick of comedy instead of intimacy," Isabel says of a friend. And this is the convention Isabel herself must work with, where danger is marked by jokes, and it is no accident that her model is Austen, the patron writer of the cloistered. The Austen method which seems so cool is not that far removed from eighteenth-century bullying: it will sacrifice anyone for a laugh. And the convent and the Catholic family need a laugh too. Thus, if Isabel's ultra-monster, Margaret Casey, seems a bit too horrible, too infallibly horrible, to swallow, it is partly because of Isabel's burning attention and need for a joke.

The heroine's chaste bitchiness adds a little something to each miserable character until we have a comedy: as Austen made comedy of the puddingy gentry of western England. And when the characters flag, Gordon takes over herself, like Austen, and *makes* them funny. "Never once in those years did I wake up of my own accord. It was Margaret, always, knocking on my door like some rodent trapped behind a wall." "Father Mulcahy was clean as a piglet bathed in milk. His black hat was brushed as smooth as the skin of a fruit; his white hair, so thin that the hard, pink skull showed beneath it like a flagstone floor, looked as though the color had been taken out of it purposefully through a series of savage washings." The cadences are grave, unfacetious: a tragedy could be written in such prose. It is as if the jokes are being paid for even as they're being made. Even at her most carefree, when she has one of her old ladies cheerily piping, "blow it out your ass," Gordon's effect is reverberantly sad.

These are the conditions Mary Gordon has set herself—that the story must be sad, the telling funny—and they appear quite inevitable. This was the style of the sardonic priest and the wry nun of the period, the ones who hid their feelings because they were so tumultuous. If God really has died as a presence to many Christians in this century, even as a grouchy demanding presence, this still seems like the best way to talk about it.

1978

15 / *Chicago on My Mind*

Last year's political conventions may have left some of the customers snoring and scratching like bums at an all-night movie, but not this citizen. At the time of the conventions I came across some pictures of myself, and they reminded me of Chicago in 1968. Now *that* was an exciting convention for you, and by the grace of God I hope never to see another one. Like an Army veteran, I swore then that if I got out of that one I would never be bored again: not by John Glenn, not by Walter Cronkite, not by anybody.

Because Chicago 1968 taught one how close any civilized country is to berserkness at all times; also how terrorism, even silly terrorism, strengthens the cops more than anyone. Yet already this European-style history lesson has been watered down by consensus into something crazy we did in the sixties, just as we "did" McCarthyism in the fifties. As if a nation changes its nature completely every ten years; as if social forces were as evanescent as hula hoops and skateboards, instead of as remorseless as glaciers.

This tendency to overwhelm history with attention and then forget it could be the death of us yet. So with this in mind, I decided to relive that week as one fringe observer: starting with those pictures where I fatuously posed in front of Chicago, as a tourist might pose with Vesuvius or Waterloo.

Embarrassed isn't exactly the word for the way I felt about the picture-taking, and bored doesn't quite make it either. It's always nice to have your picture taken by *Time:* since it usually means, by chivalric convention, that your book won't be panned. And even while your world is collapsing, life must go on.

So this photographer named Callahan came round to my hotel. Sheepish and apologetic are not quite the words for *him:* just doing his job, hustling his own fish in Armageddon. After a few absentminded snaps, in which somehow neither of us seemed to be present, we agreed to try to link our little story with the big one outside. I was to wander around Lincoln Park engaging Yippies in conversation, while Callahan shot pictures of Sheed the political activist.

But that year the peaceniks were my brothers and I simply couldn't talk to them just to promote a novel. So I settled instead for standing next to them awkwardly, jaw set, pretending to listen to something. The results, I gather, did much to drive Callahan out of photography for good. But one of his less gruesome specimens appeared in *Time* and my book sold, oh, 10,000 copies instead of nine-five—maybe a hundred dollars into my pocket from that strange day.

Make no mistake, our world had collapsed in Chicago of '68. Our peace candidate, for whom we'd screamed ourselves hoarse all year, had caved in without a struggle, and the war party had mounted in his place a china doll with dyed hair and the voice of a manic spinster. And as if that wasn't enough, our host, Mayor Daley, had decided to rub our noses in it all the way, by administering a delicate lesson in real power. For a week, his cops appeared to have carte blanche to manhandle any peace-lover they could get their trotters on. Great for department morale, no doubt; the boys went hog-wild and had a fine time of it. And we learned our lesson.

Because even then, reports were coming in from the rest of the country that *we* were causing the trouble; and later, of course, we were accused of causing Richard Nixon. All that and nightsticks too. His Honor knew his business very well. "Power comes from the barrel of a gun," one of our flakier spokesmen had said earlier, and the mayor concurred heartily. Why not? He knew where the guns were.

Yet for all that and the rueful years that followed, that week was one of the most exhilarating of my life; and veterans of it still greet each other as if they'd fought for King Harry on St. Crispin's day. Which may be why, incidentally, Callahan and I became friends eight years later in a diametrically different context—and started talking about Chicago and doing this piece.

At this point, it is necessary to backtrack a little, because Chicago was a long time in the making and it affected you in direct proportion to your own investment. My own was averagely large. As a born Englishman, I have a special angle on colonial wars (friends of mine had sweated out Malaya and Cyprus) and I was against Vietnam from roughly the first adviser on. But in the early days, the matter could still be hashed out over pipe smoke and among gentlemen. Perhaps it wasn't until LBJ described Barry Goldwater as the kind of bloodthirsty nut who would do what Johnson himself later did that the peace movement caught fire.

Once it did, the fire had no trouble keeping itself going. Every now and then, Johnson would obligingly throw another outrage on it. An escalation here, a bombing there. But by then we had each other and didn't need Johnson. After you've sung "Where Have All the Flowers Gone" and "I Ain't A Marchin' Anymore" in an open truck on a cold day, you're hooked; though of course we did march anymore, and more and more and more. And each time we drew closer to each other, the teachers and parents and kids in their Sunday best (so they wouldn't feed the Yippie image). If that closeness was scattered by tear gas and Mace in Chicago, it also reached a sort of culmination there, a death which gave a little life—at least for four more years: that's the longest lease this country allows on anything, even resurrections.

Gene McCarthy was, I suppose, a funny sort of saint to take over this brush-fire religion of peace in 1968, but at the time he seemed to suit us miraculously. Let me say quickly that I don't know if he could have done more for us politically than he did, because I don't know what happened in the top floors of Chicago, and nobody else does either, at least for attribution. But he treated us to a hell of a time on the road there. His wit sweetened the temper of the peace party and simultaneously rescued it from the Yippie humor-of-menace-and-madness. By an irony, his gentle followers were finally punished for the whacked-out rhetoric of Rubin and Hoffman, and a Marxist might argue that McCarthy had softened them up for a beating. But Chicago would have been infinitely worse without McCarthy's civility. The cops were fairly begging for a violent response to justify the blood on their nightsticks and to make an ass of the peace movement. But the ironic candidate, whose hotel room sardonically overlooked the protestors in Grant Park, fortified his people just enough for them to keep their own crazies in line: the week's most effective police action.

A thousand different roads led us to Chicago and shaped our experience there as if by our own private tailors. But one thing many of us, I think, carried through this phantasmagoria was a fear of our own side. Whether it was Abbie Hoffman levitating the Pentagon (could the Pentagon take a joke?) or those attempts to splash the Justice Department with paint, we could never set out on a march without worrying about our fruitcakes that day; and we could never watch the news afterwards without wondering how much of the camera they had managed to hog. Although the rest of us were performing prodigies of respectability, there they always were capering like loons and coaxing hatred out of the public. I'm glad that Jerry Rubin tells us he has since grown up, but he can do his apologizing to someone outside the peace movement; those who took the cause seriously and suffered for it would probably prefer he took his little book and did one of his old tricks with it.

Anyway that was the tension that gave Mayor Daley his opening in July 1968. The Yippies were promising all kinds of revolutionary wonders in Chicago, and the old bulldog spat on his paws and waited. To an old pro, they were pussycats. And the serious members of the movement could do nothing about them. Whenever a Leftist group tries to purge itself, a chortle goes up on the Right. As the Women's Movement well knows, if any two spokespersons disagree, it is taken as a sign of their basic frivolity. Therefore, grimly, we hung together. ("You have to coalesce with *someone,*" as Dave Dellinger said, explaining his association with the Chicago Seven.)

This then was the army that marched on Chicago: half a million, boasted the crazies, giving Mayor Daley an excuse to polish his tanks; more like 5,000 in fact, but the mixture still inflammable, and the tanks rolled anyway for our *opera bouffe* confrontation.

The vague figure in Callahan's pictures did not, as I recall, know the numbers yet, though the naked eye told plenty. The peaceniks sleeping in Lincoln Park the first night could not have marched on an old people's home. But the cops blind-sided them anyway, leaving their calling cards. It seems the kids had been denied a permit to sleep in the park, and the Mayor or whoever used the piffling opportunity to beat them at their own game: if they could create media events out of nothing, so could he. Let the public see the urchins get their lumps. Who was to know in those rags whether it was a Weatherman or a seminarian being belted?

The game was on. The pre-emptive first strike had gone to Daley before the convention had even started. Had I been a hawk I would have admired him. These kids had been playing at power and it had piqued his professional pride. The question now was whether the other side had enough savvy to salvage anything at all from the situation.

That was one battleground, the trenches, and we'll return to it in a moment. But meanwhile the next rung of amateurs, the Eugene's cabaret brigade, were fighting their own war. We had been brought to Chicago to do good in a vague sort of way, which turned out mostly to mean winning delegates' hearts and minds at parties. If we actually talked any of them around, I must have missed it. All the ones I met were already firmly pro-Gene. And anyway most liberals are congenitally shy and ill at ease with people unlike themselves and we wound up talking to Betty Friedan instead.

In my own case, my active service was limited to writing a speech for the actor Patrick O'Neal. That, I felt, was pretty darn gallant. The appointed speechwriter had passed out drunk or hysterical and I got a call at 2 A.M., at which time I was in much the same state as the speechwriter, and was asked to cook something up by 9. Two pots of coffee later, I'd done it somehow, and O'Neal read it splendidly. I had no idea how much an actor can do for a speech. Stuff that had people yawning and scratching when I read it myself got all kinds of laughter and applause that day. But again the audience was solidly in line for McCarthy already. And there weren't enough of them. Counting the house that day, I realized for the first time the size and certainty of our defeat.

The rest of the story was in the streets, which were heating up unbearably while our little tea party was going on. Press credentials alone entitled you to two beatings a day (I exaggerate slightly), with the result that suddenly I was able to obtain these precious items with ease. One day I was a *Newsweek* photographer, the next a *Life* editor. Festooned in these insignia, I was pushed by cops every time I stopped for a cab; once I was ordered off the street completely with the genial Brock Brower, who really was from *Life.* Brock and I were miles from any conceivable action, but three busloads of fuzz pulled up anyway and I was propelled a full block backwards by shoves in the chest.

It is this random, senseless quality that rattles one in police states, even make-believe ones. At noonday, you might see a couple of glowering cops prowling through a crowded square with their guns out; or you might be sitting later in the Hilton and hear an almighty crash, as a bunch of kids were hurled against a plate-glass window. The lobby already reeked of vomit, from a stink bomb planted by one of our crazies, and one felt one's senses gradually dissolving in the chaos.

My most vivid recollection is of an alternate delegate being dragged on her stomach out of that hotel screaming for help. I was standing at the door with an old friend, a liberal editor rendered slightly pompous by fatigue and booze (conventions overflow with both), and the odd thing is that he didn't notice the incident. It seemed they wouldn't let him in without his room key and he was exercising his American right to enter his own hotel. So the girl went screaming past with her four pallbearers, one at each extremity, and my wife and I rushed behind her to the squad car bleating for explanations.

"This is police business," said one of the goons, slamming the car door on us. He wore no identification badge. They were out of fashion that week. When we got back, our friend was still arguing about his room key.

A fraction of this frenzy lapped into the hall itself, and viewers will recall the hilarious arrests of John Chancellor and Mike Wallace, and the twisted face of Mayor Daley as he shouted curses at Abe Ribicoff. In fact, the hall was splendidly isolated, and no significant number of protesters could have got within a mile of it, but it suited His Honor to seem embattled. (Later, of course, he denied even knowing those words, but a poll of lip-readers was unanimous on the point.)

To compound the confusion, there was a taxi strike going on (which we naturally blamed on Daley) so there was a frantic scramble for the few that were running, and one always seemed to be in the wrong part of town. Hence the convention began to seem like one big rumor, and its apologists later used this. "Did you actually *see* police brutality?" they would say. Never mind. Wherever one was, one saw enough.

And you didn't need a taxi to see the troopers in gas masks lined up like spacemen between the kids in Grant Park and the pol-packed Hilton. An American street gleaming with bayonets is a sobering sight. But it was slightly reassuring to see that when the troops took off their masks they were only kids themselves, no older than their opponents. For a moment it looked as if they'd been sent to save us from the cops.

This fact indirectly occasioned one of the minor heartbreaks of that week. Phil Ochs, the folk singer, addressed the soldiers, and he did so most movingly. He told them that since they seemed to be the same generation as the peaceniks, perhaps they had more in common with us than with their masters. He added that of course they couldn't drop their guns right now and come over, but maybe they could think about it. To judge from their troubled faces, they were already doing just that.

At which point, a leading Yippie pounced up, complete with a bandage round his head and all the panache of a stage revolutionary, to drive it home. "Yeah, come on over. And bring your guns, coz you're going to need them. We're going to have 300 Chicagos." As if one wasn't enough; as if, in his sense, we even had one. This little beggar's army of his was not free even to cross the street. Yet he talked as if he'd just stormed the Bastille.

The troops stiffened, and soon had their masks back on, the masks of war, and we settled down for a grim vigil enlivened by tear gas and Mace. I guess we'd have got that anyway, but it might have seemed friendlier if Ochs had had the last word. (For the curious: Phil Ochs hanged himself this year, after an unshakable siege of melancholy, and the Yippie leader has found peace with a guru.)

Anyway, in Grant Park I hunkered down that night with my colleagues the peaceniks on a carpet of tear gas. The moment I crossed their front line, I was jerked off my feet and told to stop kicking the newspapers that lined the grass, because it stirred up the stuff and sent people wheezing home. My hosts were kind but firm. When one of their number went bananas and tried to rush the troops they quieted him as slickly as MPs. "We'll handle this," they said when someone tried to intervene and reason with the kid. A cop is a cop.

Even dormant tear gas gets to you, and in no time my whole face began to run. Your eyes burn and water simultaneously and if you're me you are wracked with sneezes. All this helps to keep your attention. Periodically the troops would lunge at us, ostensibly to get us back from the sidewalk, and more shit would be kicked up in our faces. Our marshals became masters of the orderly fall-back. We hung in there.

At some point we saw a vision: an enormous bishop in gleaming white robes bearing what memory insists on as a loaf of Wonderbread. This he proceeded to consecrate and distribute as Communion to anyone who felt like it. There was nothing pushy about him: he didn't want anyone to eat against their conscience. But it seemed theologically okay to accept Communion from an Apparition, and everyone in the area did, atheist and believer alike. Later, we found out that he was a real bishop of the Anglican persuasion, exiled from South Africa because of Apartheid and I could see why: the gummy magic bread tasted great after tear gas, and morale soared in our bunker.

That was just one night, and more than enough for me, but the others sat out all four without cracking. One afternoon Gene McCarthy came down to address them, but one could already sense the disaffection: they weren't doing it for him anymore. He had let them down, though they didn't know the details yet.

It was sad. I love McCarthy and felt that he had done more for us than we had any right to expect. But that was bitter stuff in the grass, and they were in no mood for a gentle speech from the professor.

We had all changed about as much as nature will allow in less than a week. We had arrived with the high spirits of summer still on us. It was still pretty much of a lark. I remember standing at the airport waiting for McCarthy's arrival like a kid watching a parade. I sneaked a look at Norman Mailer's notebook to see if I could learn the master's secret. "Abigail McCarthy, gracious lady," I think he had written. Oh well.

The mayor or whoever saw to it that we didn't leave town laughing. On the last night, the cops busted into one of McCarthy's rooms, on the pretext that bags of excrement were dropping from there, and roughed up the kids for the last time. Arguments ensued as to whether there was excrement at all and if so whether it could have come at that angle and finally how anyone could be certain. These were still raging as we left town. By then we knew the cops and we knew the kids, and we didn't have time to argue.

On the plane, a Humphreyite sunnily asked for our support. This seemed incredible—although many of us did warily drag our tails into that camp by November. The man got mad and called us sore losers. He had no idea what we'd been doing. Maybe nobody did. Maybe the peace movement had been talking to itself all along.

Be that as it may, the peace movement grew in strength and seriousness after Chicago. A Catholic like Daley ought to know what happens when you go around making martyrs, even bogus ones like Rubin and Hoffman. What we did with the strength—and what it did to poor Mr. Nixon's mental balance—is a story for another time. The legacy of

Chicago is wondrously good and almost fatally bad, and it is still with us like the gas on the grass.

Among the tangible effects was a radical shift in the balance between backroom and primary, so that we would never again find ourselves voting for a candidate like McCarthy only to have him brutally snubbed at the convention. At the same time domestic surveillance took a great leap forward, pushing us along the road to Watergate. Left and Right altered their judo holds slightly; as with most sports, offense and defense were making each other more sophisticated. Police slipped off the streets to turn up in people's offices, or as decoys in peace groups. The kids learned conventional politics and became conventional themselves. And on and on.

One curious fact about that week was that the blacks sat the whole thing out—a rare self-denial in the sixties. Indeed, they seemed rather amused by it. "Now you know what it feels like to be a nigger *all* the time," they said. A useful lesson in the twentieth century. A specially useful lesson as we celebrate our 200th recovery of innocence.

1973

16 / NORMAN MAILER: *Miami and the Siege of Chicago*

When the Reviewer (me) saw the Reporter (Norman Mailer's new title) in Chicago, the Reporter was wearing his glasses. Was he afraid of getting hit, with that real fear that only a brave man understands? Or was he afraid of hitting someone else and unleashing the old rage, the devil's private stomach music? He said he was looking for a television set to watch the convention on, so maybe that was it.

The above contains most of the items for a stock Mailer parody: the tendency to make too much of small things, the preposterous Fieldsian slyness, the haymaking metaphors, the damn whimsy. The latter is perhaps the best gauge to a given performance. When this formidable author goes barreling to defeat it is nearly always from trying to be funny: the one gift the gods have denied him, the one that he cannot take his mind off. Two movies, a play, and a thousand windy press conferences have suffered while Norman wrestled the old whore, Wit. So the first good thing to report about his excellent account of the conventions, printed in tandem in *Miami and the Siege of Chicago,* is that it contains less joshing, growling, and nudging than we've had in some time, and more sharp, rectilinear thinking from the old Harvard engineering major.

The glasses reappear on the dust jacket, along with a suit and a no-nonsense expression (no more boxing gloves and boozy leers), all combining to suggest a very slight tilt to the Right, which makes several ambivalent appearances in the text. Respectability would be a new Last Frontier for this author, and it seems to tempt him like sin. Although he pays his compliments to the young people and the New Politics, his imagination is really grabbed by the vestiges of the old America: the God-bless-our-land world of small-town Republicans and the jaunty turn-of-the-century corruption of unreformed Democrats.

This gives to his reporting the schizophrenia he claims to find in the nation at large. In Miami, there was not much for an outsider to do, the politics being conducted in private, except sneer at the yokels. But Mailer's sympathies are wayward and unpredictable. Since he visualizes everyone as either a possible acolyte or as someone he may have to fight on the way out, he looks closely before he sneers. And, running against the grain of his opinions, comes an unmistakable fascination with Mr. Nixon's forgotten Americans; and then, contrariwise, the line that it took a brave man to write, whatever else you may think of it: "He [the Reporter] was getting tired of Negroes and their rights."

The Miami essay is finally disappointing. Partly because of the flatness of the occasion, which no amount of nostalgia can really glamorize, and partly because the author could not, in those flaccid surroundings, track down this new split in his own consciousness. He thrashes around the Nixon question interminably, failing for once to land a good simile. In his new the-romance-of-mediocrity frame of mind, he rather likes Nixon; but remembering that he doesn't really, he strains for some subtle formula that will patch things over. (Nixon was, of course, working on this split in all of us.) Mailer's Reagan is hardly more successful: a sales manager, "an actor pretending to be governor"—weak stuff, by Mailer's standards. And of Agnew's first lowings, he writes, "he was reasonable on television . . . soft-spoken and alert." Rockefeller the alleged liberal is Mailer's sharpest cartoon; until, that is, we get to McCarthy and Humphrey in Chicago.

This was a stage where schizophrenia could really strut. The city itself excited Mailer and unleashed in him the child-observer, resident in every great descriptive novelist. He sets the scene sensually like Dickens: the smell of the stockyards, the echo of slaughtered animals, even (sure mark of the child-observer), the size of people's nostrils. At once his vignettes have imperial authority. "Some (Daley supporters) had eyes like drills; others, noses like plows; jaws like amputated knees." McCarthy's face was "hard as the cold stone floor of a monastery at five in the morning." As for Humphrey—such a psychophysical biopsy has not been performed since Dickens went to work on Pecksniff. And again the authority is unarguable. When a child says, "I don't like that man, he smells of soap," we know he's on to something.

In Chicago, the psyche had richer options to split on than Nixon's small shopkeepers and the Reverend Ralph Abernathy. Mailer had his cops to play with now—childhood totems whom most of us hadn't trembled over since grade school, but over whom we trembled plenty that week; Mafiosi real and fancied (Mailer sees them everywhere, and who's to say he's wrong?); screaming Yippies, in as many species as the angelic choirs; peace children of saintly discipline; roving bands of celebrities; snipers, wiretappers, and stink-bomb goons—enough to bring any novelist out in fever blisters. But Mailer rides herd on the scene beautifully—if too briefly.

The McCarthyites looked rather gray in the middle of this psychotic fiesta, and Mailer quickly gives them the back of his cuff. His description of McCarthy's arrival at Midway Airport is as flat as one of his Miami pieces. The people standing around, he complains, all have thin heads and thin nostrils—true enough, since he happened to be standing next to me part of the time in the press section, and I boast the thinnest nostrils in the West, but hardly the last word on McCarthy supporters. He goes on to describe a lady singer there as a typical McCarthy performer, which is not only untrue (none of us had ever seen the like) but depends for its point on leaving out Peter and Mary (Paul was sick), who were also there, not to mention Phil Ochs, Tom Paxton, and others, who had been singing for McCarthy all summer but did not have the requisite thin nostrils.

Yet novelistically, Mailer was not wrong. The war between old and young involved more primal forces, and those McCarthyites who took part in it had to march alongside political strangers and get caught up in violence that they neither initiated nor deserved. There were rather more of them in the protest action than Mailer indicates—his version comes perilously close to justifying the cops: the peaceful kids usually far outnumbered the agitators—and they were more passionate than his trite Tarzan-meets-the-egghead description suggests. Yet in the national psyche, they were the second bananas. Long hair versus short, Rudd vs. Kirk, anarchy vs. fascism, a craving for chaos and a dread of it, this was the American dream as served up in Chicago.

It is no coincidence that this matched precisely the split in Mailer's own consciousness. Mailer does not have to try to keep up with the times; he cannot help it. His early warning system, which he refers to as fear, is in fact an incredibly delicate power-gauge. In a large mixed congress of people, it flutters violently. Is there any future in this group? Can I safely march with that one?—fears that seem trifling, unless we realize that he is really checking out the accuracy of his instrument, of his responsiveness to America, which is the source of his talent.

In the end, he decides to march with the rebels, because they have courage and possibly stamina, and because he feels partly responsible for them. But he leaves his own questions unanswered, to wit, "his reluctance to lose even the America he had had . . . it had allowed him to write—it had even not deprived him entirely of honors, certainly not of an income . . . a profound part of him detested the thought of seeing his American Society—evil, absurd, touching, pathetic, sickening, comic, full of novelistic marrow—disappear now in the nihilistic maw of a national disaster." The split is still wide open.

Some readers will see all this as the inevitable stiffening of the successful middle-aged writer, combined with an attempt to hang on to his young followers: or at best a parent trying to keep in touch with his difficult children. But the point about Mailer is that he has taken the chance of opening himself to middle-class, middle-aged feelings. He was out there by himself, without his name or his reputation or last year's ideas to help, feeling what was there to be felt, willing to make himself a blood offering to the New Left or anyone else, in order to bring back the evidence.

His method is simply to stuff as much of America into his ego as will fit and then to examine the ego closely. And if you think that all that can lead to is more Mailer, you're at least half wrong. The ego is not always what it seems. The man is a born impersonator.

1968

17/ *Miami: 1972*

MIAMI BEACH, Fla.—For days the writers circled like buzzards waiting for one small rabbit to die. There just wasn't going to be enough convention to go around. "How about doing a story about the *writers* at the convention?" said the first five writers I met. The search for angles was as grim as anything in nature. Norman Mailer announced he was doing his piece in three days, presumably underwater—so that was one angle gone. Jerry Rubin and Abbie Hoffman trapped Theodore White in the lobby of the Fontainebleau (I believe they thought he was I. F. Stone) and tried to wring his secrets from him. "Do what I do," snapped White. "Make it up."

By the second day the writers were telling each other that this was the dullest convention they'd ever attended. Nothing novel about that; it's quite correct to be bored at conventions. In this case it meant that the new young delegates weren't nearly as much fun as the old warlords: they were earnest and righteous, and there was no way you could get them drunk. In fact, all that was left of the dirty old days were the writers themselves. The buzzards eyed one another narrowly: "Why don't you go home and leave this to me?"

Actually, it was a fascinating convention, but not in the usual sense.

Abbie Hoffman said it looked like an early SDS rally, and so it did in spots. But the young delegates were not going to be cheated out of a dull convention. The kids and women and blacks were fascinated with their new toy, parliamentary procedure, and so the world's freshest delegates produced the world's ploddingest politics. "It's just like a law court," my thirteen-year-old daughter said approvingly. At that particular moment the rules committee was taking a vote on whether to vote on whether to vote, and someone was objecting to the whole schlemozzle. A generation raised on *Perry Mason* had arrived and was wallowing in stuffiness.

Likewise on the floor itself, now that youth was present, the carnival flavor was all but gone. No funny hats or snake dances for this crowd, no "Kiss me, I'm a Democrat." America had come of age. "We shall overcome" was still okay, but "The monkey wrapped his tail around the flagpole" was definitely out.

Still, it *was* fascinating, in its dull way, especially for those of us who had felt the policemen's cattle prods in Chicago, 1968. As a tale of cold-blooded vengeance, it was worthy at least of a Sam Peckinpah movie. The villains of '68 were cornered and gunned down one by one. Some, like Mayor Daley, went down snarling. Others, the Larry O'Briens, recanted and promised to reform, but they were gunned down anyway. Old pros muttered about ruthlessness. The Toby Jugs with the cigars who had smirked at us in Chicago ("Grow up, kid") saw with frozen horror how well their advice had been taken. The question of the week was whether the party could stand such a bloodletting. An academic question, of course. You can't deny a revolutionary his purge.

The real story, it seemed, had taken place four years ago and had been covered by no writers at all. The McGovern committee had calmly sat down and redesigned the Democratic party, while the men laughingly called pros had dozed their long off-year's nap. The breathtaking incompetence of the pros followed them right into the convention hall. Hubert Humphrey looked at the delegations with wild surmise: the Californians, who resembled a United Nations Christmas card; New York, which might have been a class at the New School; and New Jersey, a crowd of Republican-type commuters waiting for a bus. Was this what had hit him? A cardiogram would probably have shown that the fight went out of him then and there. Only the grim, flinty labor faces from states like Indiana, Ohio, and Pennsylvania kept him company in that bright, steaming barn.

Confronted with this, the pols began feverishly to praise the wonderful diversity of the convention—what other party would let such riffraff in? Larry O'Brien welcomed the women and children as if he'd invited them himself, reminding one somehow of W. C. Fields patting Baby Le Roy on the head with a rolled newspaper containing a brick. With sour irony, the pros grabbed every chance they could find to throw McGovern's rules back at him, challenging his own apparent breach of them in California, but this merely confirmed the new rules, the new party, and it didn't even save them California.

From the first it was clear that the McGovern rules could lead only to a McGovern candidacy because he alone understood them. Even the press could not sustain the suspense for long. The rumor mill in the Fontainebleau insisted that Humphrey and Muskie were meeting upstairs to settle George's hash and even told us what they were saying. But then Humphrey and Muskie marched out of the same room and said they hadn't been meeting at all—it was like two kids caught smoking. So much for the stop-McGovern movement. Now George was in the awkward position of having no one to compromise with. If he compromised anyway, it would be from no visible pressure—unless you call Scoop Jackson visible pressure. The question, the only question for the last two or three days, was how was George using his freedom? In a temporarily open sea, would he tack to the left or to the right?

The sea wasn't really open; it only seemed that way. A word here about the triviality of history. The salamilike shape of Miami Beach stretches the hotels that housed the delegates along the longest possible line, and it was quite possible not to meet an enemy the whole time you were there. It took a long hike in a boiling sun or at least a glum taxi creep to get from the New York delegation to, say, Scoop Jackson's sarcophagus. And it was tempting to stay close to one's own pool and one's own kind. Another city and another weather forecast might have produced a different convention.

As it was, McGovern's enemies seemed somewhat unreal to his friends. To the right, there were phantom labor leaders munching on dead cigars (with George Meany owning the cartoon rights) and, to the left, the scrawny crowd at Flamingo Park—zapped-out stand-ins for the peace movement, yip-hip-zippies who could have been hired by central casting. When they marched on Senator McGovern, they conveyed just enough empty menace to make him look like quite a fellow for confronting them and to show the TV audience what dragons he had to appease on his left. But there was no real indication of what waits for him outside the dingy wonderland of Miami Beach. The state of the nation has to be guessed.

My old friends from the class of '68, two generations back as the New Politics go, seemed to feel that a slight collapse to the center would help, nationally speaking. Chicago had left them with a healthy, perhaps too healthy, respect for the power of the old bosses. They couldn't really be dead so soon, could they? "Tricks, we won by tricks," said Joe Duffey of Connecticut. "Next time *they'll* know the tricks." Duffey once sneaked a nomination himself (for the Senate in '70) and lost an election, and he knows how different the two arts are. You can pay dearly for pulling a boss's nose when you show up in his district.

That was one school of thought, very big everywhere except in the McGovern delegations. People who had limped out of Chicago more dead than alive were suddenly recommending that we try to save Mayor Daley's face and all the lesser faces that run our rundown cities—all of whom would have made invaluable allies from a '68 point of view and reputedly are still able to get the dead to vote twice, even if they can't get the kids.

Flag a passing McGovernite and you heard a different tale. The bosses couldn't get out the vote in the primaries, so why go crawling to them now? "Suppose Daley withdraws his support, and we take Illinois anyway, where does that leave the bum?" One more question: Are you drunk with power, sir? Maybe, the answer went, but a new party is a new party. If we load it up with old bosses, what have we changed? And if "boss" was a dirty word in '68, what has happened since then to clean it? If they're nicer to us now, it's only because they need us. And we have our own people to reward. Meanwhile, picture King Lear in a Humphrey button, wandering the lobbies while his children are dividing the kingdom.

More prosaically, there was some question of whether the McGovern high command controlled the delegates through too many compromises on personalities. When the famous McGovern boiler room sent up word to support a compromise plan on the Illinois delegation (one-half vote to each of Daley's people and one-half to each of the challengers), the delegates would have none of it. In fact, their greatest outbursts of stubbornness were not on issues, on which they showed a most unyouthlike willingness to compromise, but precisely on personalities: the "get

Daley" issue, the vice presidential nomination, the unseating of Chairman O'Brien.

The vice presidential mini-mutiny (Eagleton got more votes from Alabama Wallaceites than from some McGovern sectors) was a break for George, because it gave him a line for his acceptance speech about how he had not really controlled the convention at all. From all accounts, he and his boys controlled the hell out of it. A New Jersey delegate told me that they had telephone instructions on everything but how to brush their teeth. And although too many people were chasing too few phones, the system worked so smoothly that in the case of the South Carolina challenge they were able to manipulate the vote up and down until Ohio, the chief enemy, fell on its fanny.

How clever is too clever? The McGovernites have spent their lives, even as you and I, hearing about liberal losers and radical bumblers, and they could hardly be blamed for trying their hands at ruthless efficiency. As a radical bumbler of long standing myself, I was sorry to see them doing all the shabby things necessary to win—the sellout of the women in South Carolina, the apparent deal with the Wallaceites over the Alabama challenge—but I guessed they *were* necessary, and I didn't want to see the smirk on the Toby Jugs again. But occasionally the McGovern people seemed to overmanage just for the fun of it. On the abortion issue, I was told, the first signal was palms down, or "vote your conscience," but the second was thumbs down, or better forget your conscience for now. To have control of such a machine is intoxicating, and rumor has it that different boilermakers took a turn at it—Pierre Salinger over Vietnam, Rick Stearns or someone else over abortion. The very minor revolt over the vice presidency was a low growl from the beast at the receiving end.

By the last day one was so conscious of the machine that the candidate himself had all but disappeared. He was, for most writers, unavailable, but a staffer told me that he had botched the black caucus, as usual (by now he must be so self-conscious about that particular communication problem as to be completely tongue-tied), and was out of favor with Mexican-Americans, who had learned that he didn't need them anymore. Several close supporters were quite lukewarm about him personally, but this is common among candidates' staffs: As you approach the presidency, no one seems worthy of it, since it wasn't designed for a human in the first place. The striking thing about this campaign is that the leader's personality doesn't seem to matter. When McGovern finally appeared on the platform, I felt that half the crowd was roaring for Gene and half for Bobby, and that the man who had finally dragged the flag to the top of the hill was incidental.

The hot gossip seemed to bypass McGovern and land squarely on his staff. Rumors of gorgeous power struggles gurgled through the turbid air. (The crowd seemed to have absorbed all the air conditioning, and I found myself attending any press conference that was held in a cool room. Hence I have invaluable scoops on John Gilligan and Mike Gravel.) A writer who'd been chasing Frank Mankiewicz onto elevators for four days said he thought he'd been chasing the wrong man—Gary Hart had grabbed the hot crown for the moment. Others said to watch Rick Stearns—McGovern's chief delegate counter—on the rail. These rumors are self-generating. It looks as if a flock of talented adventurers, every bit the equal of Jack Kennedy's, is on the wing, and there are bound to be stories about them.

In fact, there is a whole new era of gossip, which is one of the blessings of the two-party system. Politics is basically gossip anyway, and a convention is its World Series. The women, blacks, and youth quickly opened their own gossip branches. The women, of course, had the big names, and this was some of the stuff you heard. On the first night Betty Friedan told me that Gloria Steinem and Bella Abzug were giving up too much woman power in order to help McGovern—a shrewd prophecy, since McGovern's brain trust had ordained not only the defeat of the women's challenge in South Carolina but also the precise score, in order to save George's bacon in California. But on the second night we saw Bella tearing like a red-crested mongoose into Shirley MacLaine because *Shirley* had given up too much for George by helping to dump the abortion plank. So the lines were not that clear.

Ms. Steinem lost her preternatural cool on the same issue, calling the McGovernites "bastards" for their pains, and she later caught an edge of Mankiewicz's tongue that can't have sent her home happy. Mank had just finished announcing George's choice for v.p., and Gloria asked if she could hold a women's caucus on the subject. Frank said, "You can use this hall any time you like, Gloria, and you can do whatever you like in it. But not on my time." That's the kind of thing that men have been saying to women for years, and that has caused all the trouble.

Did the women feel sold out? That depends on which women you're talking about. They got Jean Westwood as party chairman [sic], a significant wedge into the party structure, and this may be all some of them expected this time around. As usual, one felt that all the deals had been made offstage and we were watching a laborious charade. But anyone who thinks of political woman as a monolith has met only one of them, and the only thing they all agree on is that they learned a lot from their freshman (freshperson?) hazing.

It seemed that every second time one passed an open door there was a woman inside saying, "What we've got to do next time. . . ." There was some furry tongue tangling over the right to be cochairpersons, a word that will never trip lightly off anyone's lips, and some fairly wild swipes, but the general tone was one of precision and parliamentary patience, learned in the PTA wars and elsewhere. (In fact, some women now get more political practice than men, and it shows.) Some hardliners will probably never be satisfied. On the last day I heard a group complaining about Gloria Steinem's make-up. "How can she ask us not to be sex objects when she wears eyeshadow?" From a quick squint around, I would say this was like Fat Jack Leonard and Eddie the Dwarf discussing Clark Gable's uppity mustache.

Every *first* door you passed there was a Negro saying, "What we've got to do next time. . . ." In my hotel the Alabama challenge delegation held closed meetings that you could hear two floors away, and feeling ran even higher. The black caucus, which McGovern failed to dominate, degenerated into a rumble over who would be the fairest black in the new administration. (This meeting, too, was closed, but Kenneth Gibson may well have been one of the rumblers, and you have to bet that Jesse Jackson was in there somewhere. Old Jesse liked to stir things along, while remaining a cool operator inside.) The most moving speech from the platform was by Willie Brown on the California challenge, when he demanded, "Give me back my delegation," and the most moving one off the platform was by Shirley Chisholm, asking for black delegates to come on over. White observers felt that she could have led a gospel-singing march on the hall then and there, but this could be a failure to understand black rhetoric and the real purpose of Ms. Chisholm's speech. She is both bright and passionate, which is more than could be said for any of the other candidates, but these gifts were being put to the service of a clumsy stop-McGovern move, plus a bad-tasting piece of self-promotion.

Anyone who feared that the new "quota" system would flood the place with mediocrities could be assured at first glance. Prigs there were aplenty, especially in the New York delegation. But the blacks, youth, and women all looked smarter than the old pols ever did, and they sure as heck paid more attention. Television does not convey the heat and glare through which they sat for eight hours at a stretch, nor the diet of dehydrated ham sandwiches and Pepsi-Cola on which they fed themselves. The floor is a dislocating place, the kind where you suddenly wonder where you are and how the devil you got there. The din is incessant and meaningless, and there is none of the tidy organization you see on the screen. Like-minded delegations may be so far apart that coordinated action seems a miracle.

Yet for all that, the floor work of the freshman McGovernites was at least relatively smooth. Several times they broke with the old American tradition of not listening to the speeches, and they rejoiced in the crazy schedule by which numerous important issues were settled after their elders' bedtime. (When Larry O'Brien woozily suggested adjourning "until 7 P.M. tomorrow morning," they shouted for him to continue.)

The other fear, voiced or whined by a South Carolinian, that white Protestant males are now a helpless minority, also seems exaggerated. The new delegates do not form a solid bloc. A black from Pennsylvania told me that Julian Bond was a pimp. And the women and children were bad-mouthing each other just as merrily. Beyond that, blacks, youth, and women are three totally different categories of human beings, and their popular front should spring the usual leaks shortly. A Negro spoke against the women of South Carolina, pointing out that blacks had done extremely well in that delegation—we've got ours, Jack. Then the women who *had* made the original S.C. delegation "proudly" cast all their votes against their challenging sisters—we've got ours, too.

Meanwhile other minorities were chaffering. The Chicano caucus, or rather jamboree, decided that the blacks were getting altogether too much attention and that maybe a little good Chicano action was called for. They failed to come up with anything special this time, but they've got four years to think of something truly spectacular. Meanwhile organized labor could split like a firework ("George Meany is just an embarrassment," said a machinist) instead of ticking like a soggy bomb. And where were the Italians? One wound up feeling that this convention was only a rehearsal for a real blowout, with party manners suspended, which might just occur in time to catch the Bicentennial festivities in 1976.

My daughter, who'll be eighteen in time to vote that year, wants to be an alternate delegate, and I can't see her behaving that quietly.

"Bring back Chicago," said a saucy newsman. "That was a real convention, boy." This certainly was a tea party in comparison. The deskman at our hotel feared the worst. "Too many hands have been tied in this town," he said ominously. But they were tied just right. When the yippies tried a skinny-dip in Flamingo Park, the cops just said, "We'll drain the pool, son." When they wanted to march on the hall, they were allowed to march until the hot smog shredded them. After all, Hoffman and Rubin were on the other side now, with a change of T-shirts every day, and there were more kids in the hall than out. This is McGovern's basic issue. He brought the dissenters in, and he got *them* to vote against the abortion plank and against the Gay Liberation plank and the $6,500 guaranteed income and all the stuff they'd been screaming for. If the old men had done it, the place would have been in flames.

Now that the convention has dispersed, McGovern is free to make whatever deals he feels necessary with the old guard, without fear of floor demonstrations and candle-lit marches. And my guess is he'll make plenty. But his issue remains intact. The old liberal principle, co-opt the enemy, is once again being tested. Given the opportunity, the new groups did not go berserk: on the contrary, they behaved with almost humorless responsibility and were the first to discipline their own crazies. Father Flanagan would have loved it.

It's probably only a breather in this tangled nation of ours. God knows what disillusionments, new factions, brand-new diseases lie ahead. But, in the meantime, what a relief to be bored at a convention again. And after Nixon has stolen all the other issues, ended the war on election eve, and injected the economy with meltable silicone, McGovern will still have this to take to the country: Isn't it nice to have your children back again? Or, if you're sick to death of youth, women, and blacks (as many of them are themselves), he can say, behind his hand: Well, I listened. Maybe they'll quiet down now. If they get Nixon again, they'll raise the sky with their screams.

It might just do it.

1972

NOTE: *I never thought for a moment that it would do it. The oafish electioneering of that last sentence reminds me of another moment in Miami, when I chanced upon an old friend William V. Shannon, the political writer. Bill fixed me with a friendly glower and said, "Why aren't you home reviewing books?" I could only say, "End the War and I'll be gone tomorrow." It turned out that many of the firebrands of '72 felt the same way, and the 1976 convention was different in kind from Miami. A professional like Shannon would have guessed this.*

18 / *Now That Men Can Cry . . .*

In the village where I live, it hasn't happened yet, as far as the eye can see. I'm not sure the twenties happened here either, although the Depression certainly did, not once but often. Women's liberation doesn't mean much when nobody is working, or if it does, it isn't what it means in Manhattan. Long Island fishermen and their wives have to meet by appointment, while the farmers pick potatoes until they look like them, with all that that implies as to behavior. Our cleaning woman is surprised that I prepare my own lunch, and her husband is probably surprised that I have a cleaning woman.

In short, the nation is pockmarked with exceptions which all the surveys in the world haven't beveled away yet. It would be nice to list all of those between, say, Boston and Worcester, if one had grants enough and time. But before the academic storm troopers move in with their gear, there is still time for the kind of locker-room speculation that used to pass for sociology in the old days. As sociology it was probably next to worthless, but it was at least a participant sport; you got to do it yourself. And it produced livelier conversations than the Now Sound of surveys dismally butting heads. Everyone simply brought his own jug of bias and homemade opinion to the party, and a left hook or a tantrum (from either sex) was considered a perfectly respectable argument.

Herewith, then, one man's jug.

According to de Tocqueville (Oh, no! Exit wife, groaning), revolutions merely ratify what has already happened. The power balance has shifted before the first shot is fired. The rulers then make panicky concessions, which only underline how truly weak they are. Most people will join a revolution only when it is safer to do so than not. When there are finally more people behind you than in front, you storm the Bastille with menacing shouts.

Nothing that neat is likely to happen in the house-to-house fighting of sex. But for a growing class, the American husband's power has, like Louis XVI's, been more ritual than real for a long time now. The prodigious success of *Life With Father* in the thirties and forties—a play about a late Victorian patriarch whose self-esteem has to be fostered like a house plant by the rest of the family—should have told us something. First, women didn't need our strength (the very phrase seems laughable in many cases); then they didn't need our money; and if they still kept house for us, it was only out of habit and custom. And unnecessary customs live a brutally short life in America.

As upper-middle women gradually ceased washing dishes on a pedestal, they also lost the perquisites if any of mystery. With the best will in the world, it was hard for a Vassar girl to seem like a great natural force, conjuring up earth and sea. And if she couldn't be a natural force, there was no point in keeping her in the kitchen. As upper-middle housing units got smaller, this was tantamount to keeping her in a phone booth anyway.

If you belonged to this class, women's lib came as no great shock in the home. Shared housework and childrearing were in the air, even if you didn't practice them at your place. The man in the apron was a household joke in the forties; then no more was heard from him, because the people who write jokes were the first to capitulate. This aspect of women's lib was simply a democratization of how the upper-middles lived, or thought vaguely of living.

So much for the class that brewed the revolution. What about the other classes it landed on? The general understanding in a democracy is that everybody is in roughly the same boat, which makes our revolutions as harsh as they are constant. Class distinctions are something we thought we left behind in Europe, so we either don't see them or we treat them as aberrations to be flattened out, as in the Army, by uniform regulations. Thus, Freud the great equalizer and Gail Sheehy are applied evenly to all, regardless of family structure and ability to pay; and now women's lib wades bravely into the ghetto, demanding equal housework from men who haven't been seen in years.

Social classes are in fact a rational and necessary response to situation, much sturdier than they look. Machismo, for instance, is for many Americans not just a trick of style but a survival mechanism: either because their work literally demands it, or because the precariousness of low-salaried life requires effluvious self-confidence. And for the females it is serviceable, simply because they need a functioning husband.

In upper-middle myth, the working-class wife gives her man his confidence either by worshipful service or by allowing herself to be hit regularly, or both. But this is because we meet the men in bars and traffic jams and assume they act the same way at home. Despite all the jokes about wives waiting up with rolling pins, we haven't measured the space between public and private, between stranger and lover.

The fact is that machismo requires a display of *public* toughness whether you feel like it or not. Sociobiologists from the woolly regions tell us that an appearance of menace has saved many a monkey tribe from an actual fight and the same goes for barflies and cabdrivers. Anybody who has been raised among even semitough boys will remember the requirement. Although we might have been gloomily destined to become lawyers or even publishers, we all Wayned and Cagneyed as best we could to buy breathing room from the one guy in five (we didn't know which one) who really did like to fight.

For our class of secret sedentaries, women's lib brought instant, superficial relief from macho conventions. Not only could we unveil that curious interest in needlepoint, but we had it on good authority (from experts even skinnier than ourselves) that the guys who had frightened us so were really cowards under the skin, and that their bluster, which seemed so convincing at the time, was only a cover for wobbly masculinity. This was certainly good to know, as one tiptoed the streets of Manhattan, hoping that nobody was doubting his masculinity to the point of madness that night.

So the theory of women's lib was welcomed with reasonably open arms by the upper-middles. Chances are that the U.M.s had never gone in for the heavy kidding about sex differences—that mosaic of dopey broads and long-suffering men, women drivers and their husbands who sleep through the opera, which salted blue-collar conversation—if only because the U.M. wives had quite likely gone to drivers' training school and the husbands had memorized *Tosca.* Their education had gently informed U.M.s over the years that physical strength was not the Fort Knox of power anymore. Now women's lib was telling a huge new contingent of men the same thing. A whole herd of lower-middle machos was being forcibly sidelined and told that unless they actually mined coal or wrestled steers, and perhaps not even then, they just didn't need those secondary characteristics of toughness and cool. Why, you could even *cry* now.

In which case, why didn't you? What's eating you, Mac? Some kind of block? Suddenly, in the great middle-middle, where blue-collar shades into white, the macho kid stopped calling the tunes in the sixties and found himself on the run. With leaders like Bob Dylan and Timothy Leary, Aware and Talkative easily routed Strong and Silent. And the new oppressors were as relentless as the old. If letting it all hang out is the thing, then the grim-faced mob will follow you home to see that you do it: chanting, "Uptight, uptight," until hundreds of new customers climb aboard the Revolution, crying their hearts out.

But that's theory, and the upper-middles can accept theories in a twinkling. You meet so many in college that you learn to glad-hand them like a salesman. "Well, hello, there, Siggy . . . why, it's Karl." Practice is different. There, upper-middles have to move as slowly as anyone else. Racial equality, for instance, has been part of their baggage for years. Yet a black is still made more at home in a locker room than a faculty lounge. And so it goes with sexual equality. Crying, primal screaming, admitting you're weak and scared? Consider it done. But when it comes to living near *her* job instead of yours . . .

It's then that we realize that, perhaps because we had to act macho in school, certain aspects of it may mean more to us than it did to the naturals. It was our lifebelt for so long that we can't imagine what sea of sissyhood and abnegation lies underneath it. In other words, Joe Namath can model panty hose, and Alex Karras can do an entrechat in a tutu, but Prof. Walt Poffinger Jr. had better not, because he might mean it.

So instead we might expect to find the professor reacting to women's lib by working out in the gym and tinkering with the car and perhaps telling his wife sarcastically what a wide receiver is. For the first time, he will take seriously the notion that women have not produced a single

Beethoven (as if men produced them all the time, and not just in incredibly favorable circumstances) and he will covertly comfort himself that equal opportunity will eventually *prove* male supremacy. They asked for it, they got it, avers the Prof.

Since he is certainly right in the short term, as the women trip prettily over the starting gate, we can take it that the professor is a relatively happy man, by his standards, for now—so long as his job is safe. What machismo he learned in school is subtly underlined in the new alignment. He does do certain things pretty well, and he would certainly rather compete at them with his wife than with Fred Masterful next door. I doubt he is bothered much by female sexual assertion: it should be right up his alley. Appearing dominant on dates was a devil of a strain for him. And knowing when to make the first move without appearing a clod was so taxing that frequently no first move was made at all. His dream was always to find a girl with clear traffic signals, at which point he became (in the same dream) a tiger. If he doesn't in real life, it is because at the last minute he fears comparison with the other tigers who've been this way. Female sexual sophistication is much more inhibiting than female desire.

In other words, Woody Allen is no accident. But it doesn't do to caricature the Prof, who owns a piece of all of us. Owing to a standardized education, we *are* all in the same boat to some extent. We all meet the Prof and we all meet the Coach, and their influence is unpredictable. Many intellectuals enjoy instinctively the old masculine style, as I imagine many lower-middles do not. A working-class sissy has always been in a desperate fix. For him to try to cultivate the swagger of a dock worker and the glibness of a C.B. radio trucker must be simple torture. Women's lib in its stylistic aspect should come as a relief to him too, if it can get at him through his wall of buddies.

But what about the genuine hard men of the tractor and assembly line, whose toughness is by no means superfluous? Here again, with the confidence of one who knows that the data haven't come in yet, I would offer a conjecture. Which is that, while the upper-middles bought the theory of lib instantly but dragged their feet on the practice (studies show that many of them laughably exaggerate the amount of housework they do), the lower-middles might in some respects have done just the opposite.

For these latter, the theoretical hierarchy is quite likely to be sacred, because they're not used to a new theory a day, but at least some of the new practice is old hat. If they came from large families, the men's earliest memory will be of housework, with few distinctions of sex. If they are Catholic, they will also have been conditioned (whether the conditioning took or not) to help out with the children. A church that forbids birth control had better teach parenthood, and for every mythical husband spending Saturday in a bar, there are a dozen taking their kids to Coney Island or staring glassy-eyed as they fall off the jungle gym. Children are his natural environment; he's never lived in a house without them, and he doesn't find them any earth-shaking challenge (a bore maybe). Finally, if he's been in the military he has long since detached K.P. and bedmaking from femininity.

As for women taking jobs—at that income level they'd damn well better. And if they make more money, it would take a fussy man to worry about that. Money is money. It's only at the top that you can afford to write His or Hers on it. Of course, his wife's job may cost him some of her domestic services, but these may have been exaggerated in the first place. From what little I know of the Irish poor (and, since they are the finest of peoples, you can imagine the rest) the legendary wife slaving all day in the kitchen was usually either a creation of her own rhetoric or a self-confessed saint who made you pay for it with her silent suffering. Even in the days when meals still had to be cooked, a husband had better learn to fix for himself soon after the honeymoon; of course, his mother with her 300 ways to boil potatoes was another story, and he might sometimes wish he'd married her. But those mothers traditionally turned off their husbands after the children arrived for very good and compelling reasons, so he wouldn't have had her for long.

Anyway, nowadays, a husband is more likely to comment drily on his wife's peerless way with frozen vegetables or her deft handling of the dishwasher—hardly enough to make up for her potential market value. Men notoriously underrate the onerousness of such scrubbing and dusting as remain to be done. But a full-time maid is an unjustified expense now, whether you call her a wife or not, and a full-time mother is less fun for the children than a full-time TV set.

Beyond the whole debate so far lies a possibility so benign that I hesitate to broach it: namely that men, all things being precisely equal, slightly prefer their wives to be happy. Call it self-interest or call it genes whispering in code behind our back, but this minor instinct cuts across class lines and nourishes women's lib even in its foolish moments. Because, Golden Age theory notwithstanding, nameless female discontent was and is so widespread that it cannot be put down to individual neurosis. And any cure has to be looked at. An unhappy woman can destroy a man so easily that by middle age he is often in worse shape than she is, because he is always on guard against apparently meaningless assaults of rage; or he may find himself, on a sunny Saturday morning, suddenly trapped in a species of tragic wallowing that he dimly understands, if at all.

It goes without saying that, now that men can cry, they can give at least some of these lumps back. Crying is a superb offensive weapon in the right hands, an imposition without parallel, and I'm convinced that once men get the hang of it they will do it *better* than women, reducing their wives to twitching wrecks in no time at all. As, of course, they always have done, those who have a mind to; psychological warfare finds gifted killers on both sides, as if nature had chosen the teams with some care.

Decent people are rare enough in either sex, and atrocity stories can be multiplied indefinitely. But anyone who happens to be a parent or child or even neighbor knows that an unhappy parent of either persuasion is a family disease shared equally, so we watch closely across sex lines to see if women's lib makes it better or worse.

For children so far it seems to have made things slightly worse. The horrors of assertiveness training—as if the world needed more rudeness—symbolize a jungle view of life in which husband and kids form a single threat. And a child's wanton greed for attention sucks at a mother's very lifeblood and brings her consciousness banging down. The maternal instinct having been triumphantly routed, it's hard to know what you *should* feel for the little nippers. Perhaps when those over-competitive males start outmothering and outnurturing and take to commandeering the kids' affections, the mothers will get back in the game and the American child will return to the catbird seat, manipulating the pair of them to its heart's content.

But right now, the focus is on the unhappy grown-up, who, once straightened out, will presumably spread beneficence everywhere, but who may have to kick some tail on the road to health. The early stage of a revolution is always rough going; the question, as with Soviet Russia, is whether the second stage will ever come, or whether tail-kicking is too much fun to stop. The answer depends a good deal on the job market. Fathers usually don't mind looking after their children if there's nothing better to do, and women returning from the unemployment office, or even a data-processing office, may fall back on the children with relief.

As things now stand, the office is a slightly meaner battleground than the home. Male bosses seem to dominate their women underlings as they would never dominate their wives, as if women's lib has sent them a gift to make up for what they've lost at home, while women bosses must practice either a paper-thin toughness that fools nobody or a sort of crisp femininity that must be terribly hard to sustain. The male prejudice against working for women may be the last to go, and even the best women executives must sometimes feel that the men under and around them are toying with them, helping the little woman out, carrying her and tolerating her. She is there at their pleasure and could be snuffed out in an instant if they weren't such nice, well-adjusted guys with such supersecure self-images.

Increased female leadership in school may neutralize this eventually, and life may get better at the top, but it won't help much lower down the ladder, where most work is, as it has always been, paralyzingly dull, and now scarce to boot. A man who's had to fight for a job he doesn't even want is in no mood to share it with a woman, or a black, or anybody else. Having settled for so much less than his dreams, the least he can feel is indispensable; in fact, the less glorious the job, the sniffier the possessor of it, as anyone who's dealt with minor civil servants can tell you.

Yet here again, the lower-middles may, between sneers, adjust better to women's lib than the upper-middles have. The battle for thankless tasks is likely by nature to be less ferocious than the fight for those rarest of plums, *interesting* jobs. In a centralized mass-production society these are becoming fewer all the time. As networks wipe out theaters and teaching aids wipe out teachers, the best and brightest who brought you women's lib may be the first to abandon it and start clawing each other the old way, man, woman, and black alike. Solidarity is easier in good times, and movements depending on it may prove a luxury. Already the most bitter fights take place on the most enlightened campuses. Even in graduate school, that cradle of civilization, women can usually count on an elbow in the eye right along with the lip service.

The ideal solution would seem to be simply to multiply the interesting jobs. But the route we seem to be taking, as the money drains out, is to shrink the number of people trained for the jobs. This means that the kicking and gouging will start earlier in life, and the casualties will limp off earlier too, expecting less of work than their parents did. Women will and should continue to scramble for interesting careers, but there may soon be so few to scramble for that neither most men nor most women will care very much. Woman's lib must address itself evermore to the great gray mass of work that it has almost won the right to share.

The grayness of work is also of concern to an unusual group of heroes who, quite informally, have probably advanced the cause as much as anybody, namely fathers of daughters. As one of these, I feel somewhat unsung. Because at least some of us are every bit as ambitious for our daughters as for our sons, maybe more than they're prepared for. We want them to have interesting work, and every victory for women's lib is a victory for us. We know that our daughters have to be twice as good as men to get there, and we'd like to make them so. At the same time, we don't want to see them built up just to be crushed, as so many men have been, by failure. Both sexes should get some juice out of life, even if work fails them. Which means that if our daughters become drudges, or sex objects, or scatterbrained dependents, we'll be almost as disappointed about it as they are. (Even the M. Champion P. Muhammad Ali has been heard to suggest that he would shred any man who "jacked up" his daughters the way we—his "we"—jack up other people's.)

Women's lib so far has delivered us a mixed bag. It is certainly no sillier than most movements. The biggest mouths as usual hog the microphones, and one listens for the quieter voices: Letty Pogrebin, who has done wonders in the field of humdrum jobs, Eleanor Holmes Norton, even the new improved Gloria Steinem, and many others. My friend Betty Friedan was noisy when she needed to be, and anyhow has the rare knack of being noisy and sensible at the same time. As for the ones who want to mess with the language these can be handled by their own literate sisters, if bad ears haven't already driven out good, as they do in most movements. "Ms" is O.K. with me, as is the above Muhammad Ali or Brother Timothy or any name anyone wants to call itself. Why people should laugh at "Ms" and not at "Mr." is not clear. As a man, I also don't mind relinquishing my hold on the word mankind, if you can find a stronger one. I never got that much out of it anyway. "Woman" is usually better than "girl" or "lady," but "person" is a wet fish of a word that shouldn't be tacked onto anything. English prose has its own troubles these days, and I'll have no part in barbarizing it further. A debased language, unlike a debased group, may be incurable.

Beyond that, the language faddists have given the male chauvinists something to laugh at, thus easing the pressure on them. Their last redoubt is humor, and women are their last joke. If a feminist is serious, she's funny, and if she isn't, she's funny for that too, so perhaps there's no winning with them. But they shouldn't be given real jokes to laugh at. There's no harm so long as the simple fellows are still cackling over bra burning, which nobody ever stood for anyway, but rewriting the classics in bad English is something else. Those of us who have been blessed with intelligent mothers, sisters, wives, don't want the cavemen to have such live ammunition. Women's lib should give a thought to its male fellow travelers, who have to argue too, and who want the women's movement to be at least as intelligent as our mothers and sisters and wives.

Throwing the men and children off the raft is not intelligent. Nor is the light-hearted ostracism of other women. Quarreling with them is probably intelligent but treating them as baboons is not. Since women are expected to fight, they may have to do less of it, just as black intellectuals have to cut back their tap dancing. More seriously, there are coalitions waiting to be made out there. E.g., the right-to-lifers, loud mouths of course to the fore, also include many sensitive women, who may feel, for instance, that the hit-and-run male is getting off rather lightly if he can talk *them* into getting an operation on the house. Or they may feel quite a lot of things closely allied to their femininity which, without being swallowed whole, might still add something to women's lib's philosophy of Family, which is far from complete.

Even the farcical Total Woman, or black negligee movement, must speak to *somebody's* reality. It could be that the Total Woman thing is part of a class countersuit against the Ivy League ideal in which a couple haggle like lawyers over their rights prior to seeking self-fulfillment and self-gratification at the hands of opposing counsel—who isn't really needed, mind you. Granted that this is a parody. Classes normally parody each other; it's part of their equipment. But this is what the outsider sees, and women's libbers must find a more human and attractive way to present the upper-middle vision, or some more universal vision, to, e.g., men and women in labor unions who tend at first contact to split their sides over what they take to be women's lib. So far, the parodies are a standoff. Where a teacher might find a Total Woman alternatively funny and suffocating, a coal miner would probably feel the same about encounter groups.

Which doesn't mean he shouldn't have them, if they can be miraculously tailored to a coal miner's needs. The voices from the women's power center can be discouraging about this. They sound not so much insensitive as woefully inexperienced in modes of life other than their own, even within their own cities. In this, they resemble the well-meaning missionaries of legend or Woodrow Wilson at Versailles, making the world over in their own peculiar image. But who knows what local geniuses may not even now be studying the natives of Wheeling and Shreveport to find out what they really want? (The black community, so triumphantly opaque to outsiders, seems to have its own seers, if the novels of Toni Morrison and Gayl Jones et al. are anything to go by.) As with other large organizations—e.g., the Catholic Church or the U.S. Government—the dopes of women's lib probably prefer to congregate in the capital accreting jargon while the best work is done on the edges.

Whatever this work may be, it has to be good for men, whether they like it or not. You cannot (alas) play baseball all day; saloons provide moments of genuine ecstasy—but only if your soul is at peace and the rest of your life bears contemplating. Otherwise, they are palaces of misery. And anyway, you have to go home sometime. And it's a rare home, in the sane world, where one person feels good while the others don't. If the mysterious headache, that coast-to-coast blight which came over on the Mayflower, could be stamped out, men would pay a stiff price for it. And—who knows?—we might even take another look at tired blood.

Anyway, the choice is probably not between women's lib and something else but between different kinds of women's lib. The power shift has occurred, even if the movement were to blow away tomorrow, and can only be undone by another power shift. Causes seem to weaken when they leave the headlines, but headlines are not the only form of power. Property ownership is real power, social, political, and psychological, and although rich men still like to truss up their estates in trust funds, etc., women have too much money control not to have a say in the national life. Women's lib is just one way of organizing that say and drastically mobilizing it. But there will be others. A state of acute world shortage might someday restore physical strength and mobility to their old primacy. But most civilized males would also have a thin time of it in such a world.

Meanwhile the wise little pig should build his ego of brick and try to take an intelligible part in the discussion. It is even possible, since we're throwing around wild generalizations, that all things being exactly equal, women would like *him* to be happy. In which case, he must explain his erogenous zones, be they hunting or poker or having a giggle with the boys, and only hope that she understands.

Western civilization runs on curiosity, and we still seem to have enough of that. The supply of usable questions should not give out in this century. Some men at least would like to know if there are any sexual differences at all, beyond the outstanding ones. What about touch and sight, for instance? Could men in significant quantities be induced to run soap bars up and down their legs while they purr with pleasure? Could women goggle for hours simply at a display of the other sex undressing? Like Oedipus, we may be sorry we asked. But we have to ask. We even have to ask whether women are as curious as men. And women's lib is the latest gleaming instrument in the lab, the probe that can tell us what an unconditioned sex would actually look like.

Until we are conditioned not to ask questions, we have to follow this one to the end.

1977

Scott Donaldson

BY FORCE OF WILL

The Life and Art of Ernest Hemingway

This is a new sort of book about Ernest Hemingway—not a biography, not a personal memoir, not a critical study of the writing, but a character study of the man and the author. Scott Donaldson, with scholarly patience and a gift for separating fact from legend, has put it all together candidly. "Fame," "Money," "Sport," "Politics," "War," "Love," "Sex," "Friendship," "Religion," "Art," "Mastery," and "Death" are the titles of the chapters, each of which reveals another aspect of Hemingway's mind in action. Donaldson pays full attention to the contradictions in each field but ends by suggesting an underlying pattern in the character of this fear-haunted young man who displayed outstanding courage and who became a world-famous author by force of will.

Frank MacShane

THE LIFE OF RAYMOND CHANDLER

Raymond Chandler murdered more people than Dashiell Hammett did—and he murdered them brilliantly. Dismissed from his job with an oil company for heavy drinking, Chandler did not begin to write detective fiction until he was forty-four; yet within a few years he published *The Big Sleep* and created in Philip Marlowe one of the century's most popular and durable heroes. Marlowe's exploits were filmed, and Chandler himself went to Hollywood as a scriptwriter. Drawing on Chandler's voluminous yet lively correspondence and on conversations with members of his circle, Frank MacShane has given us the definitive account of the life and times of this unique literary figure.

Malcolm Cowley

—AND I WORKED AT THE WRITER'S TRADE

Chapters of Literary History, 1918–1978

Poet, critic, editor, and author of the acclaimed *Exile's Return,* Malcolm Cowley has played a pivotal part in the world he writes about. *—And I Worked at the Writer's Trade* adds further eloquent chapters to the story of American literature in our time, as it deals with figures as diverse as Erskine Caldwell, Conrad Aiken, and William Faulkner and with scenes and situations from Greenwich Village and Paris after World War I to the youth movement of the 1960s and the return in the 1970s of a religion of art. "I never read a book or essay by Malcolm Cowley that I was not instructed by. He is certainly our best and wisest student of American writing. . . . No student of our literature can afford not to know everything he writes"—Wallace Stegner.

Edited by Elaine Steinbeck
and Robert Wallsten

STEINBECK: A LIFE IN LETTERS

Here is the life of John Steinbeck as revealed in his letters, most of which have never before been published. These letters are imbued with all the passion that Steinbeck brought to his other writing. The collection opens with his early years in California, when he said, "I think I shall write some very good books indeed." It continues through the work on his plays and novels ("We have a title at last. See how you like it. The Grapes of Wrath from Battle Hymn of the Republic.") and closes with a 1968 note, from Sag Harbor, that ends in mid-sentence. To Steinbeck, who hated the telephone, letter-writing was not only a preparation for work; it was also his most natural means of communicating his thoughts on people met and loved or hated; on marriage, women, and children; on the condition of the world; and on his own progress in learning his craft. Distilled from more than five thousand letters, this book portrays him as nothing else has and as nothing else ever could.

Graham Greene

THE END OF THE AFFAIR

This frank, intense account of a love affair and its mystical aftermath takes place in a suburb of wartime London.

THE POWER AND THE GLORY

In one of the southern states of Mexico, during an anticlerical purge, the last priest, like a hunted hare, is on the run. Too human for heroism, too humble for martyrdom, the little worldly "whiskey priest" is nevertheless impelled toward his squalid Calvary as much by his own efforts as by the efforts of his pursuers.

THE QUIET AMERICAN

The Quiet American is a terrifying portrait of innocence at large, a wry comment on European interference in Asia in its story of the Franco-Vietminh war in Vietnam. While the French Army is grappling with the Vietminh, back at Saigon a young high-minded American begins to channel economic aid to a "Third Force." The narrator, a seasoned foreign correspondent, is forced to observe: "I never knew a man who had better motives for all the trouble he caused."

Also:

BRIGHTON ROCK
A BURNT-OUT CASE
THE COMEDIANS
THE HEART OF THE MATTER
IT'S A BATTLEFIELD
JOURNEY WITHOUT MAPS
LOSER TAKES ALL
MAY WE BORROW YOUR HUSBAND?
THE MINISTRY OF FEAR
OUR MAN IN HAVANA
TRAVELS WITH MY AUNT

Saul Bellow

HENDERSON THE RAIN KING

In this sparkling novel Nobel Laureate Saul Bellow recounts the adventures of Eugene Henderson, prodigious American millionaire, in darkest Africa. Henderson "is a picaresque hero in the great tradition, full of bizarre vitality, with affinities both to Odysseus and to Don Quixote"—*Newsweek.*

HERZOG

Herzog tells the story of Moses Herzog, sufferer, joker, cuckold, charmer, and survivor of disasters both public and private. First published in 1964, it won the acclaim of critics and readers alike; it was a longtime best-seller, a selection of the Literary Guild, and a winner of the National Book Award for fiction and of the International Publishers' Prize.

MR. SAMMLER'S PLANET

A wry old man, once a resident of Krakow, of London, and of a Nazi death camp, strides recklessly through New York City's Upper West Side and through the pages of this extraordinary novel. Observing everything, appalled by nothing, Mr. Sammler notes with the same disinterested curiosity the activities of a pickpocket, the details of his niece's sex life, the madness of his own daughter, and the lunar theories of a Hindu scientist.

Also:

MOSBY'S MEMOIRS AND OTHER STORIES
THE PORTABLE SAUL BELLOW
SEIZE THE DAY

Jack Kerouac

ON THE ROAD

This is the novel that put Jack Kerouac and the beat generation on the national map and the best-seller lists. Concerned with a group of exuberantly uninhibited young Americans, the narrative roars back and forth across the continent and down to Mexico in one of the most fantastic journeys ever to appear in American literature. The book is ultimately a celebration of life itself, a lyrical yea-saying outburst from one of the few truly original talents to careen down the literary pike in many a year. "A historic occasion . . . the most beautifully executed, the clearest, and the most important utterance yet made by the generation Kerouac himself named years ago as 'beat,' and whose principal avatar he is"—Gilbert Millstein, *The New York Times.*

Barry Gifford and Lawrence Lee

JACK'S BOOK

An Oral Biography of Jack Kerouac

Here, in the voices of his friends and lovers, is the fascinating story of Jack Kerouac, "the King of the Beats," the daddy of the hippie generation. In the memories of Allen Ginsberg, Gore Vidal, Neal Cassady, John Clellon Holmes, Lawrence Ferlinghetti, Gary Snyder, William Burroughs, and many others, and in the words of authors Barry Gifford and Lawrence Lee, the complex personality of the Canuck kid from Massachusetts who became a literary legend comes to light. We see Jack at Columbia University and on the scene in Greenwich Village; speeding across the tarmac of America with Neal Cassady (Dean Moriarty in Kerouac's classic *On the Road*); at home with his possessive mother; in California, drinking wine and talking Buddhism; and, finally, in Florida, where his life ends tragically at age forty-seven.